the
ROBERTS FAMILY
GUIDE TO MIRACLES
for the rest of your life

CELEBRATING 40 YEARS
1947
1987
MIRACLE MINISTRY

D1133526

by Oral and Evelyn Roberts
Richard and Lindsay Roberts

Unless otherwise indicated,
all Scripture quotations are from
the King James Version of the Bible.

Copyright ©1987
by
Oral Roberts Evangelistic Association
Tulsa, Oklahoma

CONTENTS

FIRST WEEK

I CAN HAVE A
NEW MIRACLE IN MY LIFE EVERY DAY

by Oral Roberts

SECOND WEEK

NO MATTER HOW BAD THE SITUATION, "GOD CAN TURN IT AROUND" FOR ME WHEN I TURN AROUND TO GOD

by Richard Roberts

THIRD WEEK

JESUS DIDN'T MAKE ME...OR YOU...FOR FAILURE

by Evelyn Roberts

FOURTH WEEK

I KNOW
WHO MY SOURCE IS AND HE KNOWS ME

by Oral Roberts

FIFTH WEEK

MY FAITH
IS THE MOST POWERFUL THING I HAVE

by Richard Roberts

SIXTH WEEK

GOD IS ALIVE
IN MY LIFE AND THE LIVES OF MY LOVED ONES

by Lindsay Roberts

SEVENTH WEEK

KNOWING THE NAME AND NATURE OF MY ENEMY IS HALF THE BATTLE!

by Oral Roberts

EIGHTH WEEK

THE SEVEN GREAT THINGS
I CAN DO WHEN I NEED A MIRACLE

by Richard Roberts

NINTH WEEK

GOD HAS
A SPECIAL PLAN FOR MY LIFE!

by Evelyn Roberts

TENTH WEEK

HOW I DISCOVERED GOD WILL MEET
"ALL" YOUR NEEDS AND THE WAY HE WILL DO IT!

by Oral Roberts

ELEVENTH WEEK

THERE'S SOMETHING I MUST DO TO GET FROM WHERE I AM TO WHERE I WANT TO BE

by Richard Roberts

TWELFTH WEEK

I CAN BE LOOSED FROM THE THINGS THAT THE DEVIL USED TO TRY TO HOLD ME DOWN

by Lindsay Roberts

THIRTEENTH WEEK

GOD HAS SOMETHING GOOD —
NO, SOMETHING EVEN *BETTER* — FOR ME!

by Oral Roberts

"Why This Is A Must-Read Book For You"

By Dr. Larry Lea
Senior Pastor, Church on the Rock
Dean of the Oral Roberts University
Signs and Wonders Seminary

As you read this book, **The Roberts Family Guide to Miracles,** I encourage you to expect *your* miracle to happen! I can say this because of the powerful anointing that touched me as I allowed the words of Oral Roberts and his family to penetrate my life.

Oral Roberts is the senior apostle to the Body of Christ in our day. His life and ministry have impacted the Church of the twentieth century in dimensions that truly are in preparation for the second coming of Christ. Before that great day, the Church is going to experience a mighty restoration. This mighty restoration implies the miraculous power of God flowing to the individual members of God's Church. This gets to the heart of the man Oral Roberts and his family and to this book, **Guide to Miracles.** The Roberts family wants you to learn how to live a supernatural life. As you incorporate the truths of this book, you will see miracles transform your life. Then you will contribute powerfully to the great renewal that is moving in God's Church today.

Several vital ingredients are present in this book to

help you release your faith and bring in your miracle.

First, the Roberts family has been given a unique ability to teach you how to *expect* the supernatural. The Bible clearly teaches a doctrine of expectation. Jesus taught us, "Ask, and it shall be given you..." (Matthew 7:7). Man has a responsibility and God has a responsibility. This doctrine of *expectation* really comes alive in **Guide to Miracles.**

Second, **Guide to Miracles** is profoundly simple to read and understand. At the end of each chapter you will know what the Word of God instructs you to do in order to receive your miracle. The Apostle Paul warned us against losing the "simplicity of the gospel." Steeped in the bedrock of solid biblical principles, **Guide to Miracles** flows forth as a strong, clear word from God to you.

A third ingredient that makes this a "must read" book for your faith is that it has been birthed out of the *real* experiences of the Roberts family. As Oral, Evelyn, Richard and Lindsay candidly open the secret places of their hearts to you, the miracle anointing of God is seen clearly in their day-to-day life. The word *reality* continually came to mind as I read each family member's individual contribution. The sorrows and joys that are a part of your life are reflected in the lives of the Roberts family. Yet, herein are the answers that make this *real* family a *miracle* family. Together, they have tapped into God's unlimited source of power. With honesty and a great openness, they share with you *real life* with a *real miracle-working God.*

In short, **The Roberts Family Guide to Miracles** brings the faith of the Roberts family into your life. I know your life will be changed as you read this book. As you plant your seeds and expect your harvest, you will not be disappointed. I am praying for you as you read this book, that God will truly give you the desires of your heart.

Prayerfully yours,

Larry Lea

OUR PERSONAL WORD —
AND PLEDGE —
TO YOU

ORAL

I am a man anointed of God to bring His miraculous power into your life as long as I have breath. And knowing you are reading the book you hold in your hand today, I will be in agreement with you to receive every miracle you need — every day, every hour, every second, for the rest of your life. AND I WON'T COME OUT OF THE AGREEMENT (Matthew 18:19,20) because there is NO DISTANCE IN PRAYER.

As I am in constant prayer for you, I have that strange but familiar feeling I am in such close touch with Jesus Christ of Nazareth that I know what it is to sit where you sit, to feel what you feel, and to know that I know every word in this book is a word for you where you are this second and where you will be in all your tomorrows. I feel very close to you because this book is now in your hand.

EVELYN

I have lived the TRUE and TRIED miracle principles Oral, Richard, Lindsay, and I share with you in this book. What you read is not what we "hope is true" or what we "wish to be true." You will read what we have experienced personally, helped others personally express, and which has stood the test in the low, medium, and high moments of our lives. I am excited that *you* are going to be excited when you actually see for the first time in your life that you will have miracles happening to you as they have happened to us. I send you my highest hope and expectation that you are going to come into a miracle life.

RICHARD

This book is a gift that is genuine. And, friend, it takes a GENUINE miracle to get you from where you are to where you want to be. Through the commitment of our lives to God and hearing Him speak inside us and doing things the way He does them, we have made a breakthrough into how to turn a need into a miracle — every day of our lives, and I do mean *every day of our lives.* For we as individuals and as family have been struck by Satan with tragedies, hit with misunderstandings and persecutions, beset with troubles and needs — along with our own mistakes and failures. The Roberts family is not a perfect family, but we are a learning family. We don't quit on God or on life. We don't give up when we are struck or hindered by our own shortcomings.

We are dedicated to being disciples of Jesus — learners — and then to DOING what we learn. We just keep on learning and doing day after day, week after week, year after year, like water dripping on a rock. The number-one way we *learn* and *do* is by our seed-sowing. The way we sow is out of our need...against our problems...so we have a base on which to expect our miracle for a desired result from God. We have proven that this is the biblical way, therefore the only successful way to get our needs met and get through the hard places. We are into the rhythm of Seed-Faith and we do it with our spirit and with our gifts. It is our way of serving God and "proving Him" to ourselves and to you.

This book is the real us, all the joys and laughter, the tears and heartache, and the absolutes we seek to live by with our whole being. This is why I believe you'll understand this book and get your miracle.

LINDSAY

This book is the result of Oral and Evelyn living four decades in the healing ministry that first touched my life as a girl of 12 when we made contact with them for prayer for my father who was deathly ill. How we survived that awful struggle and how I, along with Richard, survived the loss of our little son Richard Oral, but gained beautiful little Jordan and Catherine Olivia is a story written in this book in ways you can get hold of to "see you through" and to "find a way where there is no way." So this book you hold is *more* than a gift. It is the very best seed we can plant out of our lives into yours for you to become — yes, become — a MIRACLE PERSON in your own right. This book is our vote that you are going to get your miracle, and keep on getting your miracles, *and that you will make it.*

ORAL

We as a family give you this book as the "best of our lives for the best of your life," and ask you to do these three things:

First, read this book exactly like we wrote it for you: day by day. It will get you through the day like it does us. Read with your head AND your spirit, causing the words, the events, and the answers to go into the deepest levels of your being and to take root and grow as you adapt them to your own everydayness of winning in life. Then go on to the next day because you are going to need answers for tomorrow, and in this book you will get them.

Second, we ask you to do what we've done: memorize the key at the end of each day's passage. Keys are important to open the doors of your home, your car, everything that needs to be open to you. "Memorizing these keys" is very important to your unlocking your own spirit, so please do it. Say the key you find at the end of each chapter and *over and over to yourself often* throughout the day. At the end of the week you will be delighted that you can say all seven keys and see that they are working for you.

Third, with all our hearts we urge you to finish this book in 13 straight weeks. Do it! Just do it! When you finish the last chapter, 13 weeks from now, 81 days, ONE QUARTER OF A YEAR, then I ask you to turn right around and start reading it again so that you will read and absorb this book four times each year... *for the rest of your life.* Why do I ask you to do this? Because this book is totally based on God's eternal Word, the Bible, which is God's DAILY WORD to you and me. It is a written word or what we call a LOGOS word. But the Bible must leap off the pages into your spirit and mind as a living, personal word from God to you or what we call a RHEMA word. So as you read and study your Bible first and foremost and alongside it read our book DAILY, comparing... comparing... comparing ... you'll find that the Bible written thousands of years ago will come alive in the NOW of your existence in ways you've not known before.

One final word before you begin. If you will do as we tell you in this book, we know that we know SOMETHING GOOD IS GOING TO HAPPEN TO YOU...

and nothing shall keep God's goodness from filling your life. We are your friends. God has called us as a family to be His servants and your Partners to help you as though we were face to face with you, telling you personally in your deepest need, "What He's done for us, He'll do for *you*."

When you need us, write us and we'll pray and write you back.

Your Partner always,

Oral Roberts

FIRST WEEK

I Can Have
A New Miracle
In My Life Every Day

By Oral Roberts

SUNDAY

Key:
GOD MADE MIRACLES
FOR ME AND ME
FOR MIRACLES

or
I Can Expect A New Miracle Every Day!

God knows how to change a fear Satan seeks to torment you with into the faith that will give you evidence to stand on to expect the miracle He is sending personally to you.

And God knows exactly when to excite and astonish you with a WORD OF KNOWLEDGE by His Spirit that will immediately alert you that you can expect a miracle, *not* only at some specific time of urgent need *but each and every day* you live on this earth!

And I'm talking about miracles in every area of your life daily…spiritually…physically…financially…your family…and all things that touch your existence.

I witness to you today that God has already written your name on miracles on the loading docks of heaven and there's one marked "today" and "tomorrow" and "every day" for the rest of your life.

And this is true because God made miracles for you and me and He made you and me for miracles. I haven't always known that. It had never entered my mind…before one important day at the very height of my evangelistic and healing crusade ministry. God stopped Satan and his emissaries in their tracks from killing me by coming to me in the urgency of that hour with a fresh word from heaven about miracles. Here is the story.

I was conducting a crusade in a major city — to preach, to win souls, and to lay my hands on the sick and to pray for God to heal them. One morning during the crusade I got a word that a death threat had gone out on my life. A group of atheists were determined that I would not preach about miracles anymore or lay hands on any more sick people and ask God to heal them. They said that night that they were going to come in and drag me out of the pulpit. They were going to stop the healing ministry by assassinating me.

Well, ordinarily I wouldn't have paid much attention to their threat. As I've traveled over the world, throughout America and to more than 40 nations, I've had many dangerous experiences. I've been shot at — a bullet missing my head by inches. I've been confronted by madmen. I've been struck, spit on, cursed, and, like Paul in the first century, been forced to close a crusade and escape with my life. But I've been able to endure all that because I know that I know God has called me and I trust Him as my Savior AND as the Source of my total supply.

But for some reason I can't explain, I fell apart on this one. When Satan hit me, fear hit the pit of my stomach. I allowed that fear to lodge inside me.

Now when I conducted crusades like that regularly — on the road — I usually spent the entire afternoon in prayer and study of my Bible, then in late afternoon I'd take a short nap to get refreshed to preach and pray for the people that night. When the time came in the afternoon to take a little nap that day, I allowed the devil to really work on my mind. I couldn't shake the negative thoughts about that threat. I don't know why it had such a negative effect on me, but I was almost paralyzed by the fear.

I stretched out on the bed and as the devil just kept hurling ideas into my mind about how I was going to be killed, I began to think I shouldn't show up for the meeting. That way they wouldn't know where I was

3

and might call the whole thing off.

Finally I fell asleep and really slept. A half hour later while I woke up and rolled out of bed, these words came up out of my spirit: *Expect a miracle.* And then, *Expect a new miracle every day.*

And then I heard God speak, *And when you go to the crusade tonight, you expect a miracle. You tell your friends and Partners to expect a new miracle every day.*

Immediately I knew the gift of the Spirit — the word of knowledge — was giving me these words for they were not coming up out of my mind. I had been too full of fear to think of them myself. The fear literally jumped out of me as those words caused my spirit to soar.

You see, I'd never heard anything like that. You say, "Didn't you believe in miracles?" Sure, I believed in miracles. I preached a miracle-working God. I'd seen miracles...many times...right before my eyes. But I'd never heard that phrase, "Expect a *new* miracle *every* day!"

Something happened to Oral Roberts. I was so eager to get to that crusade meeting I could hardly wait. I paced the floor in eagerness for the minutes to pass. I was READY to expect that miracle I needed... and to expect a new miracle...and to tell the thousands that night to expect a new miracle every day.

When I entered the auditorium that night at 7:30 and glanced out over the packed building, suddenly the words I'd heard God say began to fade and I fell back into myself instead of upon God and His Word. As I was being escorted up to the platform, my mind went back to those people who said they were coming to get me. Fear gripped me again. But at a time of crisis I've practiced doing only one thing: stand up and face it!

I walked up to the microphone, opened my Bible to the Scripture passage I had marked earlier in the day, and I read to the entire audience, "It is of the Lord's mercies that we are not consumed, because his compassions fail not. They are new every morning: great is thy faithfulness" (Lamentations 3:22,23).

The boldness of God I felt in my spirit after God spoke to me that afternoon swept away the fear once again and pretty soon I forgot all about those people with their death threats. I preached like a man on fire. And when I invited people to accept Christ, hundreds jammed the aisles as they surged forward. Then I began the prayer line, and the first person I prayed for had a large goiter on her neck, and because the TV lights were so bright and focused on the stage, the audience could see it clearly.

What a test, I said to myself, *and now I understand the positive effects if God heals this woman of the goiter — and why the enemy doesn't want it to happen.*

In my usual emphatic way I prayed in the name of Jesus and by His power commanded the devil to take his oppressive hands off that woman's body. "You foul goiter, loose her, in Jesus' name," I prayed as my right hand clasped her forehead.

A terrific expectation washed through me and somehow I knew. I heard a gasp from the audience and opened my eyes. God had taken that goiter away immediately. It just shrank away. The woman felt for it, but it was gone. She swallowed freely. Suddenly the healing power flowed across the audience and as I sat there watching, people were jumping up like popcorn testifying that God was giving them a miracle of healing.

Friend, it was as if Jesus of Nazareth had walked in and taken over. I didn't have to do a thing except to shout encouragement the rest of the service. We saw miracle after miracle after miracle.

Out of that experience came the phrase that has been associated with this ministry for more than thirty years now, "Expect a miracle!" It excites me that it's almost a household word worldwide.

And I want to encourage you once again as you read these pages today, YOU can expect a new miracle every day. You may be just as doubtful as I was before God spoke those words to me that I, you, and everyone can have a *new* miracle *every* day. But honest doubt is good. It causes you to seek evidence for your faith to act on. People who have a pretty deep feeling in their hearts that miracles are possible but then deliberately stifle their feelings, well, they have a problem. But if you will deal with any doubt you have in an honest way, believing the Bible is real for you today, that God is personally involved in every area of your need — and if you can believe God speaks such words as "Expect a miracle!" and "Expect a new miracle every day," just let go with all the faith you have, little faith, middle-size faith, great faith — whichever — and see for yourself that the God we serve is in the miracle-working business. And He will never go out of the miracle-working business.

Start looking for your "new miracle" this very day. Because if you'll look, I believe with the force of my faith God will send it to you.

The important thing is to be in an attitude of receiving. Expecting a miracle is an act of your faith ...but expecting is *not* receiving. A woman in her pregnancy is "expecting" a baby. But there is a moment when "having a baby" becomes an action just like expecting is an action.

I'm saying this because I don't want you to stumble around needlessly as I did so many years before God showed me that expecting a miracle had to lead to the actual receiving of that miracle. The two words *expecting* and *receiving* work best together. When you think of expecting, think of receiving...GET THE WHOLE THING!

I'm excited as I, Evelyn, Richard and Lindsay take this 13-week journey together, then turn right around and do it again the second 13 weeks, and every quarter for the years ahead. You'll find we're down-to-earth folks just like you, having our share of trouble, heartache, pain — sometimes it seems we have more than our share — but we're also folks with dreams and visions, with commitment of our lives to Jesus. I haven't a doubt you'll see that we try to live what we preach — and preach what we live. As for expecting miracles, we're determined that no one — but no one — will believe God more to receive a *new* miracle *every* day than we do!

God has placed the ability in you to both expect and to receive a new miracle every day — and we're with you all the way in expecting and receiving, then giving the glory to God.

YOUR GOD-GIVEN KEY FOR TODAY

"I Expect A New Miracle Every Day... And That Means Today!"

7

MONDAY

or
How One Man Learned God Expected Him To Choose His Own Miracle

What miracle do you want from God today? Can you name it? Can you describe what your miracle looks like, feels like, acts like, *is* like? Do you know *specifically* what your heart is desiring from God and what you are believing Him for?

Yes, God as God knows all things, including the thing you need even before you name it and ask Him to help you. But He made you to interact with Him in the deepest levels of your being. Let me illustrate. Several years ago I got a call to come quickly to the hospital. My associate evangelist for more than thirty years, Bob DeWeese, was down with a heart attack. He had a second attack while he was in the hospital, and only the hardworking and alert doctors — with their great machines and fine facilities — were able to keep his body functioning. Bob actually saw the edge of heaven and started to enter it. Then Someone called him back to earth.

I knew his doctor and got permission to see Bob in the intensive care unit. Bob was happy as a lark. He was *eager* to go to heaven. He had been a pastor and he had worked with me through the years in the great crusades. He had done a good work for the Lord. And now he was *happy* at the thought of getting to heaven as soon as possible.

I prayed for Bob and left the room. As I walked out

of the intensive care unit, Bob's granddaughter stopped me. With her eyes red and swollen from crying, she said to me bluntly, "Oral Roberts, you didn't pray a tent prayer for my granddad!"

"I did the best I could," I said. "Besides, your granddad's mind is made up."

Then she went on, "I sat in the big tent crusades as a little girl. I heard you pray. I saw God heal people. And you're not doing it today for my granddad like you did then for those people."

She started to cry and between her sobs she said, "Please go back in there and really *pray*."

The Holy Spirit moved in me and I turned and asked the doctors if I could see Bob again.

When Bob saw me, he said, "Did you forget something?"

"My tent prayer."

He looked puzzled. I said, "Bob, I didn't pray for you like I used to for people who came through the healing line in our crusades."

Then I added, "Bob, how old was your dad when he died?"

"You know how old he was, Oral. He was sixty-seven. You're thinking of that, aren't you?"

"Yes, I am. How old are you now?"

"Sixty-seven."

All through the years I had heard Bob tell me and others that he was "taking after his dad" and since his father had died at 67, Bob often said, "I'll die at sixty-seven or before."

I could never understand that thinking. Bob was strong and athletic. He was an Olympic swimmer. And he was still playing racquetball in his 60s. I'd say to Bob, "We're in healing evangelism. We're trying to follow God's system, not merely man's." And Bob would listen and nod...and agree for everyone else's

9

sake…but not believe it for himself. Now Bob was struck down with a heart attack at 67.

I had also known Bob's mother. I asked, "How old was your mother when she went to heaven?"

"Ninety-two."

"Ninety-two? And you chose your dad's genes over hers?"

"Now, Oral."

"Okay, let me ask you some questions. Then I'll get out of here and let you go."

"Ask me," he said.

"In your heart of hearts, are you finished with what God has called you to do on this earth?"

"I think so."

"Are you *sure?*"

No answer.

"Bob, all these years that I've known you, you've talked about being like your father and dying when you were sixty-seven. Directly or indirectly, have you chosen your father's experience? Have you been holding on to a wrong attitude?"

"Maybe. I'm not sure."

"Bob, I'm going to level with you like I see it. Now may be your time. But it may also be that God isn't through with you and you can change your attitude and decide to believe for something else."

"Like what?"

"Like decide to believe for your *mother's* genes."

We were both in uncharted territory. The medical people were doing their job as it seemed best to them. I was doing my job too.

"If you are willing, I will pray again, Bob. But not like before."

"Go ahead."

My prayers are brief and to the point for the most part. Often they are only one or two words. But this time I heard myself saying, "Bob, do you choose your father's genes or your mother's genes?"

"Mother's," he said faintly.

"Say it so I can hear you!"

"*Mother's!*" And then he began to laugh, and when Bob laughs, he really laughs.

I prayed again, "Jesus, Bob DeWeese has chosen his mother's genes. He wants to live beyond that hang-up he's had for years about his father's death. I ask You, grant it in Jesus' name! Amen and amen."

I turned to leave and Bob's body began to shake until he nearly fell out of the bed. Charlotte, his wife, had slipped into the room along with a couple of nurses. They helped me roll his big six-foot-three-inch body back onto the bed. Again, he shook. It was not a normal shaking. It was a shaking under the Spirit of God. The entire room seemed to fill with the power of God until I thought there was enough power there to heal hundreds or even thousands.

When I left, Bob was cheerful. As I passed his granddaughter, she smiled. "He'll live. Those tent prayers still work."

"Cindy," I said to her, "it wasn't a tent prayer. You remember prayers that were positive, that expected results from God. Sometimes it's a matter of deciding what you're going to pray *for* and deciding what you're going to believe *for.* And I had to get your grandfather to make the choice, then add my faith to his."

Bob DeWeese is alive and healthy as a horse at this writing nearly eight years later.

Now I'm not going to promise you or anybody else that what happened to Bob DeWeese is going to happen for you. What I *can* say to you with certainty is this: God has put it in your control to decide what you are going to believe for.

How much health do you want to have?

How good do you want your marriage to be?

What do you want for your children, or grand-children?

How much prosperity do you want to have?

Specifically!

Name the problem in your life. Then name its *best* solution. Say it until it gets into your spirit. Like Bob, once it gets inside you, it'll come rushing out of you up to God. God will take over, then you'll experience just how large and powerful He is for you to receive your miracle.

You know, a blind man called out to Jesus one day while He was walking through Jericho. Now Jesus could see that this man was blind. He was dressed like a blind man. He was begging by the side of the road like the blind people did. He looked blind. But still Jesus asked him, "What do you want?" In other words, "What do you want *Me* to do for *you?*" Jesus wanted the blind man to name his need… to call it out…to get involved with Him for his sight to be restored by the living God.

It was only *after* the blind man said, "I want to see!" that Jesus healed him and he received his eyesight. (See Mark 10:46-52.)

Jesus wants to know today, "What can *I* do for *you?* What miracle do you need from My hand?" Others can tell God your need. But He's asking *you* to name the need… to call out your miracle by name. To focus your faith on your need and Jesus at the same time.

I've discovered time and time again God is a God of precision, of order, of exactness. He doesn't deal with us in a haphazard way. He knows that our thoughts and life patterns are often so divided we've not stopped to get hold of ourselves so we can zero in on the key issue or the main thing we need from God.

Also, in spite of the fact Jesus has a world view of carrying the whole of mankind in His great heart to deliver them, we see Him in Bible times being keenly attuned to every individual. It usually came down to Him and one person doing business together with their faith.

All people are important to God, for His Son died for all. But the offer of salvation and healing is to "whosoever will." This excites me for myself...and for you. It means the Lord has fixed a straight line between Him and you...between Him and me...and between Him and every person in the world.

The outstanding thing I learned about Bob DeWeese's full healing was to remember to get a person to be *specific* with God so I can get hold of the specific need with Him and put the full force of my prayer to work in his behalf.

But whether I pray for you in person or pray for you where you are, there is NO DISTANCE in prayer. As I write, I'm praying for everyone who reads this and my prayers are reaching you. Get specific with God about your need, call it by name as the blind man did to Jesus and Bob DeWeese did to the Lord through me that day. Don't keep it to yourself; get it out of you. The most listening ear is God's. He loves to have you talk to Him.

YOUR GOD-GIVEN KEY FOR TODAY

"I Will Call My Need Of A Miracle By Name . . . Specifically!"

TUESDAY

**Key:
GOD WANTS YOU TO
START EXPECTING
THE UNEXPECTED**

**or
I Will Open Myself Up To God's Next Great Idea!**

Many years ago while conducting a crusade in Seattle I met a man by the name of William Skrinde. Mr. Skrinde was about seventy years old at the time. He was an inventor, and one of the things he had invented was a part for the wheel of the Jeep. He had been unable to sell it, however, and had literally poured out his life and exhausted his supply of money in trying to prove the worth of his invention.

By the time Mr. Skrinde came to our crusade he and his wife were living hand-to-mouth. He was working in a convalescent home, making about two hundred dollars a month in addition to their Social Security checks.

During the crusade, the Skrindes both accepted Jesus into their lives and soon thereafter accepted the Seed-Faith principles of the Bible of "seeding" out of your need, then looking to God as the Source of supply— from both expected sources and unexpected sources. This was a new idea to him but seizing it, he found himself opening up to God to help him in a way he hadn't thought possible. His first Seed-Faith gift was $10 sown totally out of his need and a new expectation that an invisible source would be revealed to him in every area of his life, including help for his invention.

During the crusade, the Lord led me to say, "Look for God to give you ideas. In fact, there may be something God already has for you that you haven't seen. Be observant. Go up in your attic. Open your closet doors. Look in your dresser drawers. Look around! Open your eyes. See what God has given you. Be expectant even from unexpected sources."

Mr. Skrinde went home, climbed up into his attic, and found the papers that he had drawn up years before. He looked at them a long time. Then he felt led in his spirit to try one more time with the makers of the Jeep.

And this time Jeep bought the invention. Mr. Skrinde became very wealthy as a result.

At the time that my associate, Lee Braxton, asked me to meet Mr. Skrinde, he was stooped over — not only physically, but in his inner man. Gradually as he got more and more into the rhythm of planting his seeds of faith and expecting God to open His sources of supply to him, he began to straighten up. And when he came to Tulsa for a Layman's Seminar at ORU he looked years younger and was really turned on to the Lord and His miracle power. By the time he died at age 92 he had made the largest and most frequent gifts we had received to build Oral Roberts University, and he became a founding member of the Board of Regents.

In addition, he built a new church for the congregation he joined in his home city. He was on the United Way Committee and literally poured himself and his earnings into helping people for the glory of God. When I walk across the ORU campus and see his imprint in building after building, including the great pipe organ in Christ's Chapel, it's almost impossible for me to go back to that stoop-shouldered, worn-out man with his lost dreams and his pitiful little income — and the fact he didn't know the Lord.

Well, I'm saying the same thing today that William Skrinde heard me say many years ago. "Get right with

God. Start sowing into the good soil of the gospel. Then look around. Be observant. Be expectant. Look to God, your Source, who can tap both the expected and unexpected sources to help you!" God does His work on the basis of PEOPLE…and the SEEDS they sow.

If you'll just think, doubtless you've already sown many seeds of faith. But you've not been observant or expecting from the only real SOURCE of total supply there is…GOD. What are you to look for?

It may be an idea.

It may be an opportunity.

It may be a relationship.

It may be something you've inherited…or something you bought long ago and forgot…or something you started and haven't finished.

It may be special favor with someone…or a vacant lot…or an empty building…or an unused room …or a piece of equipment…or something you've given up on and put away like William Skrinde had done. God is involved in your life.

Look around! Be observant! Be expectant!

Remember that Jesus used two fishes and a few loaves to make a miracle…that fed five thousand people…when a little boy got involved with doing what He said. Another time He told His disciples that there was a coin in a fish's mouth…that they could catch that fish and take the money and pay their taxes that were due…and they were observant and did it!

Yet another time He asked a fisherman for the loan of his fishing boat to preach from and when He finished, He shocked the man by telling him there was a net-breaking, boat-sinking load of fish right there in the same waters they'd been fishing in time after time and had failed to catch anything.

The fisherman's name was Simon, which means "an unstable person." But out of this experience Simon caught a vision of what could happen to him when he gave his life to the Lord. You know who he became: Peter!

God is all around you like the air you breathe, under you like the ground you walk on, above you like the sky the planes fly in. He is the Source of all good. He knows your name, your address, your needs, your dreams and visions. All the sources of expected supply AND unexpected supply are in His hands.

Reach down into your innermost being, and by an act of your desire and your will, open yourself up to God's next great idea…His next great miracle and start doing it now!

YOUR GOD-GIVEN KEY FOR TODAY

"I Open Myself Right Now To God's Next Miracle…For Me!"

WEDNESDAY

Key: GOD WANTS TO HEAR YOU SAY THE DESIRES OF YOUR HEART

or
I Must Want My Miracle More Than Anything Else

Were you ever the one that nobody noticed? Were you always under the doorstep…the last one people called…the one nobody thought would amount to anything?

That describes Oral Roberts, the stutterer.

I remember when I was very young my brother Vaden, the middle boy, had a terrific personality, as he does today. He was the favorite of all the Roberts. When the relatives would sit around and talk about which child would grow up to be like my father, who was a preacher, they always picked Vaden. They never picked Oral. I stuttered.

I'll never forget the first day I went to school. The teacher asked all to stand and give their names. When it was my turn, I tried to say my name but I couldn't do it. My throat choked up and the words just wouldn't come. The kids laughed. Then the teacher laughed too. And a terrible thing happened inside me.

That feeling of hurt and rejection was with me through all my growing-up years. It was there the day my Uncle Willis threw a birthday party for Vaden's twelfth birthday. Aunt Eve baked a big cake. Everybody was invited — except me.

I stayed alone in our little house down the road from Uncle Willis' big house and my desire for a piece of that cake got bigger and bigger. It began to represent *everything* I ever wanted in my life...all the dreams of my heart...the burning inside me to amount to something.

Finally I got up and walked barefoot up the road to my uncle's house, kicking the dirt and saying, "I want a piece of that cake. It's not right for them to give my brother some cake and not give me any."

I knocked on the door but nobody came. So I sat down on the edge of the porch, swinging my feet and saying, "I want a piece of that cake." Finally, Uncle Willis came out and said, "Oral, what in the world are you doing out here?" I blurted out, "I want a piece of that cake!"

He said, "Well, come on in!"

Aunt Eve cut me a big piece of cake and gave me a chair and a fork. I finished and said, "Aunt Eve, you got another piece of cake?" Let me tell you, when I got through, *I had a piece of cake!*

The Bible says, "What things soever you desire, when you pray, believe that you receive them, and you shall have them" (Mark 11:24). WHAT THINGS YOU DESIRE!

We need to ask ourselves, "What is it I desire at the gut level of my being? What do I desire from the crown of my head to the soles of my feet?" Your real desire is more than a passing thought. It's more than a whim. It's deep and strong within you and it just won't go away. You know why? God put it inside you. He made you to have great desires that are designed to make you soar!

Recently I heard my friend Dr. Jerry Savelle tell of a young man who wanted to be a success in his life. And one of his greatest desires was to get to know the most successful man in his city. He figured if he could just get a chance to talk to him, he'd learn the secret of success.

One day this young man carried his fishing pole down to the creek and whom do you suppose he found there? The most successful man in town. The young man said, "Do you mind if I fish here with you?"

The successful man said, "No." So the young man sat down.

After a while, the young man couldn't hold in his desire any longer. He said, "Sir, I've wanted to meet you for a long time so I could ask you a question. How do you get to be successful?"

The man stood up so the young man stood also. Then the successful man pushed the younger man into the creek and jumped in after him and held his head under the water.

The young man flailed his arms and came up gasping for a breath, only to be pushed under again.

Again, he fought against the water, struggling to come up to breathe. He had a fight on his hands — a fight for his life!

And again the successful man let him up for just a gulp of air. Then he pushed him under a third time.

By this time the younger man was frantic. He was thrashing around in the water with all the energy he had — almost in a panic. When the man let him up, he gasped long and hard for air, taking in big gulps until finally he could talk.

"What did you do that for?" he said to the man, exhausted and mad.

"Son, when you want success as much as you wanted that last gulp of air, *then* you will be successful."

And, friend, that's true for you today. It's true for me. Miracles don't just happen. Miracles must be *made* to happen. The desire for a miracle is deep inside you, stirring you all the time. You've got to want to make it happen more than you want anything in life. I know, I've been there hundreds of times, and it's the same every time.

What do you do when you want a miracle that much?

You start desiring it until you get yourself believing God it will happen. This will arouse your faith every time. You already have the faith — the ability to believe. Jesus compared your faith to a mustard seed. He said in Matthew 17:20 when you sow your faith like a seed you plant, then you get yourself to SPEAK TO YOUR MOUNTAIN (of need, of opposition, of things held back from you)... and tell it to be removed from your life! Jesus says in Mark 11:23, "Whosoever shall

SAY unto this mountain, Be thou removed, and...cast into the sea; and shall not doubt in his heart, but shall believe that those things which he SAITH shall come to pass; he shall *have* whatsoever he SAITH."

Speak out to God your need. "Sickness, I want you to go."

"You evil force breaking up my home, I want you to go."

"Unemployment, I speak to you to go."

"Money, I call you into my life."

"Love, inside me, I speak you into action."

"Faith, in my spirit, I speak to you to be released to God in my behalf."

"Satan, I speak in Jesus' name, take your hands off God's property — me!"

I urge you to speak out against the thing that is holding you down...pulling you back...pushing you further behind!

Ask yourself, "What do I want from God today?"

Speak it out!

Desire it with all your heart.

Be willing to take action to get it.

Rise up against the need with your words.

Do as I did when I got up and walked up that dirt road to my uncle's house saying, "I want a piece of that cake." Remember, I didn't stop saying it until I got it. As I think back dozens of years to that tough moment, I still feel the words rising up, "I want a piece of that cake."

Remember the young man who was pushed under the water over and over until he wanted to succeed as much as he wanted that last breath.

God's in business with you. It's time you decided to get in business with Him!

Write here what you really desire in your spirit for God to do for you, right now, this very moment:

1. _____
2. _____
3. _____

Think about it. Examine your heart. Ask yourself: Do I want these things more than anything else in my life? Yes or no!_____

Do I believe God will do this for me?
Yes or no!_____

Now speak out against your need:

"(Need), I command you in Jesus' mighty name, *GO*, be removed from my life...and don't touch my life again — in the name above you, the name of Jesus Christ of Nazareth!"

Say it, say it like you mean it! And keep on saying it until God does it in your life!

YOUR GOD-GIVEN KEY FOR TODAY

"I Will Speak Out The Desires Of My Heart Until I Know God Hears Me And I Receive My Desires."

Key:
THERE IS NO LIMIT TO WHAT GOD CAN DO FOR YOU, EXCEPT THE LIMITS YOU PUT ON GOD

THURSDAY

or
I Won't Hold God Back From Blessing Me!

All of us face struggles in life. *I did.* I do.

I am a man who has faced suffering, personal crises, and family loss. I have been called upon by God to build a university, a seminary, and a medical school and to take His healing power throughout the earth to my generation, including sending medical missionaries worldwide to open the nations to the gospel...and for our full Healing Teams to bring salvation and healing to the people. In all these things, I've struggled, struggled, struggled.

I want to share with you today three powerful ideas that enable me to face up to these difficult struggles, and to continue to emerge stronger and stronger each time. They are ideas for YOUR deliverance as you face your struggles today, and they come from Moses' struggles as told us in Hebrews 11:23-27: "By faith Moses, when he was born, was hid three months of his parents, because they saw he was a proper child; and they were not afraid of the king's commandment. By faith Moses, when he was come to years, refused to be called the son of Pharaoh's daughter; Choosing rather to suffer affliction with the people of God, than to enjoy the pleasures of sin for a season; Esteeming the reproach of Christ greater

23

riches than the treasures in Egypt: for he had respect unto the recompence of the reward. By faith he forsook Egypt, not fearing the wrath of the king: for he endured, as seeing him who is invisible."

FIRST, SEE THE INVISIBLE

This is an idea as old as God, yet so new it may come to some like a totally new discovery. As we read about the new state of Israel, its people drawn like a magnet from the nations of the earth to that priceless little piece of land that is the geographic center of the earth and what the Bible calls "The Promised Land," we are once more inspired to remember that a new idea of God was sent like a rocket to the ends of the earth: God as the invisible God. Yet, mystery of mysteries, *you can see the invisible!*

The Bible tells about a man, Moses, born in slavery, yet rescued by the princess of Egypt to be raised as the prince of all Egypt. At the height of the suffering of his people, the children of Israel, Moses remembered what his mother, Jochebed, had poured into her child's mind: "Moses, there is a God who is unlike the gods of the Egyptians or of any other people. He is not a visible God made of inanimate things and without life or power. His name is Jehovah and He is invisible. And someday, my son, you will develop the faith to see God. Not by your natural eyes but by your spirit, and it is this God who is the one God, the only God, the God who will deliver us. Your faith will see beyond the visible barriers that cloud the vision of all people without faith — and there'll be a moment of destiny for you and for all mankind: you will see the invisible so that the ways of the invisible God are made more real than anything in this world, and the light will shine upon every man."

If you have reached the point in your life where visible things can only do so much for you, and you are still limited to the point of frustration and heading toward utter hopelessness, let me tell you there is a way for you. You can take the limits off God by believing inside yourself there is a God…He is invisible…but more real and alive than the breath in your nostrils.

What is faith? Faith is seeing the visible things around you and believing that back of every one of them is the invisible One who made them all. Faith is allowing yourself to feel again that deep feeling you first felt as a little child that there is *Someone* out there beyond your physical sight…at the edge of your finger tips. Faith is your taking hold of your *will* to determine you believe in this God, that He's all-powerful, all-wise, everywhere present at the same time — and that He is a good God who created you and sent you a Savior, Jesus Christ of Nazareth.

Faith is yielding your spirit to its God-inbuilt urge to allow the Holy Spirit supernaturally to empty you of doubt of God's existence, or doubt of His goodness, or doubt of His care about you…and to fill you with a knowing that you know that you know God is real — and He is your God!

I faced all of this as a 17-year-old boy while struck down by tuberculosis when there was no medicine to cure me or very many Christians who believed God could heal me through prayer. Like Moses, I had parents who believed and lived by the invisible God.

They talked to God so intimately that when I was a small child I actually thought God lived at our house.

I foolishly ran away from home, fell in with the crowd to whom God didn't mean anything. They believed only in what they could see or touch. Soon any thoughts of the invisible God my parents knew

25

better than they knew anyone in the world faded from my life.

I developed tuberculosis and collapsed in a basketball tournament, hemorrhaging to death. Then my coach, Herman Hamilton, picked me up, put me in his car and said, "Son, I'm taking you home to your parents."

Those five death-dealing months of being bedfast gave my father and my mother another chance to awaken in me belief in God. Within days before I surely would have died, Papa knelt to pray for my soul to be saved. Kneeling at the front of my bed, he raised his face and talked to God as if He were in that bedroom. He told God about me while tears ran off his face. And suddenly there was a light on Papa's face and in that light *I saw the invisible.* I knew it was God. No one had to tell me. I knew. Faith leaped in my spirit.

Immediately I heard my own voice calling upon God to come into my life... to let me live... to be His child. I couldn't see Him with my eyes, but all the senses of my being came alive inside me. God came inside me and I knew Him and He knew me. And that was the new beginning of a whole new life for Oral Roberts. And I am alive today — excited, anointed, dreaming dreams and seeing wonders of this invisible God. The God Moses saw, the same One everybody who has seen the invisible sees today.

Although God was invisible to Moses, yet in Hebrews 11:27 we're told he "saw him who is invisible." And it was Moses walking in that light of God's presence inside him and all around him that captured the imagination of two million slaves in Egypt, causing them to throw off their shackles and follow him to the land of Israel.

It's in this generation — yours and mine — that by

our faith we see beyond all limitations of spirit, mind, body, and circumstances. Your faith's sight of God goes beyond 20/20 vision. You see things in perspective. But to see the invisible you have to reach down into your inner self — your real self inside your body called your spirit — and choose to see. The light and the evidence for you to see the invisible is everywhere. Work on your faith, work *with* your faith, let it soar within you to see beyond all things visible to Him who is invisible — and who is the only reality you will ever know.

I'll tell you this: Moses didn't start trying to do the impossible! He "saw" the invisible within his inner self and THEN he set forth to DO the impossible.

Before Moses saw the invisible he was deep into the life of Pharaoh's court, becoming "learned in all the wisdom of Egypt," being trained to take Pharaoh's position, while his own people, the Israelites, were under the cruelest bondage they could suffer. The king's palace, the crown held out to Moses, the promise of all he could see happening to him and his future were in sharp contrast to those enslaved dear ones. They were perishing, soon to be blotted out from all history, a people that would never be while Egypt with its treasures and boundless future would live forever.

But when Moses saw God, the invisible One seen only by faith in his heart, he came to a fork in the road. He had to trust the invisible enough to give him strength to take the next important step in life and choose the imperishable. The Bible tells of Moses' choosing to suffer the afflictions of the people of God rather than to enjoy the pleasures of sin for a season (Hebrews 11:25).

Moses, in seeing the invisible, saw things as they really are. When he compared giving himself over to

27

sin, to disobeying God's Word and separating himself from God's people even though they were in slavery, he clearly saw suffering for God's cause and His people far greater than any visible benefit that could come to him because of any sin he committed.

Moses admitted there is a degree of "pleasure" in sin but only "for a season," or a temporary time and then like a puff of wind such pleasure would be gone and, like the bite of the most poisonous snake, sin would kill.

Everything and anything you choose to do to separate yourself from sin and to identify your life with God is literally imperishable. Neither you nor it will ever perish.

SECOND, CHOOSE THE IMPERISHABLE

When we see the invisible God, suddenly we have a choice to make about our lives. Do we choose God and that which is imperishable, or do we choose sin and its pleasures, which are temporary and perishable?

It's like being at a fork in the road.

I grew up on a farm and I know what those little country roads are like. Most of them are unmarked, and when you get to a fork in the road, you have to trust your sense of direction and your instincts to make the right choice to get where you want to go.

Moses had to make such a decision. On the one hand were God's people. On the other hand was the king's palace. He was raised in Pharaoh's house as a prince of Egypt. He had all the opportunities anyone could ever have had to enjoy the pleasures of sin.

Moses, BY AN ACT OF HIS FAITH, CHOSE THE IMPERISHABLE. He chose to give up the treasures and pleasures of Egypt to believe God, to live his life in a way that was pleasing to God, and to help his people to escape bondage.

When we choose to turn away from that which is sinful — but only lasts for a little while — and turn TOWARD God, we are choosing the road that leads to an everlasting reward. The things of God are eternal. They go beyond the pleasure of the moment. They last forever and ever and ever and ever. Without end.

The Bible says it's "by faith" that you make these choices…and you *can* choose by your faith. No matter what kind of life you're living or how much you've longed to really know God and hear Him speak in your heart and yet don't have that close relationship, you have the faith to choose it to happen to you.

You can do it! And I'm believing with you to do it!

THIRD, DO THE IMPOSSIBLE

The entire Jewish race in every generation since Moses, as well as the whole human race, looks back on Moses doing the impossible as no mortal man has ever done. But I doubt if anyone at the time believed this individual person could do these mighty acts. No one believed…but God!

You know, God is the greatest believer in us human beings. A man said to me, "Oral Roberts, it's so hard for me to believe in God."

I replied, "That used to be my trouble also, but not anymore."

"How did you come to believe in God?" he asked.

I said, "If God can believe in Oral Roberts who has lost his health, has nothing to offer Him, and is soon to leave this world, then surely I can believe in God who is eternal and is the only One who can and will save my life."

If you're having trouble believing in God, just turn

it around and realize how difficult it is for God to believe in you.

Now consider Moses doing the impossible. When he heard God speaking in his spirit, he literally obeyed...trying each time to put God's way and God's plan above his own. That took commitment.

Recently a noted heart doctor walked up to me on the golf course. "Oral," he said, "will you write a little book on how a person can hear God's voice...really how I can hear Him in my spirit?"

I told him, "You'll be surprised just how simple it is to hear God speak inside you. In fact, you have to uncomplicate yourself, get simple in your thinking like a child, and LISTEN!"

He said, "You mean if I will listen I will hear God speak to *me?*"

I said, "Yes. Try it. And you'll hear God because He speaks to everyone."

But again it takes commitment to listen.

I've been four decades in this ministry, of seeing God in my spirit, of choosing the imperishable with all my heart, and — yes — of doing the impossible. And the older I get, the simpler I believe it is. If I had it to do over, I'd listen more inside myself. I know I would have heard God more often...and more clearly. I praise Him that I have listened to His voice. Because of it, He brought me out of nothing and made my living worth something. And the rest of my life I'm committed — absolutely — to listen, listen, listen.

One thing I want to point out that's very important to you is that Moses did those things through *struggle*. Moses struggled to STOP playing around with sin and with trying to become a prince in Egypt where all the so-called glory was. He struggled to get down in the trenches with his suffering people, the children of Israel, under Pharaoh's whip. He found no easy way, no short cuts, no free lunches — just plain struggle. If he hadn't used his faith to see the invisible God…to choose the imperishable…he couldn't have done the impossible.

I tell you on the authority of the infallible Word of God, out of the experience of every believer who's accomplished anything, and out of my own entire life, you do the impossible through struggle. I've often called myself Oral *"Struggle"* Roberts — because struggle is so much a part of my life and accomplishments it seems like it should be my name.

I'm honored that I've traveled this far through faith and struggle and seen God enable me to do things totally impossible, and that He still lets me do it. I exalt Him in it.

No! I don't like struggle or persecution or any of the stuff Satan and men throw at me constantly. But they always overplay their hand, particularly when I choose to reach down inside my inner self and declare I will be God's man, I will obey God, I won't quit, and I won't be defeated.

If this sounds like bragging, it's not; it's simply truth, the same as Moses' experience with God was truth, the same as yours is or will be truth.

Only you can hold God back from blessing you or limit Him, or fall apart inside yourself. He created you with the inner ability to SEE THE INVISIBLE… CHOOSE THE IMPERISHABLE…DO THE IMPOSSIBLE. Like getting in your car, turning the key in the switch to start the motor, shift into forward gear and drive, you can turn your faith loose this instant and go over the top… with God.

Make up your mind to start doing it NOW!

31

YOUR GOD-GIVEN KEY FOR TODAY

"I Determine To See The Invisible God...
I Choose The Imperishable Life...
I Will Do The Impossible
With God's Help."

**Key:
DON'T LET SATAN TRICK
YOU INTO INTERRUPTING
YOUR FAITH OR TO COME
OUT OF YOUR FAITH**

FRIDAY

**or
How My Mother Taught Me
One Of The Greatest Lessons I Ever Learned**

Friday is for most people the end of a working week, when they can walk away and look forward to the weekend and to rest, recreation, a change. Whether your workweek ends on Friday or some other day, you get what I'm saying.

Well, miracles have to be made to happen just like your workweek has to be made to happen — by you! God isn't going to have His Son die again, or rise from the dead again, or put any more miracle power in your world. God, the full God, is here. But once you use your faith to start a miracle, you must set your faith to keep the miracle happening, then not take off any weekends with your faith.

If you interrupt your faith with anything, or you take off some time not to use your faith, the miracle you got going will STOP!

I know, I've been there time and time again. And I

still have to remind myself: Oral, stay in faith; Oral, keep believing God; Oral, never give in; Oral, never interrupt your faith!

Shortly after my healing from tuberculosis began at age 17, I became aware that the excitement was dying down and the surge of new health in my lungs appeared to be waning. At that time I didn't know why but I entertained the idea that my healing was a flash-in-the-pan — my miracle wasn't going to last, or my strength wasn't coming back fast enough.

I really couldn't grasp what was happening and I came terribly close to interrupting my faith or shutting off the very believing I had begun to do the night the man of God laid his hands on me and prayed these words, "You foul, tormenting disease, I command you in the name of Jesus Christ of Nazareth, you come out of this boy...you come out...and enter him no more forever!"

But now doubts struck me, I felt weaker and weaker. Then I learned one of the greatest lessons in life.

My mother discovered me one afternoon sitting with my back to the wall against the side of the house and she said, "Oral, you're beginning to believe you weren't really healed, aren't you?"

"Well, Mamma," I replied, "why do I still feel so weak? Why don't I feel strong like I did the other night when I was prayed for?"

"Oral, don't forget you've been sick a long time. You've been five months in bed and lost the power to walk. The tuberculosis had taken root in your lungs before that. God has begun to heal you and your miracle has started. You've got to remember two things."

"What are they?"

MAMMA SAID I HAD TO
REMEMBER TWO VERY IMPORTANT THINGS

"First, each day when you feel weak, think back to the power of God you felt surging through your body and opening your lungs to breathe free again and remember that was God's *touch, His instant touch of healing in you.* But it may take weeks, maybe months, for the miracle of complete healing to happen so you'll get all your strength back. You'll have to start doing some light work so your strength will grow."

"Well, Mamma, why do I get so weak I have to lie down some during the day?"

"Oral, that's the second thing I want to tell you. It's all right for you to be down an hour or two a day for a while. But don't take off your clothes and put on your pajamas. Just lie across the bed with your clothes on."

"What good will that do?"

"Son, if you undress, get into your pajamas, and get under the covers, the whole image of your five months in bed will come back in your mind. You'll see this thing coming back on you. If you lie down on top of the bedcovers fully dressed, you'll think you're only resting to help get your strength back. Do it like I tell you and you'll fully recover. And you will learn what started can be completed."

Mamma was right. I did exactly like she said. With every discouragement — and there were lots of them — I remembered the night God's healing power entered my body and opened up my lungs and let me breathe all the way down without hemorrhaging. I lived it in my spirit and mind over and over. When I took naps during the day I didn't crawl under the covers but lay with my clothes on across the covers. Slowly, but surely, I felt my strength renewed. And within 12 months I had regained my weight from a skeletonlike 120 pounds to a robust 165 pounds.

There was a flash in my eyes, a lift to my shoulders, a spring in my step, and faith in my soul. And I had preached my first little sermon!

Time after time I've looked back and tried to understand the wisdom my mother gave me. I believe she was telling me not to interrupt my faith…not to take a weekend off this most important thing in my life…not to stop the making of that miracle to restore my life — and keep it restored.

WHEN YOU
START YOUR FAITH — DON'T LET UP ON IT

I believe my mother was saying God's truth that your faith can start your miracle and letting up on your faith can retard that same miracle or stop it altogether.

When anything strikes at my health now, I get serious about it instantly. I have developed an attitude, a lifestyle, a habit with the way I use my faith. I can't say it's perfect, but it beats any other way I know. First, I start getting hold of myself, I mean my inner self — my spirit — and shift the gears of my mind to think on great things God has done for me, like that first burst of healing energy in my tubercular lungs.

It's amazing how many miracles God has done in you that you can't explain in rational terms — but you *can* bring them into your thoughts and literally THINK ON THEM.

There's a Scripture I often turn to and read over and over. It's Philippians 4:8. "Finally, brethren, whatever things are true, whatever things are honest, whatever things are just, whatever things are pure, whatever things are lovely, whatever things are of

35

good report; if there be any virtue, and if there be any praise, think on these things."

It's the devil's business to tempt you to forget God and all His providences in your life or family — and to have you think only on the bad things. But greater is God who is in you than Satan who is in the world, the Bible says, and here God strongly tells you to think on whatever is

> true...
> honest...
> just...
> pure...
> lovely...
> of good report...
> virtue...
> praise...

both in your past and in your NOW.

He says, "THINK ON THESE THINGS."

The good thing is you have the God-given power to think like this. I know when I do it I am enormously strengthened in every way.

I TRY TO GET INTO AGREEMENT — AND NOT COME OUT OF IT

Second, when my health is attacked I try immediately to get people who believe God heals to pray for me...to start agreeing with their faith joined with mine — and not to come out of the agreement — that I will be able to overcome.

It's sometimes hard to pray for yourself, especially when you're in pain...or have received a bad health report...or you get real ill. This is why the Bible says to "call" for prayer and not wait until someone finally discovers you're sick or in trouble.

I literally practice James 5:14-16, "Is any sick

among you? let him call for the elders of the church; and let them pray over him, anointing him with oil in the name of the Lord: And the prayer of faith shall save the sick, and the Lord shall raise him up; and if he have committed sins, they shall be forgiven him. Confess your faults one to another, and pray one for another, that ye may be healed. The effectual fervent prayer of a righteous man availeth much."

I ask for the anointing oil and hands laid on me in believing prayer, just like the Bible says. And with whatever faith I have, little faith or middle faith or great faith, I give it all. I've got to get well.

The churches that practice James 5:14-16 and are eager to get involved with you in your healing and wholeness can really help you — if you let them by bringing your needs to their attention and cooperation.

Television programs coming directly through the screen into your home — or wherever you are — that present Jesus in whole-person salvation, healing, and biblical prosperity are very important to your total well-being.

The Bible and good books on God's delivering power are also very helpful.

I hate sickness with a passion and love health with a passion. I'm *not* going to turn away from anything God has put on earth for my health and wholeness — spiritually, physically, financially, and in my family and work.

Third, and this one can be first or second, depending on any number of factors: I get hold of my physician, by phone, or by having someone call for me, or I get there as quickly as I can AND I faithfully follow my physician's orders. Another thing I do, I pay my doctor bills, not only because it's right, but because only then have I completed my part of what he and I can *do together* for my recovery. I find in

37

getting well and staying well that it's important to follow through — all the way.

I love God who heals me and in only a slightly lesser sense I love the people who pray for me and the physicians who medicate me. To be frank, I make no difference in my faith in God to heal me through prayer or medicine or by both at the same time. To me, the Source of my healing and health is GOD. People who help me with their prayer and faith and medical skills and prescriptions are all instruments God uses. They can't heal me themselves but God through their loving ministrations *CAN!*

YOU HAVE TO MAKE THINGS HAPPEN

The bottom line of *GUIDE TO MIRACLES,* as far as I am concerned, is that *you have to make things happen,* they don't happen by themselves. That's why you have God, His ministers and other health-care helpers, His divinely implanted ability in you to think on good things and to plant good seeds, and every other thing that is based on His Holy Word for you to live by on this earth.

This may sound trite but remember, you live in your physical body 24 hours a day, every day. In addition, remember inside that body is the real you: your spirit, your inner self made in the image of God. Your spirit and body are tied together in some mysterious way by your mind, your intellect, your brain power. You're not just a body, or a mind, or a spirit — you're all three; a whole person-to-be!

Keep your faith moving. Don't interrupt its action or go on a weekend binge from it or on a vacation.

The Bible says, "We live by faith!" and we can add: we can't live without it!

I hope you'll remember what Mamma told me,

"Don't put on your pajamas." I hope you'll remember her telling me, "Remember how you felt when you felt God's healing power when you were prayed for and keep this in your mind." I hope you'll remember Philippians 4:8 and James 5:14-16 and I pray you'll get on your own case immediately when something goes wrong and call for help as well as help yourself. Make prayer agreements with other believers, also with good physicians, and don't come out of agreement that things are going to work out in your life.

YOUR GOD-GIVEN KEY FOR TODAY

"Miracles Have To Be Made To Happen And By My Faith, God And I Will Make Them Happen In My Life..."

SATURDAY

**Key:
GOD WORKS HIS MIRACLES ACCORDING TO A "DYNAMIC TENSION" OF THE NATURAL AND SUPERNATURAL**

**or
I Will Put Myself In Position
To Use All Of God's Methods For My Miracles**

Early in this ministry I began to apply the principle of what scientists call "dynamic tension" to the healing of the sick...and to helping people get their needs met in every area of their lives. And it has

39

worked fantastically so that now I can bring it strongly into your thinking and practicing for your miracles.

I'd like to illustrate this by telling you when I was growing up on a farm in Pontotoc County, Oklahoma, we didn't own a washing machine. Mamma used an old number-two tub and a rub board. It was my job to stretch the clothesline for her so she could hang our clothes on it to dry them.

I'd climb the clothesline poles and pull so the lines would be tight enough to hold the wet clothes. Now if I pulled too tight, the line would break and the clothes would fall to the ground. Mamma would say, "Oral, you pick those clothes up." Then she'd have to get that old rub board and rinse them again.

On the other hand, if I didn't tighten the line enough, the clothes would really start to flap when the wind began to blow — which it can do in Oklahoma — and pretty soon the clothes would drag on the ground and get dirty. Again, Mamma would have to rewash them.

Well, it didn't take me long to understand how important it was to tighten the line in proper balance or Mamma would be "after me" and I'd have to do it all over again.

When we built Oral Roberts University I discussed this principle of things being in balance with our engineers. They told me there's a principle called "dynamic tension." It's that point where something is pulled together just tight enough to do the job. Not too tight. Not too loose. Just tight enough to be in balance.

JESUS' INCARNATION
WAS IN "DYNAMIC TENSION"

We are learning more and more in the spiritual

and physical realm of God's delivering power for our lives that it was in this perfect state of "dynamic tension" that God sent His Son to earth in what we call in theology, the incarnation: God himself dwelling in the flesh of Mary's son, Jesus.

The divine nature of Jesus came from God. The human nature came from His mother, Mary. God-incarnated-in-Jesus made Him fully God and fully man at the same time. Fully human to sit where we sit and feel what we feel. Finally, God to have the power to deliver us from our hurts and ills — to save us!

The incarnation is a mystery and you and I will never understand it by our human reasoning but only by our faith.

Thank God for faith!

Well, I began to understand through the Word of God — and out of my own faith in God — that when Jesus came to earth He created the "dynamic tension" for miracles. As the Son of God He took the supernatural power of God from heaven and as the son of man He took the natural power of God in earth *and He joined them together.*

So, put it the way I helped Mamma with the clothesline. Jesus stretched the supernatural and the natural line until they were in perfect balance — just right for us to get our miracles.

At 17 in my illness the very first thing my father did was to call our family doctor to treat me and people to come and pray for me. Someone said in jest, "The greatest thing one can do is to choose his parents." One thing I know, I had the right parents. Papa was very strong on medicine but still with a belief in prayer and Mamma was very strong on prayer but still with a belief in medicine. In reality, they never divided them and I never learned to look to doctors alone or to prayer alone. They taught me it is God who heals, no matter what method He uses.

I've had this balance all through the years and I've been able to help millions of people to get into a state of "dynamic tension" in the supernatural and natural power of God to heal and to meet their needs.

Only God knows how many people have suffered sickness too long or died needlessly because they tried to force God into a box, because they insisted they would get well either by medical science alone or by prayer alone.

JESUS SHOWS YOU WHAT THE FATHER IS LIKE

Now, let me say something that can really help along this line. If God had divided the supernatural from the natural we never would have had a Savior, our Lord Jesus Christ. And most of us never would have understood God as well as we do today. For example, when Philip, one of the twelve disciples of Jesus, asked Him, "Show us the Father and it will satisfy us" (John 14:8), Jesus answered, "Philip, if you have seen Me, you have seen the Father."

In other words Jesus was telling us: *I've come to show you what God is like.*

For me, Oral Roberts, I was totally incapable of seeing or understanding in my spirit God who is invisible. The great Hebrew prophets cried, "Hear, O Israel: The Lord our God is one Lord" (Deuteronomy 6:4).

From our Hebrew fathers in the faith we've learned that God is one God, a God so holy, so powerful, so awesome, that we scarcely dare say His name.

When we look at the history of the children of Israel, whose father Abraham was the first to discover that God is the most high God, in possession of heaven and earth and is the One who delivers us from all our enemies (Genesis 14:20), we see them having a proper reverential awe of God yet they have a lot of fear about just how to approach a God they couldn't see or of whom no graven image was to be made.

But "in the fulness of time" (Galatians 4:4) God knew the only way mankind as a whole would relate to Him in a close, personal, intimate way was to send His own Son in human flesh and for Him to do the things that God does to show us what God is like: a good God, a near God, a prayer-hearing-and-answering God, a miracle-working God, a God who works with things He created both in earth AND heaven to meet our needs, a "God who is the Source of our total supply, a God who is the way, the truth, and the life for each of us."

MY MEETING WITH TWO JEWISH RABBIS

Recently two Jewish rabbi friends of mine and I were discussing Jesus. He is almost incomprehensible to our Jewish brothers and they made me see that very clearly. Being a Gentile I was having difficulty in being of any help to such learned men in Old Testament Hebrew and Jewish life to which we owe so much.

Finally it hit me. I said, "If nothing else, remember I wasn't born a Jew with the inborn link back to Abraham, Isaac, and Jacob, Moses and David, and all the great Jewish prophets. I was born a part of that vast Gentile world of billions who had little or no connection with the God of the ancient Jewish patriarchs and kings and prophets. The Gentiles worshiped gods totally unlike the God of Israel, the invisible and eternal God. I certainly couldn't grasp God because I hadn't seen Him. I couldn't visualize

Him and at the point of death with tuberculosis as a 17-year-old I was without hope. Only when God gave me a vision in which I saw a flash of Jesus in my father's countenance did the true God become real to me. When Jesus became real to me the Father became real to me and I was converted and healed and given a healing ministry."

The rabbis indicated this was a view they hadn't thought of. As a result, there seemed to be a warming up and a better understanding of appreciation come among us. I really appreciated that they prayed to God for me and I had the privilege of praying to God for them.

The only way I know it and can explain it is that Jesus, in "the brightness of his glory, and the image of his person" (Hebrews 1:3), is the only One who makes us see the Father and relate to Him by His Holy Spirit!

And that means neither you, nor I, nor anyone can divide the spiritual from the natural. We must relate to God to work His wonders in us ANY WAY HE CHOOSES.

GET EVERYTHING GOD OFFERS FOR YOUR HEALING

In my illness I got everything medicine had to offer at a time before the antibiotic drugs had been discovered which can cure tuberculosis today. And I got everything prayer could do for me at a time when not many preachers or other Christians of our generation believed it was God's will to heal supernaturally. In both instances — medically and in prayer — it came down to one doctor, then two others that my family knew, then to one preacher who prayed the prayer of faith for me although many were praying in one way or another in my behalf.

But not once did my parents or I question that my healing — or my cure — came directly from God as the Source of healing and wholeness.

During this period in my life, just one block from where we lived there was a friend of my brother's whose bodily functions became clogged. His family called the same doctor who had treated me but the man refused to let the doctor treat him on the grounds he wanted to "trust God" for his healing and be healed by prayer only. He died 21 days later.

After his death I heard our doctor tell Papa, "Ellis, we have a simple medical procedure which I could have used to help this man in minutes. I'm convinced that he died needlessly, leaving a wife and seven little children. As you know, I believe in prayer too but didn't the Almighty put things in the earth and help us doctors learn to use them?"

I heard Papa agree with him and say, "Some day there will come a new understanding that all healing comes from God. He only uses different methods."

I never forgot that and I'm excited that gradually we are seeing the merging of God's healing streams and that we are more and more seeing God as the Source of our healing and wholeness.

I've heard some doctors say privately and a few say on television, "I don't believe God heals through prayer. I don't accept the idea of miracles."

I've also heard some preachers and other Christians say privately and a few on television say, "I believe God heals by prayer and faith only. I don't need doctors."

The tragedy of this kind of thinking is that when we go too far in dividing the natural from the supernatural it's like cutting Jesus up into two separate parts of being divine without being human and human without being divine, and the tragedy on a personal level is that more people don't get well and some die needlessly.

LINE YOUR THOUGHTS UP WITH GOD'S WORD

It's really up to you and me — to all of us — to line our thoughts and beliefs up with the Word of God and Jesus in the incarnation, which is to say we get into the state of dynamic tension of the supernatural and the natural force of God in our lives.

The publishing of this book is a celebration of four decades of this healing ministry. I can tell you many, many miracles have occurred. Perhaps the greatest one to me personally is that I am alive and healthy and ready for 20 more years. But it's no accident. It's no happenstance. I've fought for every breath I've breathed, every ounce of health I've had, and I am in constant dynamic tension with strong prayer and good medical care. In fact, I call people to pray for me or I write them or I ask them in person. I also call my physicians and I carry out what they share with me very carefully and continually.

Both those who pray for me and medically treat me have been kind enough to say I'm their prime example of a person believing God wants us all to have top health and to prosper spiritually, physically, and financially.

YOU HAVE TO LIVE
IN YOUR BODY 24 HOURS A DAY

When something starts going wrong in my body, I get on it immediately — and I stay on it! I have to live in this body 24 hours a day and I want to be well and whole!

When the physicians who help me and I have a

chance to talk, I always sincerely show my deepest appreciation but they know I give the credit or the glory to God. I've never seen one of them offended by this. They tell me, "We serve you with our best in medicine but we too believe it is God who heals."

To those who pray the prayer of faith for me, I say: "Thank you for praying for me and I give the glory to God."

The main thing with me is to be grateful to those who pray, to those who medicate, to those who help me in any way at all...and to praise God as the Source of the help I receive. To me there can be no dividing up of the supernatural and natural for it is God who said, "I am the Lord that healeth thee" (Exodus 15:26). And it was the Apostle Paul who had Dr. Luke, the physician, join his evangelistic/missionary team in the first century to spread the gospel of Jesus Christ of Nazareth to the nations (Acts 16-28).

Let me ask you, "What do you think, what do you say, how do you react to help you receive from those who minister spiritually to you for your health and wholeness and to physicians who minister the medicines that come out of God's earth to you?"

Maybe my practice will help you. I'm in constant prayer and in a ceaseless attitude of faith that both prayer and medicine are blessed of God to heal me. I tell myself this over and over. I cultivate the idea GOD IS MAKING ME WELL THROUGH THESE, HIS INSTRUMENTALITIES.

I say again to you, work with the dynamic tension God has made possible through His supernatural and natural forces. It's to your advantage in every need of your life in every moment of your existence to have your faith in action toward God to work His miracles in you both supernaturally and naturally. I

47

encourage you in this and I stand with you with the full force of my faith.

YOUR GOD-GIVEN KEY FOR TODAY

Say this over and over on a daily basis.

"I Am In Dynamic Tension In My Spirit, Mind, And Body With God's Supernatural And Natural Power!"

FIRST WEEK

I can have a new miracle in my life every day.

SUNDAY I EXPECT A NEW MIRACLE EVERY DAY... AND THAT MEANS TODAY!

MONDAY I WILL CALL MY NEED OF A MIRACLE BY NAME...SPECIFICALLY!

TUESDAY I OPEN MYSELF RIGHT NOW TO GOD'S NEXT MIRACLE...FOR ME!

WEDNESDAY I WILL SPEAK OUT THE DESIRES OF MY HEART UNTIL I KNOW GOD HEARS ME AND I RECEIVE MY DESIRES

THURSDAY I DETERMINE TO SEE THE INVISIBLE GOD...I CHOOSE THE IMPERISHABLE LIFE...I WILL DO THE IMPOSSIBLE WITH GOD'S HELP

FRIDAY MIRACLES HAVE TO BE MADE TO HAPPEN AND BY MY FAITH, GOD AND I WILL MAKE THEM HAPPEN IN MY LIFE

SATURDAY I AM IN DYNAMIC TENSION IN MY SPIRIT, MIND, AND BODY WITH GOD'S SUPERNATURAL AND NATURAL POWER!

SECOND WEEK

No Matter How Bad The Situation, "God Can Turn It Around" For Me When I Turn Around To God

By Richard Roberts

SUNDAY

**Key:
I CAN SURVIVE THE
EXPLOSIONS OF MY LIFE**

or

**How, In The Midst Of A War-Torn Nation,
God Showed Me That He Knows
The Layout Of The Devil's Minefield
Against Me...And He Can Reveal It To Me**

Several years ago, God spoke to my heart that He was going to send me to 40 nations across the earth to preach the message of His gospel and to pray for the sick. One of those nations was war-torn Northern Ireland, where I conducted a crusade in 1985. God taught me something very important while I was there that I want to share with you. Because in this uncertain time we live in, it's vital that we remember that no matter what explosions the devil brings against our lives, Jesus knows the layout of the devil's minefield and He can reveal it to us and deliver us from it.

God brought that truth home to me as I was ministering in and traveling throughout Belfast, one of the most violent, dangerous cities in the world today. It's a city that has had explosion after explosion. As I traveled, I saw places that had been bombed out and still were in ashes, piled high with rubble. As I saw those places, God began to speak to me about the explosions the devil sets for my life and for your life...and how we can survive them.

One of the people who explained a great deal to me about the bombings and attacks in Belfast was our dear friend, Pastor Leslie Hale. He knows from personal experience what it's like to live in a "war zone."

51

I'll never forget one story in particular that he told me. This is what he said:

"Years ago during the height of the bombings and terrorist activity in Belfast, I was in Tulsa visiting the Oral Roberts University campus. While I was at ORU, I bought a reproduction of a painting of Jesus and took it home with me. In Belfast, I took the painting to a shop to get it framed so I could hang it on my wall.

"The days passed and I forgot about the painting. Meanwhile, bombings and explosions were happening with great intensity all over the city.

"Then one day I remembered the painting and I drove to the shop to pick it up, wondering all the while if it would still be there. When I arrived at the shop, I discovered that the shop had been completely destroyed by an explosion.

"I jumped out of my car and saw the man who owned the shop standing in the rubble. When he saw me, the shopkeeper said, 'My wife and children and I got out safely. But everything in the store has been destroyed — every painting, every frame, every picture. Except one.'

"Then I watched as he walked over to a burned-out corner of what had once been his shop, reached up on a shelf, and pulled out a picture. As he unrolled it I could see that it was my picture of Jesus…with only a few marks on it. The shopkeeper held the picture out to me and said, 'Only Jesus survived the explosion.'"

As Leslie told me that story, I thought to myself about the explosions of life that you and I face every day. No matter what country we live in, or who we are, or how old or young we are, we all face things that go wrong every day.

I thought about how the devil fills people's hearts with hatred, violence, and such despair, how he would like to destroy the nation of Northern Ireland, and how he would like to destroy *you*...and me. Sometimes he brings the explosions in the form of sickness and disease ...sometimes in the form of marriage and family problems...sometimes in your relationship with God, in your finances, or in your emotions.

But then...I remembered the good news! And I want you to remember it too. For with *Jesus* in your heart and at the center of everything you do

YOU CAN SURVIVE THE EXPLOSIONS OF LIFE!

Jesus alone knows where the explosions in your life will happen next. He understands the layout of the devil's minefield. And with Jesus in your heart, He lets you see the layout of that minefield. Suddenly you know what to do to avoid many of the explosions the devil would like to use to destroy you. And if an explosion has already hit or if one takes you by surprise, you can *survive* it.

You know, I don't have many long-term plans for my life. I know I have to stay in constant communication with Jesus so that with each day that comes I'll know what step to take. And if Jesus doesn't talk to me, I don't know which way to go.

Is it that way with you? If it's not, I believe you need to get into a relationship like that with Jesus so that you can be led by Him. Because, friend...

the devil's minefield is
out there waiting for you.

You may need to change the way you've thought before because life is serious. It's tough. And nowhere in the Bible does it say that it's going to get any easier. In fact, it says that as we come nearer and nearer to Christ's returning to this earth, it's going to get even harder.

We all need the security of knowing that we have Someone who can guide us through the devil's minefield and who can help us survive the explosions of life. That Someone is Jesus Christ of Nazareth.

I WANT TO PRAY WITH YOU RIGHT NOW

Father, I pray for that one reading these words who does not have a personal relationship with You through Your Son Jesus Christ. Move on their heart, Lord, to open their life to You today and say, "Jesus, come into my heart. I accept You as my personal Lord and Savior this day. Give me the security that only comes in knowing that You will show me where the devil's minefields are and that You will walk with me through every explosion of life that I face."

And, friend, if you already know Jesus, I pray that day by day you will become more sensitive to His voice and His Spirit within you.

I come against that explosion in your life — whether it be physical, financial, emotional, or in the family — and I command it to loose you and let you go free, in Jesus' mighty name. Amen and amen.

Jesus has already done His part. Now you must do yours.

YOUR GOD-GIVEN KEY FOR TODAY

"I Can Survive The Explosions Of My Life."

Then believe it!

MONDAY Key: I CAN CALL FOR HELP

or
Jesus' Disciples Asked The Burning Question, "Is There Any Sick Among You?" And Jesus Has Called Me To Ask It Of You Today

"Is there any sick among you?" That's the question I asked the tremendous crowd that filled my most recent visit to Madison Square Garden's Felt Forum. And that's the question I'm asking you today: Is there any sick among you?

That phrase was the burning question of the early Christians to one another in the first century after the death and resurrection of Jesus. Those men and women had been with Jesus. They had heard Him preach. They had seen Him lay hands on the sick and they had watched the sick recover.

They had watched Jesus as He multiplied the loaves and the fishes, and they had also heard the story about how He took the money out of the fish's mouth to pay the taxes. They knew about the centurion whose servant had been healed and the woman with the issue of blood who said, "If I can only touch the hem of His garment, I will be healed."

They had seen Jesus crucified. They had seen that stone catapulted from its socket when Jesus was raised from the dead. They'd seen Him in His unlimited form by receiving the Holy Spirit. They'd experienced His power and His touch in their lives.

When they walked into the temple or into someone's home as they walked along the seashore of Galilee, the first thing that would come to their minds was, "Is there any sick among you?"

Is there any sick among you spiritually? Is there anyone who does not know Jesus as your personal Savior?

Is there any sick among you physically? Is there anyone who needs healing in your body?

Is there any sick among you financially? Meaning, "Is there someone who is in need financially?"

Is there any sick among you emotionally? Is there someone fearful or discouraged or in despair?

Wherever the disciples went, that was the burning question they asked. And that question was recorded by the Apostle James in the Bible.

After James had asked the question, "Is there any sick among you?" he went on to say, "Let him call for the elders of the church; and let them pray over him, anointing him with oil in the name of the Lord: And the prayer of faith shall save the sick, and the Lord shall raise him up" (James 5:14,15).

"Is there any sick among you?" was the burning call of the early Christians because they lived in perilous times. They were oppressed by the Roman government. They were aware that at any moment they might lose their lives. Many of their meetings were held behind locked doors, in catacombs, and in caves because of their fear they might be arrested. And many *were* put in jail, while others were boiled in oil, decapitated, or fed to the lions in the Roman Colosseum. Some, like the Apostle Peter, were even crucified.

So you can see that after Jesus' death and resurrection, the early Church was totally immersed in the healing ministry. Then something happened that changed that.

OUR THINKING ABOUT HEALING GOT OFF THE TRACK AND SOMETIMES IT'S STILL OFF TODAY

In the fourth century when Constantine took over the Roman Empire, he stopped the persecution of Christians and declared that the state religion would be Christianity. And something happened to those believers when their persecution ended. It's the same thing that often happens to you and me when our life suddenly becomes too easy: we become complacent. We lose the drive inside us to persevere...to "win" in spite of the hardships we encounter. And without any real problems to plague us, we sometimes invent new ones.

When the early believers were no longer persecuted for their faith in Jesus, their zeal for evangelism grew cold. The burning fire in their heart to pray for the sick grew cold. They stopped asking the question, "Is there any sick among you?" and they started looking for a new way to suffer for the Lord.

Someone came up with the idea, *We'll suffer for the Lord through our sickness.* They decided, *It must be God's will for us to be sick. And if it's God's will for us to get sick, then God will heal us IF it be His will.* And that thought still pervades the Church today.

How many times have you prayed — or heard someone else pray — "Lord, if it be Your will, heal this person," as if God had not already made up His mind about healing His own children?

MY OWN FATHER WOULD NOT BE HERE IF SOMEONE HADN'T HAD THEIR THINKING STRAIGHT ABOUT GOD'S DESIRE TO HEAL

I remember so many times hearing my dad give his testimony of how he was healed of tuberculosis...

57

hearing him tell how a minister came to his home where he had been in bed for five months hemorrhaging to death with tuberculosis. And the minister, as well intentioned as he probably was, came in and prayed, "Lord, if it be Your will, heal Oral Roberts." Then he looked at my dad and said, "Son, be patient."

Well, my dad has said many times that if he had been patient he would have died! It wasn't until his sister Jewel came to him and said, "Oral, God is going to heal you," and until another man of God laid hands on him and prayed — with the authority of God behind his prayers — "Thou foul, tormenting disease, loose this boy and let him go free," that my dad believed he could be healed …and *was* healed in a way that's lasted to this very day.

And, friend, I'll tell you, if my dad had died of tuberculosis as a teenager, Richard Roberts never would have been born. Millions of lives never would have been touched with the power of the gospel as they're being touched through the ministry God has given me today.

I don't know about you, but that's a very sobering thought to me.

WE CAN'T BE PATIENT WITH SICKNESS

Friend, don't let the devil deceive you. Sickness is *not* your friend; disease and destruction are not from God. These things are from our enemy, the devil. God isn't pleased with our suffering; He's provided a way for us to be healed and made whole. That way is JESUS. Through Jesus' death on the cross and His resurrection we can be healed. First Peter 2:24 says, "Who his own self bare our sins in his own body on the tree…by whose stripes YE WERE HEALED." That tells me that God wants us to be healed!

But before God can heal us, we have to get impatient with our sickness. WE'VE GOT TO COME AGAINST IT IN THE NAME OF JESUS. We've got to get into action against our sickness and take advantage of all of God's avenues of healing that are available to us — such as the prayer of faith, medical science, good nutrition, to name just a few.

We've got to get back into the mind-set that the early Christians had where we know that sickness is not from God and where we are not hesitant to say to one another, "Is there any sick among you?" and then to lay hands on the sick and pray, *believing* that they will recover.

I believe with all my heart that this ministry was raised up for one main reason — to lift up a standard and once again begin to ask the question, "Is there any sick among you?" and to pray the prayer of faith...to let people know that God is still God of your life and my life today, that He's real, that He's alive, that He hasn't changed.

Malachi 3:6 says, "I am the Lord, I change not." People change. Circumstances change. Things change. But God does not change. He's just as real, just as powerful today, as He was when Jesus walked the dusty roads of Judea. And He's reaching out to you today with healing for you — body, mind, and soul — but you must also reach out to Him.

"LET HIM CALL..."

In the Bible, James went on to say something else we must do when we are sick. Because you and I must do our part; God will never do it all for us. James said that when we are sick, we must "call"...or *ask* for help (James 5:14). That WE must call. God's Word doesn't say that someone else will do our calling for us. It says, "Let him call. Let her call."

This ministry has a 24-hour-a-day, 7-day-a-week telephone prayer line that you can call for prayer any time you're sick or hurting. When you call, a member of the Abundant Life Prayer Group — someone who knows how to pray and touch God for your need — will pray with you and then pass your prayer request on to me and my dad and we'll pray for you also.

The number is (918) 495-7777.

Or another way you can "call" for help is by writing me or my dad a letter, where we can write you back an encouraging word from the Bible and pray the prayer of faith over the needs you have shared with us.

Our mailing address is: Richard Roberts or Oral Roberts, Tulsa, OK 74171.

You can ask your pastor to pray for you or perhaps a friend who knows the Lord and who believes in the power of prayer as you do. But whatever you do, don't become complacent toward your sickness. Don't be patient with it. Reach out for your healing as God's Word tells you to do. Call out for help. There *is* something you can do.

And I believe that when you do it, you'll experience God's healing power in a way you've never known it before.

YOUR GOD-GIVEN KEY FOR TODAY

"I Can Call For Help!"

Then believe...according to God's Word...He will *hear* your call and *answer* it! (See Isaiah 65:24.)

TUESDAY

**Key:
I CAN FIND GOD'S
MIRACLE METHOD
FOR SOLVING
MY PROBLEM**

or
**How A Friend Of This Ministry
Learned That God's Miracle Methods
Come To You When You Need Them Most**

Have you ever had a problem that seemed to have
no solution? You've pondered the situation for days,
weeks, months, or even years and yet have no answer.
You've attacked the problem from every conceivable
angle, and still you find no workable solution to it.

I think everyone's been in that position from time
to time and knows the frustration that comes from it.
As human beings, we often just throw up our hands
and say, "It's impossible! There *is* no solution to the
situation I'm facing."

But the good news is: that for every problem *you*
have, *God* has a miracle method for solving it. The
Bible says it like this in Matthew 19:26, "With God
ALL things are possible."

A guest on my daily TV program who is a regent of
Oral Roberts University and a farmer from Rocky
Ford, Colorado, shared how he learned that truth one
day. His name is Frank Holder and he was one of the
first major producers of little white pearl onions in
this country.

This is the story Frank shared about how he
discovered God's miracle method for solving his
particular "unsolvable" problem.

"When we first started growing pearl onions,"
Frank said, "we had trouble separating the tiny onions

61

from the dirt that had been dug up with them. We tried everything we could think of — a shaker, a drum, a vibrating screen — but nothing worked. We had the biggest mess you ever saw with dust all over town and a huge pile of dirt, but still no solution.

"Then one day one of our field trucks overturned and, by accident, dumped a whole load of onions into an irrigation ditch full of water. I'll tell you, I was so discouraged at that point that I just sat down and cried! When I calmed myself enough to look up, I noticed that there were little white objects floating on top of the water. Suddenly I realized, 'Those are my onions! And the water has separated them from the dirt!'

"In the midst of what appeared to be hopeless, the Lord had given us the answer to our problem. He had turned a situation of apparent defeat into one of victory."

Frank Holder is a man who believes in miracles and who knows that sometimes when things look the darkest, God's miracle answer is right around the corner.

Jesus used many miracle methods for solving the problems of people who came to Him for help. Sometimes He spoke the word of faith and storms became still. Sometimes He reached out His hand and lepers were cleansed. Sometimes He used the elements of nature that He had created and blinded eyes were opened. *Whatever* method He used to meet the needs of people who came to Him, it was a MIRACLE METHOD. It was the right method at the right time for the right person and it met a need that could not be met any other way.

And God has a miracle method for the problem that *you* are facing!

I don't understand fully how faith works. I just

know it does. We don't have to understand how God brings His miracle methods into our lives. We just need to know that when we've done everything we know to do and we've exhausted man's methods for solving our problem, God is there with His *miracle* methods. As we seek Him and refuse to believe that the situation we're facing is impossible, we can discover God's miracle method for solving it.

YOUR GOD-GIVEN KEY FOR TODAY

"I Can Discover God's Miracle Method For Solving My Problem."

Then, calm yourself, dry the tears from your eyes, and begin to see that your "onions" are floating in the ditch.

**Key:
I CAN KNOW
THAT GOD
SEES ME AS
A SUCCESS,
EVEN WHEN
I SEE MYSELF
AS A FAILURE**

WEDNESDAY
or
God Knows The End From The Beginning And Out Of Your Greatest Mistakes Can Come Your Greatest Successes

Some of you reading these words may know me through my live, daily TV program. Some of you may know me, at least partly, by the reputation of my father. And some of you may not really know me at all.

But I know me! I know me very well. And I want to tell you a little bit about me in this chapter. Not because I think my life is the most fascinating thing you could ever hear about, don't misunderstand me. But because I know where I've come from…and where God has brought me to today. For if anyone's life has ever been a miracle, Richard Roberts' is. And it's all because of God …because God created me to be a success. He sees me as a success, even when I see myself as a failure.

And for most of *my* life, that's exactly how I saw myself — a failure. I had failed…and failed…and failed again. Because, in the pursuit of my own goals and my own dreams, I had missed the wonderful plan that God had for my life.

I can say that it was a *wonderful* plan because in the last seven years I have been living in the unfolding reality of that plan and I know from personal experience how wonderful it is. As the little boy said to his mother when she questioned how he was so sure that the green apples he had eaten had given him a stomachache: *"Trust me. I have inside information!"*

But I can also say that the plan God has for my life …and for *your* life…is wonderful because God tells me so in His Word. "For we are his [God's] workmanship, created in Christ Jesus unto good works, which God hath before ordained that we should walk in them" (Ephesians 2:10). And "For I know the plans I have for you, says the Lord. They are plans for good and not for evil, to give you a future and a hope" (Jeremiah 29:11, *TLB*).

God has *good* plans for our lives. But when we choose to make our own plans, rather than following

God's, we get into failure. And we begin to see ourselves as failures, rather than as a person who has failed and who can repent and start over again with God's help.

It wasn't hard for the devil to convince me that I was a failure. You see, I know about Richard Roberts' shortcomings. I know all of my faults and problems. I know all about the mistakes I've made…even the ones that have never been told in books, magazine articles, or the newspapers…and believe me, many of my mistakes have!

I know the failure that was in my life. I understand what it's like for your life to fall apart, what tragedy is all about in a marriage and in a family because I've been through what more than half the adults in this nation have been through — a divorce.

I've failed just about as miserably as a man *can* fail. And yet…because of a family who loved me and who believed that God was not through with my life, and because of a God who looked at me through the eyes of love and who saw me for what He'd make me to be instead of for what I'd become…I'm living in obedience to God and in victory and *joy* today.

But that victory wasn't easy to come by and it may not be easy for you, my friend. But from personal experience I can promise you that it will be worth it.

THE FIRST THING YOU MUST DO TO SEE YOURSELF AS A SUCCESS IS TO ADMIT YOUR MISTAKES AND ASK GOD TO FORGIVE YOU

If you're living in failure today, it may be because you've never really admitted your mistakes to God and asked Him to forgive you.

I'll never forget how, when my divorce first hit the

newspapers and the broadcast media, the critics of Richard Roberts seemed to appear everywhere. I mean they literally came out of the woodwork! I'm sure many of them were good people who thought what they were doing was right. They thought they needed to let me know, and let the world know, that I had made a serious mistake.

But no one had to tell me that I had made a mistake. I *knew* I had. I knew there were mistakes on both sides of the relationship. But I knew I had to take responsibility for my part in the failure.

The first thing I did — and the first thing you must do, my friend — was to get down on my knees before God and admit what I'd done wrong and where I'd failed. I asked God to forgive me and I determined not to make the same mistakes again. I told Him that I didn't believe He wanted to throw me away because of what I'd been through, but that He still had something He wanted to do with my life. I determined that no matter what anyone said about me or did to me, I would not strike back. I was going to serve God in whatever way He wanted to use me.

And God began to turn my life around.

He brought my beautiful wife Lindsay into my life, who stands beside me in my work for the Lord and who loves me with a love only God could have given her. Then He called me to begin preaching His Word and praying for the sick, which I had never done before. I had sung for the Lord for many years in my dad's ministry, but had never felt called to preach during that time. And as much as I had always loved to see people healed in my dad's crusades as a young boy and had dreamed a child's dream of perhaps one day praying for the sick in my own ministry, I had never allowed myself to believe that it was really possible for me to have a healing ministry.

But God knew that it was possible! And He had put that desire in my heart all along because it was part of His "good plan" for my life.

You see, God saw me as a healing evangelist long before I ever could see myself that way. He saw me as what He had created me to be rather than what I had become in my own eyes. I saw myself as a failure, but God saw me as a success!

And God sees *you* as the success He created you to be, even when you see yourself as a failure.

If you've failed, my friend, don't try to hide from it. Don't try to deny it. Don't try to run from it. Or you may be hiding, denying, and running the rest of your life. Turn your failure over to God. Confess your mistakes to Him and ask for His forgiveness.

Then believe that God has forgiven you. Quit worrying about what other people think about you or try to do to you. Link up with God's plan for your life. Walk in the "good works" that God has destined you to walk in and, I promise you that based on the Word of God and on my own personal experience, you'll begin to see yourself as the wonderful success that God sees you as and has always intended you to be.

YOUR GOD-GIVEN KEY FOR TODAY

"I Can Know God Sees Me As A Success Even When I See Myself As A Failure."

Then determine that with God's help you'll get out of the failure you're in and get into success...into doing what God has always planned for you to do.

THURSDAY

**Key:
I CAN TRUST
GOD TO DO
WHATEVER IT
TAKES TO REVEAL
HIS WAY TO ME**

**or
How God Spoke To Me
About Praying For The Sick
Through A Dream Of A Man's Big Toe**

Did you know that when you believe God has called you to do something, He also has the power to make His will clear to you and to show you how to accomplish it? I often say in my ministry that it's important to remember that there's something for *us* to do in following God. Sometimes it's an action we must take or an attitude we must change or a seed we must plant. Sometimes it's simply a matter of letting God *be* God to us and not trying to do what only God can do.

Often, when God calls us to do something — especially the big things in our life — we don't know how to do it in the natural. We may be able, in our spirit, to picture ourselves doing what He asked us to do and we may be perfectly willing in our heart. But in our mind and in our natural man, we just flat out don't know how we're ever going to get from point A to point B.

We *strive* to do God's will. We *struggle* to do God's will. And when we reach a certain level of frustration — sometimes before we even take one step toward the thing we believe God is calling us to do — we wonder if God is going to leave us out there on a limb…confused …without really giving us the confirmation that we need and the direction that He wants us to take.

That's pretty much the situation I found myself in after Lindsay and I were married and I began to preach the gospel and to feel that God wanted me to also begin praying for the sick. Though I knew it in my spirit and felt it in my heart, I wondered for a long time how a healing ministry would ever come about.

Lindsay and I prayed about it every day. Then we would thank God for bringing His healing ministry into our lives, but nothing seemed to happen. And I didn't know how to move into it if it *did* happen.

My dad has always felt the anointing of God in his right hand, and so he laid his hands on people as he prayed for them. Most of the people I had ever heard of who prayed for the sick did the same thing. And I thought maybe that's what would happen to me someday. But I wanted to follow what Jesus had for *me*, Richard Roberts, not what He had had for someone else. I didn't feel impressed to lay hands on people and pray, but that was all I'd ever really seen.

I didn't know what to do. I needed confirmation from the Lord that He had indeed called me to pray for the sick and direction about how I was to do it…how He wanted to move through me.

About three months later, I was preaching in a service one night, and as I was closing the service in prayer I felt a strong urging to speak the words, "Lord, heal that man's toe."

And as soon as the words came out of my mouth, I thought to myself, *Well, what'd you say that for? It's the silliest thing I've ever heard. And in front of all these people!* But not knowing what else to do, I just finished my prayer, closed the service, and flew back home to Tulsa.

About a week later, I received a letter from a man

who had been in that service. In his letter he said:

"Remember in that service when you said, 'Lord, heal that man's toe'? Well, *I was that man!* My toe was broken. I'd had it x-rayed, but there wasn't much they could do.

"During the service when you said, 'Lord, heal that man's toe,' *my* toe snapped, and suddenly I could move it again without pain.

"When I went back to the doctor, he x-rayed it again and compared it with the old X ray and guess what? My toe was completely healed!"

He closed by saying, "Richard Roberts, what did you do?"

What did I do? I thought to myself as I sat down to answer him. "I didn't do anything," I told him. "In fact, I felt stupid when I said that."

That night when I went to bed and closed my eyes... and many nights thereafter... I dreamed about a man's big toe! Even when I woke up in the middle of the night and sat up in bed, all I could see was a man's big ol' toe! And it went on like that for the next two weeks.

Finally, when the dream persisted, it began to dawn on me that maybe it was God and He was trying to tell me something. So I decided to tell Lindsay what had been going on. As I told her about my dream, night after night, of a man's toe, she said to me, "Richard, maybe this is the beginning of the healing ministry that you told me you've dreamed of all your life."

And I heard myself say back to her, *"It just could be."*

You see, no one had ever said anything like that to me before. No one had ever encouraged me to believe that my dream could really happen someday. And when she said it, it struck something down on the inside of me.

And we prayed together asking for what He wanted me to do next.

As time went on, I began to understand how God wanted to work through me in praying for the sick. I began to realize that He gave me signs in my own body — feelings and pains in places where I don't usually have them — to show me what His Spirit was doing for someone in my services...or over television...and that I was to speak those words of knowledge out loud and people would be healed. I discovered that as I did that, I felt the anointing of God come into my chest and into my voice and I became more and more confident in what I was to do as I obeyed each leading of the Lord.

I think one of the most important things I learned through that experience was that God had something very specific in mind for Richard Roberts' ministry. He was well able to reveal what that something was when I trusted *Him* to do it and quit striving to figure it all out myself.

Friend, if you believe in your heart that God has called you to do something, believe also that He will find a way to confirm it to you. He'll do whatever it takes to reveal His way to you...even if it means something as unlikely as giving you a dream about someone's big toe!

YOUR GOD-GIVEN KEY FOR TODAY

"I Can Trust God To Do Whatever It Takes To Reveal His Way To Me."

Then begin expecting God to do what only He can do. Let God *be* God in your life.

FRIDAY

**Key:
I CAN TRUST GOD
TO MAKE A WAY
WHERE THERE
SEEMS TO BE NO WAY**

**or
When You Wait On God To Make A Way,
He Will Take You In Through The Front Door**

When God first spoke to me about sending me to 40 nations throughout the world, and gave me the names of the nations, I said,

"HOW?"

I said,

"WHEN?"

I said,

"WHO WILL CONTACT ME, LORD?"

And I will never forget what God said back to me. He said, *Richard, you leave that up to Me. For where I call you to go, I will make a way for you there.*

When I wrote down the ones I was to go to someday, I knew there would be no way in the natural for me to go to some of them. In some cases I had no contacts in the country...or I knew very little about the country...or the government of the country was not particularly friendly to America. How could God make a way for me in *those* countries?

But then I remembered that God says in His Word that He could make a way "even in the wilderness" (Isaiah 43:19). GOD can make a way even when there seems to be *no* way!

So I relaxed and left the way into those nations in God's hands. And through the years of my ministry, I've learned that when it is *God* making the way for you rather than man, you don't have to ease your way into where you're going by barely sneaking in the back door. No! God opens the *front* door for you and you walk through it as if you belonged there all along.

LET ME GIVE YOU AN EXAMPLE OF HOW GOD HAS OPENED THE FRONT DOOR FOR US IN THIS MINISTRY AND HOW I KNOW HE CAN DO IT FOR YOU

In 1984, God opened the door for me to conduct a crusade in the African kingdom of Swaziland. Swaziland is a very small nation but in spite of its size we attracted large crowds to our public crusades and were able to reach many, many people with the message of the gospel. But God showed me that was not the only purpose for my trip there.

The real reason for my trip to Swaziland was to preach to the prime minister, the deputy prime minister, all the government ministers of state, and the entire Swazi Parliament. They set up a special meeting and I thought I would have just a moment to greet them. Instead, they insisted that I preach and pray for their nation and for their personal needs to be met. As I prayed and ministered to them, two key people in top government offices were healed by the power of God.

Later in my trip I was summoned to preach to the queen of Swaziland and members of the royal family. I preached and prayed with as much anointing as I have ever had and several members of the royal family accepted Christ during that service. Then God spoke to my heart and told me to lay my hands on the queen and pray for the royal family and the entire nation. Not knowing much about protocol, I explained to the queen's interpreters what the Lord had told me to do and she agreed. When I laid my

73

hands upon her and prayed, she eagerly accepted my prayer and was genuinely grateful. Then she invited me to return to her nation soon.

After the service in the queen's residence was over, I was told that as far as anyone knew, I was the first white man ever to lay hands on a king or queen of Swaziland.

Why did that happen? Well, the original invitation to Swaziland had come from the Swazi royal family. Prince Jwabu, son of the late King Sobhusa II, and the Swazi ambassador to the United Nations had flown to Tulsa to personally invite me to conduct healing crusades in their country. Not because of Richard Roberts, but because God opened the door for me to go. And when God opens the door, no man can close it. He opened the front door of that African nation to me and I walked through it. He went ahead of me to deal with the hearts of the queen and other leaders of the country and as they received my ministry, miracles happened.

My dad and I are both beginning to experience this kind of "front-door openness" from many nations, particularly those where God is leading us to send our medical missionary teams. Not long ago when my dad went to Kenya with our friend Evangelist Jerry Savelle, he was allowed to meet with the president of that nation for several hours. At one point my dad even had a private audience with President Moi at the president's request.

My dad has been in Africa many times over the years and his ministry has always been to the common man. But as the time to preach the gospel throughout this world and to place our ORU medical missionary teams has arrived, God is moving on the hearts of the leaders of nations to receive Oral Roberts' ministry in a new way. He's making a way where there seemed to be no way before.

You say, "Richard Roberts, that's wonderful for you and your dad, Oral Roberts, but what does any of this have to do with me?"

Friend, it has everything to do with you.

If God can make a way for a man like Oral Roberts from Bebee, Oklahoma — who nearly died from tuberculosis as a young man and who never wanted anything to do with God until his life hung in the balance — to deal with the leaders of nations...

THEN HE CAN MAKE A WAY FOR *YOU!*

If God can make a way for a man like Richard Roberts — who has been divorced and remarried and whom many people wanted to throw out with the garbage not very many years ago — to minister to a nation in a way that no white man has ever had the opportunity before...

THEN HE CAN MAKE A WAY FOR *YOU!*

"God is no respecter of persons" (Acts 10:34). That means that what He has done for Richard Roberts, He can do for you.

Perhaps there is a family member you have been trying to reach for the Lord for some time, yet there never seems to be a time when you can share on a very personal level — away from other people or loved ones.

If God has spoken to your heart about witnessing to that person, then God *will* make a way for that to happen.

Perhaps there is a business opportunity you have felt strongly impressed to become involved in. Yet financially, you can't see how it could ever work.

If God has spoken to your heart about becoming involved in a new business venture, He *will* make a way financially for you to do it.

You see, friend, the problem is not with *God's ability* to make a way where there seems to be no way, but with *our own inability*, at times, *to trust Him to do it. And to be willing to WAIT on God's timing.*

Start trusting God today to open the front door into whatever it is that He's laid on your heart to do. And no matter how impossible it seems to you, remember that nothing is impossible with God. He can make a way where there seemed to be no way before!

YOUR GOD-GIVEN KEY FOR TODAY

"I Can Trust God To Make A Way Where There Seems To Be No Way."

Then be willing to wait on God's timing. When the time is right, He will open a door for you that no man can close.

SATURDAY

**Key:
I CAN LOOK FOR
GOD TO DO A NEW
THING IN MY LIFE**

or
How God Brought Something Good Out Of The Loss Of Our Son, Richard Oral

Have you ever had a heartache — a problem or struggle from your past — that you needed to be free of? If so, listen to this word from God in the book of the prophet Isaiah.

"Remember ye not the former things, neither consider the things of old. Behold, I will do a new thing; now it shall spring forth; shall ye not know it?" (Isaiah 43:18,19).

God gave Lindsay and me this Scripture in 1984 after we had gone through something so painful that we didn't know if we'd ever be able to really be excited about our future again. I want to share it with you in this book because she and I know that *only God* could have brought something good — a new thing — out of something that Satan had meant for our destruction.

You see, on January 17, 1984, our first child — a beautiful little boy we named Richard Oral Roberts — was born into this world. And, oh, how we rejoiced at the miracle God had given us! I say "miracle" because Lindsay had been told from the time she was 18 years old that, because of a physical problem she had, she would never be able to have a child. It was only after two miscarriages early in our marriage that Lindsay was finally able to conceive and carry this baby to full term.

Richard Oral was a dream come true for both of us — for Lindsay because she had wondered if she would one day hold a child of her own in her arms, and for me because I'd always wanted a son. Now our dream was a living, breathing reality and we couldn't have been any happier.

Then, just 36 hours later, our little boy was dead. And Lindsay and I felt our world falling down around us.

Had it not been for our faith in Jesus and our dedication to each other, I don't know if we would have made it through that time. Losing a child is a pain that I don't believe you can understand until you've been through it. It hurt like nothing I'd ever felt before.

Lindsay and I were filled with confusion and with questions: *Had we done something wrong during Lindsay's pregnancy?*

No. Lindsay had had a good pregnancy. Our son had been born perfectly healthy. We couldn't have known this might happen.

Had we not prayed enough when, only hours after his birth, we learned about the problems he had developed?

No! Lindsay and I had prayed for Richard Oral constantly. We had called my dad and mother to come to the hospital and to pray, and we knew other men and women of faith were praying. I had been around the anointing of God long enough to know that there was enough faith and enough healing power in that intensive care room to have raised the dead.

But, somehow, the circumstances were just beyond our control. And just 36 hours after he was born, our precious Richard Oral died and went to be with Jesus in heaven.

How do you make it through something like that? A son you've dreamed of . . . a child who never would have been conceived without the power of God?

In our grief, Lindsay and I turned TO God . . . NOT AWAY from Him.

Kneeling at our son's bedside, weeping, I heard myself almost shouting, "Though God slay me, yet will I trust in him," (Job 13:15), the same words Job had said when the devil took away *everything* from him. I knew that Lindsay felt the same way I did.

WE COULD HAVE MISSED
THE NEW THING GOD WANTED
TO DO IN OUR LIFE

A few weeks after the death of our baby son, I was scheduled to conduct a month-long healing crusade in Nigeria, West Africa. The devil tried to talk me out of it. The first thought he'd put in my mind after our baby's death was: How could I help someone else when I couldn't even save my own child? Now, Lindsay and I made the commitment that we *would* go. We determined in our hearts to let the world know what we were made of. And we believed that as we gave to others out of our own hurt and let them see us when we were down — just the same as we let them see us when we are up — God would bring a great healing into our life.

During the time we were in Africa (part of which we spent in Swaziland as I wrote about in the last chapter), Lindsay and I and our crusade team saw more healings and miracles of God than we had ever seen in our crusades before. When I preached and prayed for the sick, I felt a fresh, new anointing on me and we saw the results of that anointing in the lives of people that were changed. And God began a great healing in our own lives as Lindsay and I set aside our personal pain and focused ourselves on Jesus and on other people who were hurting.

In time, God has made that healing more and more complete — particularly through the birth of our daughter, Jordan Lindsay, in April of 1985, and our new baby, Catherine Olivia, who arrived March 17 of this year.

Have we forgotten Richard Oral?

No, we've not forgotten him; we will always remember our firstborn son because Lindsay and I are human beings. But what she and I will *not* do is to live our lives centered around the tragedy of his death.

Why?

Had we allowed ourselves to continue to focus on the past after Richard Oral's death rather than living in the present and looking toward the future, we might never have gone to Africa in 1984 and thousands of lives would have missed the miracle touch of God He had planned for them.

I would have missed the new anointing that God wanted to place on me.

Lindsay and I would have missed the supernatural healing power of God for our broken hearts...and we would have been bound up in such pain and fear that we might never again have tried to have children of our own.

God wanted to do a NEW THING in our lives...and through us, in the lives of many people, but we could have missed it all. The choice was ours.

Perhaps right now there's something in *your* life that you need to stop focusing on so that God can do a *new thing* in your life. Maybe it's the loss of a child — like Lindsay and I experienced — or an area where you've failed in some way — your business, your marriage, your relationship with someone you cared for. And just about the time you feel you're ready to break loose and step out of the past, the devil brings that painful experience to your mind and says that you'll never get away from it.

If I've just described you, friend, quit listening to the devil's voice telling you that *your* situation is beyond redemption and that your life is over. Listen to the voice of God saying to you:

"Remember ye not the former things, neither consider [meaning: focus upon] the things of old.

Behold, I will do a new thing; NOW it shall spring forth; SHALL YE NOT KNOW IT?"

When did God say it would happen? NOW! That means that God's NEW THING is on its way into your life today.

My question to you is this: Will you accept it or will you let it pass you by?

YOUR GOD-GIVEN KEY FOR TODAY

"I Can Look For God To Do A New Thing In My Life."

Then trust God to bring something good into your life beginning today.

SECOND WEEK

SUNDAY	I CAN SURVIVE THE EXPLOSIONS OF MY LIFE
MONDAY	I CAN CALL FOR HELP!
TUESDAY	I CAN DISCOVER GOD'S MIRACLE METHOD FOR SOLVING MY PROBLEM
WEDNESDAY	I CAN KNOW GOD SEES ME AS A SUCCESS EVEN WHEN I SEE MYSELF AS A FAILURE
THURSDAY	I CAN TRUST GOD TO DO WHATEVER IT TAKES TO REVEAL HIS WAY TO ME
FRIDAY	I CAN TRUST GOD TO MAKE A WAY WHERE THERE SEEMS TO BE NO WAY
SATURDAY	I CAN LOOK FOR GOD TO DO A NEW THING IN MY LIFE

THIRD WEEK

Jesus Didn't Make Me... Or You... For Failure

By Evelyn Roberts

SUNDAY

**Key:
I CAN KNOW
GOD DESIRES
GOOD THINGS FOR ME**

or
I Can Tell
If Something Is From God Or The Devil

Have you ever questioned whether something in your life — an illness, a tragedy, a loss — was from God or the devil? If so, then John 10:10 can settle the question in your mind once and for all. It says, "The thief [the devil] cometh not, but for to steal, and to kill, and to destroy: I [*Jesus*] am come that [you] might have life…more abundantly."

I have found a simple way to help us understand what John 10:10 is saying. Take a piece of paper and draw a line right down the middle of it. On one side write "the devil" and on the other side write "Jesus." Under "the devil" put what he does.

First of all, the devil comes to steal. What does he steal? He steals your finances. He steals your peace and joy. (On Tuesday of this week I tell about having my joy stolen.)

Next, the devil kills. What does he kill? He kills your desire to read God's Word. He kills the friendships you have. He kills your very life.

Last of all, the devil destroys. What does he destroy? He destroys the faith that you have in God. He destroys the love in your family. He destroys your health.

Anything that steals, kills, or destroys does not come from God. It comes from the devil. It's the *devil's* desire for you, not God's desire.

Then under "Jesus" on your paper put what He

does. What does Jesus do? Jesus said, "I am come that [you] might have life, and that [you] might have it more abundantly." Jesus gives you abundant life! He saves you. He heals you. He helps you in your problem. It's His desire that you be whole in body, mind, and spirit, that your needs be met. That surge of joy that had come to me was the abundant life of Jesus welling up within my spirit and the depression was gone.

James 1:17 says, "Every good gift and every perfect gift is from above, and cometh down from the Father." *Every* good gift comes from God. Not one good gift comes from the devil. However, I believe God delights in taking the bad that the devil does and turning it into something good for our lives.

My husband Oral has always said that in every tragic accident or in every mistake we make, there is a seed of equivalent benefit. It's like Joseph in the Bible said to his brothers after they had sold him into slavery in Egypt, "You thought evil against me; but God meant it for good, to bring about that many should be kept alive, as they are today" (Genesis 50:20, *Amplified*). Again, when we lost our daughter and son-in-law, you'd think there was no way God could turn this for good. But Oral said from the beginning, "One thing I know for sure, and that is God didn't take our daughter and son-in-law. The devil did. And out of this is going to come something that will glorify God."

I knew that God didn't do it, and that the devil certainly did. I felt it was an attack on us and our ministry as much as it was on our family. So we just trusted the Lord and tried to find out what we were supposed to do to turn it for good.

During this time, we went out to the desert where we oftentimes go to pray and meditate and write. God

85

began to talk to Oral about building the City of Faith. I well remember the evening we were having dinner and Oral began to write on a paper napkin. Finally he said, "Evelyn, the Lord is giving me words so fast I can't get them all. Excuse me, I must go write this down." It was the article he called "I'll Rain on Your Desert," and it told how the City of Faith would look and how to build it. We had been through a desert and God was bringing us out. The devil took our daughter and son-in-law, but he couldn't steal the plans that God gave us! And out of this has come something that glorifies God.

Planting of Seed-Faith doesn't keep us from suffering losses, for this is not a perfect world we live in. It does, however, give us a mighty stability in our losses, a mighty Source to look to — and assurance in our heart that God has placed within every seed of faith planted the potential for a miracle greater than any loss Satan causes us to suffer.

Say to yourself:

God desires only good things for me and the devil desires only bad things for me. I will not blame God for the bad the devil does.

I will take John 10:10 and decide what is from God and what is from the devil and refuse to give the devil credit for the good God does or blame God for the bad the devil does.

YOUR GOD-GIVEN KEY FOR TODAY

"God Desires Only Good Things For Me."

MONDAY

**Key:
I CAN KNOW
GOD'S DIRECTION
FOR MY LIFE**

**or
There Are Several "Lights" That Will
Line Up If I Am Following God's Direction**

I once attended a spiritual retreat in southern Oklahoma. I had been with this group on other occasions and particularly enjoyed a unique part of their service called "devotions-in-motion."

During their devotions-in-motion, everyone moves to music and acts out certain portions of the song we are singing. This time our leader asked us to find a partner, close our eyes, and let our partner lead us about the room while we sang, "Where He leads me I will follow."

My partner was a dear lady who graciously began to lead me around the room as I sang, "Where He leads me ..." I was following with my eyes tightly closed when I began to realize the room was full of people doing the same thing we were doing. Fear gripped me. I thought, *Suppose I run into someone else! Suppose I trip over someone's foot!*

Suddenly I realized that is what I do sometimes when I'm supposed to be following Jesus. I doubt that He will keep me from falling. "Lord, do I fear following You this much? Do I give You the feeling that I don't trust You to lead me the right way?"

"Where He leads me, I will follow. I'll go with Him all the way," came wafting across the room.

Tears were streaming down my face by this time. I was having my own battle right in the midst of a spiritual service. My guide sensed something was wrong so she stopped.

"Evelyn," she said, "when I was legally blind I took hold of a person's arm like this to be led..."

Legally blind! I had no idea she'd ever been legally blind. No wonder she was so sensitive to my moves and my spirit. It was as if Jesus were saying to me, *Oh, yes, Evelyn, you can trust Me! You see, I even chose the right person to be your partner.*

As I took the arm of my guide and began to follow her again, "Where He leads me I will follow" took on a new meaning. My confidence began to return.

"Yes, Lord," I prayed. "I see how You planned this to take away my fear. I am now free to follow You all the way without fear. I may bump into mountains occasionally or trip over a problem, but I have hold of Your everlasting arm, Jesus. In fact, I'm leaning on it!"

God promises to give us His guidance. Proverbs 3:5,6 says, "Trust in the Lord with all thine heart; and lean not unto thine own understanding. In all thy ways acknowledge him, and he shall direct thy paths."

Whether God reveals His overall plan for your life or directs you one step at a time, rest assured He will not lead you astray. You can trust Him and He will let you know the direction you are to take.

I read a story once about how a harbor pilot navigates his ship into port in the darkness. He locates a light and maneuvers his vessel toward it. But he doesn't go by the guidance of that one light alone, or he could wind up on the rocks. He locates another light and another and waits until he can line up all the lights. Then he knows he is in the harbor channel and can safely dock the ship.

The procedure is similar for us when we face a decision. We have several "lights" that line up to guide us and assure us we are on the right path.

One of these is *God's Word.* The vast majority of

God's will is already revealed to us in His Word. It is important to remember that nothing can be the will of God that contradicts or goes against what He says in His Word, for the Word is His will written down for us. When you keep your life in line with God's Word, you will go in the right direction.

A second "light" to guide us is our *inner voice.* The inner voice is what we call feelings or impressions which we receive from God. Everybody hears the still small voice of God in some way. Sometimes it's through hearing a sermon, listening to a song, reading the Bible, praying, or simply thinking. A strong, deep impression of guidance will come to you and not leave. It is an impression that is for your *good.* This is God talking to you.

A third "light" is *outer circumstances.* God often guides us by matching our inner feelings with an open or closed door of circumstances. Suppose you have a feeling you are to leave the job you now have. So you go apply for a new job. But you are told no applications are being taken. The door is closed for you at that time. However, a month later, if you still feel you are supposed to have another job, and try — this time the door may be open and the job is yours.

And a fourth "light" is *guidance from others.* Your husband, wife, parents, a counselor, a trusted friend, or your pastor can often help you. God's Word says, "Without counsel purposes are disappointed: but in the multitude of counsellors they are established" (Proverbs 15:22). You cannot rely upon others altogether, but they can help you.

A calm, Spirit-controlled consideration of all the facts involved is very important in making decisions. When you feel you have God's direction in regard to a particular decision, then do your part to accomplish it. You may not understand everything about His direction. God seldom gives the whole picture to you at one time. It may not be exactly what you expected and to carry it out may seem hard but, remember, as God reveals His will to you He will give you the strength to act upon it. Your part is to walk in faith and act upon His directions.

YOUR GOD-GIVEN KEY FOR TODAY

"I Can Know God's Direction For My Life."

TUESDAY

Key: I CAN HAVE JOY EVEN IN SORROW

or
Turning Your Thoughts From Your Grief To God's Love Can Restore Joy Even In Times Of Sorrow

Religious music and hymns have always given me a spiritual uplift. They relieve me of depression and loneliness, and bring me joy.

One time in my life when I had allowed the devil to rob me of joy, they served as a powerful point of contact to bring joy back into my life. It was after the accident that took our daughter Rebecca and her husband Marshall to heaven. About six weeks after it had happened and the time had come for me to readjust to life again, I realized I was really ill. I had no strength. I felt tired all the time. My body hurt and I was depressed. So I went for a checkup. The doctor said I was anemic and he gave me some medication which I was glad to take.

Later one night I was reading my Bible in bed, as is my custom, when a Scripture just seemed to jump out at me. It said, "The joy of the Lord is your strength" (Nehemiah 8:10). I put the Bible down and said aloud, "Lord, have I lost Your joy? Is that why my strength is gone?"

Then I began to ponder — joy! What brings joy to me? Music! Why, of course. I hadn't been listening to music. Now all of my life music was one of the things that gave me a lift and brought joy into my life, but as I pondered my feelings that night I realized I hadn't actually listened to spiritual songs since Rebecca's death. I had allowed Satan to rob me of the very thing that brings joy into my life. I said to him right then, "All right, Mr. Devil, you've had it. You tricked me once but you won't do it again."

The next morning I turned on records, tapes, the radio — anything that had spiritual music — and my strength and joy began to return. I had an inner healing that made me whole again.

I believe a healing of your spirit is just as important, if not more important, than a healing of your body. For when your spirit needs healing, there is an absence of joy in your life…and without joy you don't have strength or desire to do the things that you need to do for yourself and others.

Coping with the death of a loved one robs one of joy as no other scheme of Satan I know about. But even in sorrow, God's healing power can restore joy in your life when you turn your mind from yourself to the Source of your total supply — God.

YOUR GOD-GIVEN KEY FOR TODAY

"I Can Have Joy Even In The Midst Of Sorrow."

WEDNESDAY
Key: I CAN HEAR GOD'S VOICE

or
If I Don't Hear God Speak To Me In An Audible Voice, I Will Listen For Him In The "Everydayness" Of Life

Both my husband Oral and I received our prayer language of the Spirit many years ago, but we were taught that a person speaks in tongues at the moment he receives the Holy Spirit and he might or might not ever speak in a prayer language again. And until Oral undertook the tremendous task of building a university, we had only used it when we were elated or in deep distress.

When Oral began to build Oral Roberts University, he discovered that he could interpret back to his mind what he had spoken with his prayer language. He had never done that before.

He shared this with me and we both began interpreting, but I never felt I did this as well as Oral. In fact, I've argued with the Lord because I thought He was showing respect of persons by talking to my husband audibly when He didn't talk to me that way. So one day as I was discussing this with the Lord, He said to me in my spirit, *I won't talk to you like I talk to your husband because I haven't given you the job to do that I've given to him. But I will speak to you in the everyday things of life.* And that is the way the Lord usually speaks to me — in my spirit. I don't hear His audible voice.

We were in Dallas this summer in a ministers' meeting and Oral was speaking on this subject of speaking in tongues and then interpreting it back to your mind. When he finished he said, "Now I want us all to pray in the Spirit and ask the Lord to give us a new language. Then ask the Lord to give you the interpretation of what you said."

I prayed, "All right, Lord, here I come again. Maybe this time You will speak to me audibly." As I prayed, the Lord again spoke to my spirit, but it was as clear as if it had been audible. He said to me, *You are resisting the Holy Spirit.*

That pricked my heart because the last thing I want to do is to be resistant to the Holy Spirit. I asked, "Lord, how am I resisting the Holy Spirit?" He didn't tell me how. He just said, *If you will go on the long trips with your husband, I will give you your health.*

My husband was getting ready to go to Africa at that time. We had decided that I would not go because on those long airplane trips overseas always before my feet and legs would swell until I couldn't even feel my feet. When I got there I would have to go to bed and stay for 24 hours before I could walk. So we both had decided it was best for me to stay home. I didn't go with him to Africa, although I should have because Oral loses everything. He's a good preacher and he can build a university and the City of Faith, but he needs help keeping his clothes together. The Lord knew that I needed to be with my husband and that's why He said to me, *If you will take these long trips with your husband, I will give you your health.*

When the Lord spoke that to me, I first thought,

But I already have good health. I don't need that promise. Then I thought, *Maybe the Lord means He will keep my feet and legs from swelling.* Another thought that came to me was, *Maybe He sees something down the road that I don't see that's going to happen to me, but if I go with my husband, it won't happen.*

I said, "All right, Lord, I will obey You and I will do what You ask me to do."

When Oral began to plan a trip to the Orient, I called his secretary and said, "I'm going to Japan and Korea with my husband. I'm going to be obedient to the Lord." And I went. Not only was I believing the Lord to take care of the swelling in my legs and feet — but I also went to see my doctor and he gave me medication to help with the problem.

When we got off the plane in Tokyo to walk around before changing planes, I had a little swelling in my feet. When we got back in the plane to go to Osaka, the swelling was going down. When we arrived, I had no swelling whatever.

I'm giving the glory to God for this, but I have to give some of the credit to medicine and some to prayer. I did pray a lot on that trip. I kept reminding the Lord, "You know what You said. I'm holding You to Your word." I reminded Him all the way. And I took the medication. So medicine and prayer really worked together to give me the miracle I needed.

I was able to tell the Japanese people who desperately needed miracles what God did for me. The Lord kept His word as He always does if we believe Him.

I believe God speaks to most of us as He does me — in the "everydayness of life." If you don't hear God's audible voice, that doesn't mean God is not speaking to you. Listen for Him in the words of a song, in a verse of Scripture, in the voice of a friend, or a line in a book, or in a multitude of other ways God may choose to communicate with you. You can be assured that whatever He chooses will be a way that is right for your personality.

YOUR GOD-GIVEN KEY FOR TODAY

"I Can Hear God's Voice."

THURSDAY

**Key:
I CAN BE
A SUCCESS
IN GOD'S EYES**

or
I Can Be Freed From A Lifestyle That Keeps Me From Accomplishing Something For Jesus

I'm thankful for the opportunity I have to present Jesus to hurting people. One group of hurting people I have a deep burden for are homosexuals because I know they have a desire to get out of that lifestyle.

One day when I was a guest on Richard's program, we were talking about this concern and I just looked into the camera and said to homosexuals who might be viewing the program that day:

"I know that you who are homosexuals have a desire to get out of that lifestyle. Don't let anybody deceive you; it is not something that God let you be born with. The devil tells you, 'Oh, you were born with this and you can't find any way to get out of it'. But you can! The devil's a liar. Jesus will heal that disease — and it is a disease — as much as He will heal any other disease."

A young woman in Louisiana named Christy was watching the program that day, and God used those words to turn her life around. I'd like to share her testimony with you as she shared it on *Richard Roberts Live:*

"For years I struggled with the sin of lesbianism. But now, at the age of 27, I have finally won the battle.

"As a child I always felt close to God. I talked to Him and worshiped Him from an early age, and I grew up going to church. But I always felt like there was something different about me. Whenever I would play house with my little girl friends, I always tried to be the daddy. When I'd watch movies and television, I always tried to copy the mannerisms of the hero… not the heroine. And I learned from that how to treat a woman like a man would treat her.

"All my life I was too masculine to be feminine and too feminine to be masculine. People didn't know how to relate to me, and I didn't know how to relate to them, so I didn't have many friends. It was horrible. I felt like a man in a woman's body.

"As I entered my teen years, my attraction to other girls became very strong. And while attending a girls' school I had my first lesbian experience at the age of fifteen. Shortly after that I repented and was able to stay away from further involvement for a while. But by the time I was twenty, I had become fully active in the gay lifestyle.

"It was in the gay bars of New Orleans where I live that I first felt comfortable and accepted by other people. So naturally I thought I had finally found 'my kind of people'. Nobody was talking behind my back or condemning me for the way I looked and acted. In fact, many of the girls there thought I was attractive.

"One reason I had a hard time breaking away from the gay life was that the devil had deceived me through the gay churches I attended. The gay preachers I heard would take Scriptures out of context to make it sound like there wasn't anything wrong with homosexuality. They said that if I committed myself to any person, even someone of the same sex that I was, it was just like being married.

"The devil told me that I was supposed to have been born a man, and that there would never be any hope for me to live a normal life as a woman. Not knowing the real truth, I believed him and blamed God for my situation. Many a night I cried myself to sleep because of what I thought God had done to me.

"I even went to doctors and asked if I could get an operation that would turn me into a man. But they told me that the operation wasn't available in New Orleans. It was during that time of intense frustration with my sexual identity that I seriously contemplated suicide.

"Through the years I gradually gave my life over to the lies the devil had filled my mind with. But it wasn't without a struggle. I had a lot of pressure from my family, from their church, and from society to go straight. So from time to time I would try to act straight.

"I know a lot of homosexuals go through that. They come under so much pressure that they try to go back to a heterosexual lifestyle for the wrong reasons — and then it doesn't last.

"One thing I really thank God for is that through all those years my family never forsook me. At first they argued with me and preached at me about how wrong it was to live like that. But when they finally realized I was so confused that their arguments didn't even make sense to me, they started praying for me instead.

"I guess their prayers started working too, because gradually the bondage I felt started to break. And I came to realize what a hellish life the gay life really is.

"While I was sitting in the darkened gay bars watching women dance with each other, Scriptures I had read started coming back to me. One that I remembered was, 'The Light from heaven came into the world, but they loved the darkness more than the Light, for their deeds were evil' (John 3:19, *TLB*). I even started telling my gay friends that I didn't think that was the right way to live.

"Then one day while I was visiting with my mom, we were watching a game show on TV. After it was over, I started switching stations and noticed that Richard Roberts was on. So I said, 'Look, Mom. Let's watch Richard Roberts.'

"Mom agreed and then she said, 'You know, I haven't seen Evelyn on TV for a long time.' And what do you know? The next thing Richard said was, 'And now I'd like to introduce my very special guest for today...my mother, Evelyn Roberts.'

"They talked for a while and I can't even remember what they were talking about. But all of a sudden Evelyn looked into the camera — right at me — and said, 'I know that you who are homosexuals have a desire to get out of that lifestyle. It is not something that God let you be born with. And don't let anybody deceive you about that. The devil tells you, "Oh, you were born with this, and you can't find any way to get out of it." But you can. The devil's a liar. Jesus will heal that sickness — and it is a sickness — as much as He will heal any other sickness.'

"When Evelyn spoke that word from the Lord, I felt the power of God touch me and a flood of joy rushed through my body. I started crying because I knew that God had meant that word just for me. After all those years I knew that I was finally free from that miserable bondage.

"Most people who are involved in the gay life don't want to be that way, but they don't know they can be any different. They go from one relationship to another, searching for love and getting nothing but heartache and pain.

"Now I have new friends to fellowship with at my new church. The Lord has led me to a church that preaches the true Word of God and where I can minister to the sick and the shut-ins through their women's group. That gives me a lot of satisfaction.

"Also, I was really blessed to hear that after my testimony was shown on Richard's program, people were calling in to report that they were being delivered from homosexuality. I praise God that lives have already been touched through my testimony."

I know there are many hurting people today who are like Christy was, and if you are one of those hurting people — if you're homosexual or if you are an abused child or if you're a battered wife or if you're someone who's hurting for some other reason — Jesus can help you. I pray that you will let Him come into your heart and heal your hurt and bless you.

Then I pray that you will ask Jesus to give you a place to minister to others as He has Christy, and that you will have a burning desire to live the rest of your life with a purpose and goal to become, with His help, that joyful, successful person He created you to be.

YOUR GOD-GIVEN KEY FOR TODAY

"I Can Be Free Of The Bondage That Keeps Me From Being A Success In God's Eyes."

FRIDAY
Key: I CAN RECEIVE THE MIRACLE I NEED

or
God Wants Each One Of Us To Have Miracles To Meet Our Needs On A Regular Basis

I don't understand why, but apparently some people think if my husband Oral or son Richard prays for them, all their problems will be solved at the snap of a finger. Somehow they've gotten the idea that a miracle is something that comes totally out of the clear blue sky when some "man of God" prays. Now I thank God that Oral and Richard pray for people. As a result of their prayers, many miracles from God *have* occurred in people's lives. But I believe God hears *everyone's* prayers and wants each one of us to have miracles to meet our needs on a regular basis. The Bible says, "The effectual fervent prayer of a righteous man availeth much" (James 5:16). Righteous simply means "in right standing with God." If you have accepted Jesus Christ as your Savior, then you are in right standing to receive miracles.

But miracles are not just something that happen out of the blue. The Bible teaches there are some things we need to do if we are going to receive the miracles we need. I think one of the greatest stories in the Bible that teaches us how to receive the miracle we need is found in 1 Kings 17. It's about a prophet of God named Elijah.

The first thing that we learn from Elijah is to

OBEY GOD

Elijah was a man of obedience and faith who knew that God could provide for him...and God did provide for him. In a time of terrible drought and famine in the land, God gave Elijah specific directions to go to a little brook. The Bible says that Elijah did what God said. Thank the Lord that Elijah obeyed God, because if he hadn't we would never have read about the miracle that took place later at a widow's house.

When Elijah obeyed God, He sent ravens with meals of bread and meat to feed him. When we obey God — when we do what He tells us to do and only what He tells us to do — He will bless us with the miracles we need in our lives.

I was in Washington a few months ago for a women's leadership conference. When the meeting ended, a young couple met me in the hall and said, "Evelyn, we have received inspiration for our ministry at this conference, but we want to ask you something." They said, "The Lord has impressed us to build a college and also to build a hospital. Now, what advice do you have for us?"

I said, "My first advice is this: Make sure God told you to do it. Make sure He told you to build a school, and especially make sure He told you to build a hospital, because that's the hardest thing in the world to do. I know. God told Oral to build Oral Roberts University and the City of Faith Hospital! I advise you to get on your knees in prayer and make sure. If you're sure He told you to do this, then obey

Him. But if you're not sure He told you to do it, don't undertake it.

"If God tells you to do something, and you're being obedient to Him, He will somehow make a way for you to do it," I told them. And the same is true for you and me also.

A second thing that we learn from Elijah is to

LOOK TO GOD AS OUR SOURCE OF SUPPLY

Elijah had prophesied that there would be no rain in the land...and, sure enough, there was no rain for three years. After a while, the brook to which God had sent Elijah dried up. The prophet had no water to drink.

Many people think that preachers don't have a need in the world, but preachers have needs just like everybody else. Oral and I have needs because we are human beings. We have problems just like the person does who has lost his job or can't pay his bills or hurts inside from a broken heart.

Many times I have said, "Lord, how are You going to get us out of this mess we're in?" The Lord always does if we have faith in Him, obey Him, and look to Him as our Source of supply.

God supplied for Elijah. He sent him to another city where he could have his need met. It's hard for us to see that God will do for us what He did for the great men and women of God in the Bible — but He will.

A third thing we learn from Elijah is to

TRUST GOD

The Lord told Elijah to go to a certain city for He had commanded a widow there to provide for him. Elijah didn't know the widow's name, he didn't know how to find her, but he arose and went into the city. Elijah believed God when He said that a widow in the city would help him even though he didn't have many details. When he came to the city's gate, the widow of whom God had spoken was there gathering sticks. (See 1 Kings 17:9,10.)

Sometimes we have to trust God when we don't have all the details we would like to have. Last spring after the annual graduation ceremonies at Oral Roberts University, Oral and I were so very tired. "We need to get away," I said, "but we don't have reservations on a plane." We didn't know how we were going to travel.

"I'll just trust the Lord," Oral said. "He'll help us." Not long after that, a couple we know invited us to ride with them on their plane to California for a rest. Oral said, "See, isn't that just the way the Lord works?"

I wish God would do things for me long before I feel I have to have them done. But He doesn't. He doesn't because He wants you and me to live by faith every day of our lives. I like that about Him. I like knowing that even though I don't have all the details about how or when my miracle is coming, God IS going to give it to me in His perfect way and time!

A fourth thing we learn from Elijah about receiving the miracle we need is to

FEAR NOT

Elijah asked the widow he had just met for a drink of water and a little bread, but she answered him, "I have but a handful of meal in a barrel, and a little oil in a cruse; and, behold, I am gathering two sticks, that I may go in and [cook] it for my son and me, that we may eat it, and die" (1 Kings 17:12).

Do you ever feel like the widow — that you don't have anything?

Sometimes we get so low spiritually, financially,

and in many other ways that we feel like we are absolutely empty. The widow Elijah met was so low that she was gathering sticks to bake a little meal one last time and then die.

The Bible says, "Elijah said to her, Fear not." We're so afraid at times. We fear that we're going to lose everything, that nothing good will ever happen to us again. God knows when there is great fear in our heart and He says to us, "Fear not."

Why is it important to get rid of fear? We can't really believe God for a miracle with fear in our heart. Fear absolutely destroys faith if it remains in us. We need to say, "Devil, I command you to flee! Fear, in the name of Jesus, I command you to leave me so that I can believe God!"

And finally, a fifth thing we learn from Elijah is to

GIVE TO GOD

Knowing that the widow had only a handful of meal in a jar and a little oil in a bottle which she was going to use to bake one last meal for herself and her son, Elijah said something that sounded cruel. He said, "Do as you have said; but make me a little cake of [it] first and bring it to me, and afterward prepare for yourself and your son" (1 Kings 17:13, *Amplified*).

A preacher was asking a poor widow to take the last thing she had and give it to him first! But it really was not cruel at all for him to ask this. Elijah was just telling her how to get her needs met. He went on to say, "For thus says the Lord, the God of Israel, The jar of meal shall not waste away, or the bottle of oil fail, until the day that the Lord sends rain on the earth" (1 Kings 17:14, *Amplified*).

The widow did as Elijah asked and, not only was his need met, her need was met. She had food throughout the time of famine that was in the land as

God had said would happen. I have been told that the famine lasted another year, yet God provided her needs every day.

And when we give to God first, He will give us the miracles we need. He will multiply our seeds of faith that we sow, and give back to us more than enough to meet our needs.

YOUR GOD-GIVEN KEY FOR TODAY

"God Will Make A Way For Me To Receive The Miracle I Need."

SATURDAY

**Key:
I CAN WAIT OUT
THE GROWING
TIME OF
MY MIRACLE**

or
**I Can Wait Confidently Because I Know
God Is Changing My Seedtime Into Harvesttime**

Not long ago someone reminded me of a statement I had made in a book several years ago. I had written: "One yearning of my heart has not come to fruition. I know God must have a reason. I asked Him for one child to be in full-time Christian service."

When I wrote that, I didn't have any children in the ministry. It didn't look like I ever would either. But just one year after I wrote that, Richard came to work with us in the ministry of music. And since that time he has been called and anointed with a powerful healing ministry as well.

It has been so exciting to see how God has moved in Richard's life. God's timing in his life is far more perfect than anything I could have imagined.

Sometimes God's timing may be different from ours, but we can be assured He loves us and He will answer our prayers in His perfect way and in His perfect time. But what are we to do in the meantime? That's what I would like to talk to you about today.

First of all, we need to remember that there is a growing time for every seed that is planted. And that includes our seeds of faith — which are anything of value we contribute to God's work or to other people's lives such as money and time we give to God or prayers we pray for other people. Anything good we do is a seed and, when we wrap our faith around it, it becomes a carrier of life, a carrier of miracles.

One of the things I learned from the vegetable gardens we planted when I was a child is that very seldom could we plant anything where the harvest came quickly. This has helped me to have patience through the years for my harvest to come from the seeds of faith I plant.

I was so glad not long ago when Oral prepared a little plaque for our Partners that gave five things to do after we have planted our seeds of faith — what to do in the growing time of our seeds. I'd like to share these with you for they have been a help to me and I believe they will be to you also:

1. In the growing time of your seed, confess with your mouth, "I have given to God my tithes and offerings of every dollar I've earned to date and they are in God's hands as seeds of faith."

It took me years to throw off the old teaching — or lack of teaching — that I was to give but expect nothing back. When I finally began to see that God himself is the "good soil" — soil I can't see but which is eternal and ever abundant and faithful in reproducing my seed sown into harvests for me to receive — I began to get excited because I could see God would grow and multiply every seed that I sow. Not one would fail to produce so long as I believed it and expected the harvest to come.

2. In the growing time of your seed, confess with your mouth, "My seed is sown and God is growing it invisibly, but absolutely."

Your seed-planting is an expression of your faith. It is your belief in the Word of God, in the seed system of God. You're saying, "I'm expecting a miracle. I'm expecting a desired result."

When your tithes and offerings have gone from your hand, they become invisible. You can't see them, yet God is growing them invisibly, but absolutely.

What do we say of the woman who is pregnant? For the first few weeks after the seed is planted in her body it is invisible and her body remains the same, but we say, "She is expecting." She is expecting a harvest — a child. That's the perfect example of what takes place when we plant our seeds and we're expecting seedtime to change to harvesttime.

3. In the growing time of your seed, confess with your mouth, "God is changing my seedtime into harvesttime."

You can't see it, but God is changing the seed. It's growing up. It's becoming greater.

When Jesus was put on the cross God said, "That's MY seed to save human beings." When they buried Jesus, where was the seed? It was growing, invisibly, absolutely, and three days later God raised Jesus from the dead. A few days later He poured out the gift of the Holy Spirit — the unlimited, invisible

107

presence of Jesus that is now in this world and in you and me.

When you have your seed in, even though you can't see it, understand that it is growing absolutely.

4. In the growing time of your seed, confess with your mouth, "God is rebuking the devourers for my sake."

The literal Greek meaning of the word *rebuke* in our New Testament is "stop it, that's enough." God is saying to the devourers of *your* life, "Stop it. That's enough!"

5. In the growing time of your seed, confess with your mouth, "My giving is causing the windows of heaven to unlock...to open...and God is pouring out ideas and insights into my mind greater than I can contain about what to do and how to make miracles happen in my life."

When you talk about bringing in your tithes and offerings and God opening the windows of heaven and pouring you out a blessing you cannot receive, God is not talking about raining dollars out of heaven or a new house or a new car. He's pouring ideas into your mind. He's sparking your imagination. He's giving you dreams to dream and things to vision that will change your life. God is changing your seedtime into harvesttime. That's the eternal law.

After we have planted our seeds of faith, we are to wait upon the Lord. That's where the faith part of Seed-Faith comes in. We call it Seed-Faith because our faith enables us to wait expectantly during the growing time of our seeds. Every day expect, expect, expect! until the harvest comes.

YOUR GOD-GIVEN KEY FOR TODAY

"I Can Wait Out The Growing Time Of My Miracle."

THIRD WEEK

SUNDAY GOD DESIRES ONLY GOOD THINGS FOR ME

MONDAY I CAN KNOW GOD'S DIRECTION FOR MY LIFE

TUESDAY I CAN HAVE JOY EVEN IN THE MIDST OF SORROW

WEDNESDAY I CAN HEAR GOD'S VOICE

THURSDAY I CAN BE FREE OF THE BONDAGE THAT KEEPS ME FROM BEING A SUCCESS IN GOD'S EYES

FRIDAY GOD WILL MAKE A WAY FOR ME TO RECEIVE THE MIRACLE I NEED

SATURDAY I CAN WAIT OUT THE GROWING TIME OF MY MIRACLE

FOURTH WEEK

I Know Who My Source Is And He Knows Me

By Oral Roberts

SUNDAY

**Key:
I KNOW GOD SPEAKS
TO ME AND
I WILL RESPOND TO HIM**

**or
How You Can Have A
Faith-Connection To Get "On The Line" With God**

If you could see into the world of the spirit — the spirit realm — you would see a LINE connecting you directly with God and you would know you can make daily contact with Him, telling Him exactly what you need. It would make all the difference in your life.

Now God from His end of that LINE sees you with absolute clarity — and with a caring that you've never known from any human being or earthly source. His words are coming across the LINE. If you are in connection AND if you are listening, you can hear Him in terms you understand right at the point of your need.

Now here's a good way to understand this in your spirit and mind so you can "get on the line" with God and stay in connection for your miracles to be flowing toward you every day of your life.

"I CAN FEEL IT TUGGING ON THE LINE"

A little boy was flying a kite. He kept letting out the cord he had in his hand connected to his kite until after a while it literally soared so high it went out of sight.

A man walking by saw the little boy standing there with his hands stretched high holding to what looked like a string and looking up. But there was nothing in sight. "Sonny, what are you doing?" the man asked.

"Flying a kite."

"Flying a kite?"

"Yep."

"I don't see any kite."

"It's up there."

"Well, I can't see it."

"It's up there."

"Well, if you can't see it, how do you know it is up there?"

"Mister, I can feel it tugging on the line!"

That story means a lot to me because it describes so well how you and I can know God is up *there* because we feel Him speaking to us in our inner being down *here*. Or if it's not actual words, it's an *impression* inside us that is different from any human expression because it is drawing us toward God or pointing us in the right direction for our lives.

A critic jumped all over me one day when I told how I feel God's presence or how I hear Him in my spirit or how His gifts of the Spirit, such as the word of knowledge or the gift of healing, manifest themselves in me to help someone.

He said, "Oh, that's not possible. You're deceiving the people."

I said, "Sir, I don't know how big you think your God is, but the God I serve created the universe. He created man. In fact, everything visible came from the invisible hand of my God. That means He's bigger than all He created.

"Now, I'm just a man, a mere little spot in the universe. If God is bigger than what He created, including my tiny little self, I have no problem believing He can reach where I am and deal with me on my level...and when He does, I feel Him, I hear Him, and it fills me with a knowing that God is and He is my Savior...and nobody, you or anyone else, can ridicule or talk me out of what I know that I know that I know."

To my surprise he said, "Oral Roberts, do you really believe that?"

"I know it," I replied.

"Will you pray for me that I can know God like that?" he asked.

"Yes, I will," I answered and we had a beautiful time of prayer together.

I've seen this man many times since and he assures me he's "on the line" with God, and I believe it.

GOD STILL SPEAKS TODAY: HE SPEAKS TO YOU. ARE YOU LISTENING?

If there's a doubt in your mind that God speaks or that you can hear Him or if His speaking to you is to be a part of your success on this earth, look at Mark 9:7. Those who witnessed John the Baptist baptizing Jesus in the river Jordan heard the Father say: "This is my beloved Son, hear ye him."

God was speaking. They heard His words. They understood that God speaks. He speaks to people. To every person. And Jesus went about talking to people and they "heard" His words.

On one occasion Jesus said, "Let my words sink down into your ears" (Luke 9:44). In other words, be listening so intently that you actually hear what I'm saying to you and you will know the way of God and the power of God in your life.

King David said, "Today if you hear His voice, harden not your heart." Be ready to *hear* God and to be open to His words.

In the days when the telegraph system was first invented and the Morse code with its dots and dashes carried man's voice across the wires to people across the nation, there went forth a great cry to employ those who had learned to be telegraphers. The railroad companies and others were almost desperate to find young men and women who understood what the dots and dashes meant when they were being tapped out and who could send messages in Morse code themselves.

A young man hastened to apply for such a job. When he arrived at the company's office, the outer room was filled with applicants. As he stood looking around, he cocked his ear and began listening intently. Then he marched through a door and soon reappeared saying, "You folks can all leave. I have the job."

Angry voices said, "What do you mean, you have the job? We've been here all morning and you've just walked in."

He said, "Didn't you hear the dots and dashes that were sounding when I came in a few minutes ago?"

"Oh, we heard a noise."

"Well, that noise you heard was saying, 'Do you read me? Do you read me? Do you read me? If you do, come in; you have the job'. I have learned the Morse code. I know what the dots and dashes mean, so I rushed in and I have the job."

The first time I *heard* God's voice and *understood* He was speaking to Oral Roberts was NOT really the first time God spoke to me. It was the first time I was in position to LISTEN and to UNDERSTAND. You see, He had been speaking to me before but either I didn't believe God spoke or I didn't care or I wasn't listening. How do I know?

When He spoke and I understood His words, *Son, I'm going to heal you and you are to take My healing power to your generation,* there was a certain way it sounded inside me, a certain effect on my being. It occurred to me I had heard that kind of sound and felt that effect inside me before but had paid no attention to it. I was not connected "on the line" with God as my Lord and my God.

TRAIN YOURSELF TO RECOGNIZE GOD'S VOICE

Since that time I've worked on training myself to listen AND to recognize that voice. Each time I've heard Him speak it's always in the same familiar voice. Jesus said, "My sheep hear my voice" (John 10:27).

Since God does speak to you, you must choose to hear, to have a listening heart. You, like me, may not get it every time or you may not always understand it at once.

The Bible says, "Try the spirits to see if they are of God" (1 John 4:1).

You can try the voices you hear by studying the Word of God, by being filled with the Holy Spirit, both of which will "witness" in agreement to your spirit if what you're hearing is from God.

Jesus said, "When the Holy Spirit is come, he will testify (talk) of me" (John 15:26).

Think back in your life and you'll probably recall inner impressions or actual words in your spirit from God that you paid little attention to or ignored — or even rejected. And it's not always an audible voice. Sometimes I hear God audibly, at least in my spirit I hear Him audibly. But most times I get a deep impression that will not go away. And like I do when I believe I hear His audible voice, I check these impressions with the Word of God and by the Holy Spirit who indwells me as He does all believers (1 Corinthians 6:19,20).

Sometimes I check these with certain people I trust to be in line with God to get a "sounding" from them.

Ultimately I have to make the choice that I believe I

heard God speak to me or felt His impression in my spirit. Then I must take responsibility for my actions. The real test, as I see it, is whether the message I believe I hear or feel glorifies God. Does it help people? Does it extend God's kingdom? It can never have hatred, bitterness, or destruction in it. God is a good God and He never says anything to us or impresses us to do something that is not good in the sense of God's goodness.

HOW TO DEAL WITH THE COUNTERFEIT

One of the things we face is the counterfeit and this disturbs a lot of people. They hear of some person or group who claims God told them to do certain things and they turn out to be way off line with the Word of God. A few times they kill people under the guise, "God told me to do it."

I deplore that along with every right-thinking person and I will have no part with such proclamations. But I stand unmoved in my absolute conviction that my God is alive. He speaks. He speaks to His people, including Oral Roberts, and the counterfeit happens because the devil is trying to duplicate what God does and CAN'T do — so he uses the counterfeit.

Years ago when I visited the United States mint in Washington, D.C., the guide told us that the workers who handle the bills are allowed to handle only the genuine, never the counterfeit. They learn only the feel of a genuine United States bill so that if a counterfeit bill comes into their hands, they know the difference instantly. In other words, they don't start with the counterfeit to learn the genuine.

In the same manner, I think people who get hung up on the bad and terrible things some people do in the name of God may never get into the genuine power of God. As for me, I'm committed to God, to His voice, His words, His ways, His salvation and deliverance. Those I know personally and intimately. When I run into anybody or anything that is opposite from the Word of God or His Spirit, I know the difference and I put distance between it or them and me. But I will NOT give up the real Jesus because some deceived person or group brings dishonor to Him by their ungodly words or deeds.

As Joshua of old said, "As for me and my house, we will serve the Lord" (Joshua 24:15).

When it's all said and done, God is a good God and you'll discover He will only hold you accountable for what you say and do, not for someone else's words or deeds. When you've obeyed Him, you needn't be concerned that anybody masquerading in the guise of God can effectively hurt the work of God or your own Christian life.

"Greater is he that is in you, than he that is in the world" (1 John 4:4).

HAVE YOU A LISTENING HEART?

Far more important to you is to have a listening heart, to really humble yourself to make hearing Him your top priority.

A railroad engineer of the past had to depend on accurate timing to keep his train on schedule. He relied on what was called a "railroad watch," a pocket watch that could really be depended on.

Ultimately one of his grandsons, a carpenter, inherited the watch and he always carried it on the job with him.

One day after climbing all over a construction project, he reached for his watch and discovered he had lost it. His fellow workers knew how he loved his watch so they helped him look for it. By quitting time it could not be located and he went home very depressed.

After dinner he returned to the site. Hours later when he came home, he called to his wife, "Honey, I found my watch."

"Oh, what did you do to find it?" she asked.

"I returned to the site and climbed all through the structure looking for it. I even walked the ground in the area around the site. Then I did the one thing I hadn't thought to do before."

She said, "What's that?"

He said, "I got down on my hands and knees and crawled through the construction and even wriggled my way on the ground. Every few seconds I'd stop and listen. Finally I heard a ticking sound. I reached out toward it and picked something up and, sure enough, it was my watch."

The watch was there all the time, ticking away, needing only for its owner to hear the ticking and pick it up. God is here…God is there…God is everywhere…and He is speaking…impressing himself in people…in every person in the world …me…you…

Jesus said, "He that hath ears to hear, let him hear" (Matthew 11:15).

YOUR GOD-GIVEN KEY FOR TODAY

"I Am Cultivating A Listening Heart…For I Know God Is Speaking To Me, *Flo Dranger.*"

(Write your name here.)

Key:
TO GET THE ANSWERS
TO MY "WHYS"
I MUST KNOW THERE
IS A DEVIL BUT
THAT GOD IS
GREATER THAN HE IS

MONDAY

or
How To Stop Blaming God For
All The Bad Things That May Come Your Way

I've discovered the word *why* is often the most powerful word in the English language. Beginning in childhood, *why* is the word that we use to learn about life. You can see yourself as a wide-eyed little child asking your daddy or mommy, "Why?" and having it explained and another "Why?" to the explanation. As we grow older, *why* is the word that we usually say first when something really bad happens to us. If you are like me, you hear this word *why* come tearing out of your very soul when you or a dear one is struck down by illness or financial reverses or a spiritual problem or family upheavals.

When my coach picked me up off the floor in a basketball tournament when I'd collapsed, hemorrhaging from my lungs, and put me in the back seat of his car and drove me the long trip home back to my parents, and Papa called the doctor and I was told I had tuberculosis and I knew there was no medicine then to cure me and I didn't know anyone who might pray a miracle down on me, I remember I cried until my body shook and shook and I fell into my father's arms.

I remember.

I remember I cried out to the top of my voice:

"WHY? WHY? WHY HAS THIS HAPPENED TO ME? WHAT HAVE I DONE TO DESERVE IT?"

Since that hour I've said the word *why* thousands of times and find at times, in spite of all I've learned since, I still say WHY when things don't go right.

And...I hear this question asked me every day by someone in person or by letter.

Why me, God?
Why my family, God?
Why my business, God?
Why my job, God?

IT'S YOUR CHOICE

You may like what I'm going to say to you or you may not. It's your choice. But if you read on, I must say it or I fail God, I fail you, and I fail myself.

It's this: There is a devil. The devil is real. And if you deny the devil exists or is a mean devil, you have to deny God, the Bible, and all human experience. You have to say everything is by chance. When something goes wrong you have to say, "I'm just unlucky...or the stars are against me...or life is not worth living."

If you say any one of those things and really believe it, you are in trouble, bad trouble, and you've got to get hold of yourself and declare in your spirit and with your words: "I am going back to the God who created me and who sent His Son to die for me on Calvary and to rise from the dead to give me life and give it to me more abundantly. I am going to set myself in agreement with God to bring me out of this mess and make me a whole person, even in spite of everything the devil is trying to do to me."

That's for starters.

Next, you're going to have to take a step with your

faith above and beyond every doubt you've ever had, every negative feeling you've given birth to, every lie about God you've ever entertained and make the commitment (I mean you, yourself, will do it) that God is a million, billion, trillion times greater than the devil, that He loves you with a love that spiritually and literally surrounds you...and...He is closer to you than your breath and is right now

SENDING MIRACLES
TOWARD YOU...OR PAST YOU!

And it's your choice to reach out and "receive" your miracle, or it's your choice to let it "pass you by."

There are two powers in life, not three or four or more — just two: God...and...the devil.

So let's do what Jesus did first when He was in human flesh like you and me and all things totally bad and wrong were hurled at Him by Satan:

First, identify the devil as the power, the personality, who is hurling every bad thing possible against you. Don't accuse God of doing it or blame Him as if He did.

Jesus knew the devil had once been the archangel Lucifer, the highest, greatest of all the archangels, the one closest to God's throne, the one who actually was the hovering presence over the Father. Lucifer was the son of the morning, the most trusted angel, the one given the greatest powers and responsibilities...who allowed envy and covetousness to enter his spirit so that he turned against God, and attempted to be *above* God, take His place and become what God alone is: King of the universe! (See Ezekiel 28, Isaiah 14:12, and Luke 10:18.)

God told Lucifer he had "sin" in his heart — He would cast him out of heaven, deny him his place with the other archangels, Gabriel and Michael, cast him down to earth, strip him of his heavenly body and reserve him in spiritual darkness until the final day of judgment, then cast him forever into the "burning lake of fire" (Revelation 20:10).

Later when God created man — Adam and Eve, our foreparents — and placed them in the garden of Eden with the power of choice, God had to limit himself in order for them to be man instead of robots. God *gave* them the power to decide whom they would serve. They could choose God or the fallen Lucifer, the devil. God does the same for us. He does not force us to choose Him, but He shows us in His Word how much more profitable it will be if we do.

Jesus was there when Satan was thrown out of heaven. He saw it all happen and was part of the triune God who placed the devil as "the prince of the powers of the air" (Ephesians 2:2) and the "god of the world" (2 Corinthians 4:4), but reduced him to one who became "as a roaring lion, seeking whom he may devour" (1 Peter 5:8).

Lucifer is *not* the Prince of Peace — who is Jesus Christ of Nazareth. Lucifer is *not* the King and the God of the universe — who is the eternal Father. Lucifer is *not* even a lion but "as a roaring lion" — one that can roar but with no real power except what man chooses to give him by deciding to serve the devil instead of God.

DO LIKE JESUS DID — CALL THE DEVIL WHAT HE IS

That's it in a nutshell. Jesus knew all this about the devil and more. So when the bad came against Him, He called the devil what he was: a liar (John 8:44), killer, thief, and destroyer (John 10:10), deceiver

(Revelation 20:10), and many other names that characterize him as being totally evil and without probability of redemption.

In other words, Jesus knew who the enemy was and I, along with you, must know this too.

Second, Jesus knew the Word of God. When Satan tried to say the Scriptures to Jesus, he either added or misquoted or took part of it away — and Jesus knew it and gave him the Scriptures straight (Matthew 4:3-10). Satan came at Jesus just as he comes at you — at the beginning of His ministry, before He had time to establish himself and when times were difficult. But Jesus confronted him with the same things available to you — the Scriptures and His faith in God.

You're always faced with identifying people in your life on this earth. You must identify the devil for who and what he is: evil incarnate and totally against you.

You're always reading or spending time in learning about life and daily things. You must read and study God's Holy Word, the Bible — and not make excuses for not doing it any more than you would make excuses for not eating and die because of it.

For years in my life I read everything I could get my hands on except the Bible. When I did read some of it, I didn't seek God to help me understand it. It meant nothing…zero…to me.

So when I was hit by tuberculosis in the final stages and cried, "WHY?" I wasn't able to identify the devil who had sent sickness as "the oppression of the devil" on me (Acts 10:38).

I cried, I questioned, I got mad at God, I wasn't nice to my parents or anybody, I wouldn't cooperate at first with the doctors, and when people came to pray for me I didn't even look at them much less receive their prayers.

I BECAME A PAIN

I wasn't only in pain, I was a pain. Not only was my body sick, I was sick. Not only were my lungs full of corruption, my soul was corrupted.

I don't enjoy saying this about myself but it's the truth and the Bible says only "the truth will set you free" (John 8:32). I'm telling you what God loves, the truth.

When Jesus was hurt He identified His enemy, the devil. I didn't. I blamed God for letting this sickness come on me. And it got me nowhere but to the edge of hell on earth!

As I lay there five months sick unto death, having to live with one of the foulest diseases ever put on a person — TB, I finally "came to myself" and began listening to my parents as they read the Word of God to me day by day by day...until I began to get hold of it with my spirit and mind and got in position to hear God speak to me through my sister Jewel, "Oral, God is going to heal you," and then hear God's own voice inside me confirming it.

Paul says, "Faith comes by hearing, and hearing by the WORD OF GOD" (Romans 10:17).

YOUR FAITH COMES UP BY THE WORD OF GOD

Faith comes to you in many ways, but the most powerful, the most sure, the most effective is by the Word of God as you read and study it with an open mind and hungry heart, or hear it preached and taught, or see God "confirming the word by signs following" (Mark 16:20).

You say, "Oral, how does all this help me with *WHYS?*" I'll tell you how it helps. It takes you to your *SOURCE: GOD!*

You say, "Will looking to God as my Source and only to Him answer ALL my WHYS?"

I reply vehemently, "YES!" Some of your whys will be answered instantly and dramatically. Others will be answered over a period of time and others will be answered by a miracle and the *why* will be gone forever.

Then it will give you a hope of heaven nothing else can, that in heaven all your *whys* will be answered for the simple reason that when God raises you from the dead in the resurrection — there will be NO MORE WHYS… because there will be no more devil to have to face! You will be with God forever!

There *is* an answer to "WHY?" It's faith in God.

YOUR GOD-GIVEN KEY FOR TODAY

"In All My 'Whys' I Will Look To God As My Source Of Deliverance!"

TUESDAY

Key: WHATEVER YOUR SITUATION IS, GOD KNOWS MORE ABOUT IT THAN YOU DO

or
Only God Can See The Beginning From The End Of My Problem

I began the year 1977 with God's words ringing in my heart, "There is to be a breakthrough from heaven in '77." I saw breakthroughs for the people, especially for my Partners. I saw breakthroughs for myself in this ministry.

Then came the devil on February 11 to strike with tragic force. Evelyn and I faced the worst struggle our family had ever experienced.

That night, a plane exploded over a Kansas wheat field in the middle of a severe thunderstorm. Our daughter Rebecca and her husband Marshall were killed instantly.

The next morning, Evelyn opened our door to find my long-time associate, Collins Steele, standing there with a policeman. Evelyn called to me, "Oral! Oral! Will you come in here right now?"

The sound of her voice made me drop everything and hurry to the door. Evelyn was in a state of shock. She tried to tell me what they had told her, but she couldn't get through it. Finally the policeman said, "Mr. Roberts, I've come to tell you that your daughter and son-in-law are dead."

Collins told me about the plane crash and then handed me the morning newspaper. The headline across the front page screamed the words: "ORAL ROBERTS' DAUGHTER KILLED." It went on to tell of Marshall and Rebecca and the other two couples that were killed.

I can't tell you the grief, the anguish that swept over Evelyn and me. We grabbed each other and held each other tightly. We didn't know what to do.

Then Evelyn said, "Honey, we've got to hurry and get dressed and go over to Rebecca's house and tell the children before they hear it any other way."

Brenda, 13...Marcia, 8...little Jon Oral, only 5. How do you tell children that their parents aren't coming home?

Another of my long-time associates, Ron Smith, had arrived by the time Evelyn and I were ready to leave the house. He offered to drive us over to

Marshall and Rebecca's home where the children were. On the way I said aloud, "God, You know something about this that we don't know."

Over and over I said it as Evelyn held my hand and Ron drove, the tears filling his eyes too. "God, You know something about this that we don't know."

The next day the news media picked up those words God had said to me, "God knows something about this we don't know," and thousands of people picked up on it in their tragedies and losses. I received telegrams and letters from everywhere of prayer and support, but also of what it meant to them to look to God for what He knew that they didn't know.

Without even asking, I know you have suffered a terrible loss, or you are hurting badly now, and there's the thought that something else may come along against you. And I, Oral Roberts, say these words to you,

_____:

(Write your name here.)

GOD KNOWS SOMETHING
ABOUT THIS YOU DON'T KNOW

It's been ten years since the loss of Rebecca and Marshall and although it still hurts and at times Evelyn and I and our family members still cry, the good part is that we've had time to understand a lot of that "something God knows about this" that we didn't know.

First, some remarkably good things have happened to our three grandchildren. The oldest, 23, our first-born grandchild, is in college, working hard, is a dedicated Christian, and is becoming a person of self-worth in her own right. Also, she's been able to cling to the absolute fact that SOMETHING GOD KNOWS about her parents' death is slowly being revealed to her and she is at peace about it, even though the pain is still there.

The middle child was 8 when she lost her parents, and she was bewildered more than her older sister or younger brother.

Marshall's brother Bill and his lovely wife Edna gladly took all three children into their family and poured their love into them. But Marcia couldn't adjust anywhere, including school, and we almost lost her in the rebellion she felt in her heart.

A CHRISTIAN SCHOOL HELPED

One major factor in Marcia's getting hold of her life was Victory Christian School here in Tulsa, founded by graduates of Oral Roberts University, Billy Joe and Sharon Daugherty, who also have built a great 9,000-member church, Victory Christian Center, that meets in Mabee Center on the ORU campus. In this superb Christian high school, Marcia has been awakened spiritually and academically and is making her mark for God. She went last summer as part of a youth healing team to the Far East and became involved in winning souls and healing the sick. She's still very excited about it.

Our younger daughter Roberta — who by the way just got her law degree from ORU — and her husband Ron and their family have had a remarkable spiritual influence on Marcia also. The important thing Marcia did was to open up her spirit to receive the good things God was sending her way.

Jon, 15, is an honors student, is gifted in computer science, and is devoted to the Lord and to His plan for his life. He loves his Uncle Bill and Aunt Edna but treasures everything he can get his hands on about his parents.

All three children love their grandparents on both sides. Evelyn and I not only love them, but thoroughly enjoy them when they come to our home or travel with us. Talking about Jesus around them is just as comfortable as it was with Rebecca and Marshall.

All the children have been taught Seed-Faith and sow their seeds with a joy I've seldom seen in children.

Another thing is that Rebecca and Marshall are in their eternal home. Often Evelyn and I envision them talking to the Lord about us and what we're doing down here. I believe they're more alive than ever before and are waiting for the homecoming of all of us.

HEAVEN IS VERY REAL

Heaven is very real to my family. My oldest son, Ron, while in the service during the Vietnam War got into drugs and somehow it seemed chemically to have destroyed his brain. Here we had ministered to thousands of other people's children and were not able to help our own son. When his life ended, we knew pain unlike the plane crash of our daughter and son-in-law.

Dr. Kenneth Hagin ministered to us as God gave him a "word of knowledge" about our son who could no longer cope with life.

God knows something about Ron's death too that we don't know. It's mighty comforting and strengthening to know that we know the One who knows.

You say, "But just knowing God knows, how does that help?"

Well, consider the alternative. What if God hadn't told us He knows? Can Satan help us? Can people? Is the limited knowledge of the mysteries of life sufficient? Is tormenting ourselves about what we can't understand any answer? Is blaming God going to solve it for us?

Right here is where we really discovered the *depths* of our faith. We believed with all our hearts and all our life's experiences we had faith. We knew we did. But there is a difference when part of you is snatched away and there are no human answers. The fact that I *didn't* lose my faith and that it has increased even through the worst Satan could ever throw at us, is a life-force to us that keeps us going.

One of the things that helped was to talk about it and not go off and hide with our grief being our master. And we believe it was good to let others know that we who are prominent in God's work suffer Satan's onslaughts too.

The very moment self-pity or abnormal grief seeks to enter us, we sow another seed of faith and command the mountain to be removed, as Jesus teaches us in Seed-Faith (Matthew 17:20).

In fact, I literally do not know how we could have lived without having known the three key principles of Seed-Faith.

#1. God is our Source.

#2. Sow our seed out of our need.

#3. Expect a miracle from God.

I must admit that the pain of the loss of half our family is never out of our minds or hearts. Only heaven will be the complete victory.

It helps, oh, it helps, that our other children are close to God and work with us. We have so much to be thankful for and we praise God for it — every day!

A DEEPER CAPACITY TO PRAY FOR OTHERS

And I must not forget to tell you that we have a much deeper capacity to pray for others…to believe God for them…to sow our love and faith and expectations for miracles in them. This is something you can't put on. People know the difference. No day passes that we don't get to share with someone who has suffered as we have or even more. They know we know and that we know God knows something about it that He will reveal at the hour when it's most needed.

I really believe God can see the beginning anew for me…for you…in each problem, each hurt, each loss…and that what He sees He's going to let us see.

I love that old hymn:

"Trust and obey
for there's no other way
to be happy in Jesus
but to trust and obey."

YOUR GOD-GIVEN KEY FOR TODAY

"God Knows Something About My Losses I Don't Know."

Key:
GOD IS
BIGGER
THAN ANY
WEDNESDAY **PROBLEM**
I HAVE

or
How God Showed Me
That He Was Bigger Than My Biggest Need

The City of Faith stands tall today, rising out of the rolling hills of Tulsa, Oklahoma, as a beacon to hurting people everywhere who want both PRAYER and MEDICINE working side by side, blended together with faith, for their healing. Thousands of people a year receive miracles here, and most often there is a merging of medicine and prayer in their recovery.

That wasn't always the case.

The nearer we got to the completion and opening of the City of Faith, the more God warned me that we had to follow a strict policy of PAY AS YOU GO and to open it FREE OF DEBT on the building. He had shown me how the devil would try to take His City of Faith away from us and change its God-ordained purpose. This was the first medical and research center in history, as far as we know, to be built solely for the cure and healing of the whole man, unashamedly putting PRAYER into the very heart and core of the most excellent medical treatment possible.

You can't imagine the depth of the opposition from all sides. Personal attacks were made against me and attacks were also made upon my Partners for standing with me and for building the City of Faith.

First, they laughed and said it couldn't be done.

133

Then when we started, they said it must NOT be done and they got mad. And then when we "topped out" the construction — the tallest building, the clinic, rising some 60 stories from its foundation — they literally used about every method to stop us.

WHEN YOU HAVE YOUR UPS AND DOWNS

I must confess I had my ups and downs. But I knew that I literally had to obey God no matter the persecution…the misunderstanding…or how heavy the going. I refused to give up!

One afternoon I drove over to the City of Faith and stopped my car where I could get out and stand there and look at the entire complex — the 30-story building to the right that would be the hospital, the 60-story clinic in the center, the 20-story research and continuing education building that would be to the left. The floors were all in place, but much of the outer surface still needed to be finished, not to mention all of the inside work which, as you know, is just as extensive and as expensive as the basic construction.

I felt low in my spirit. I was discouraged. I didn't see in the natural how we could finish the City of Faith by the date that God had given me for its opening. I couldn't see where we would get the money.

The time passed and pretty soon it was almost seven o'clock on that May evening, 1980. The sun was starting to go down. I closed my eyes for a brief second and when I opened them, I saw something more than the 600-foot City of Faith rising up in front of me. I saw Jesus emerge and He was about a size and a half as large as the City of Faith, at least 900 feet tall.

In the vision, I saw Him bend down and put His hands UNDER the unfinished City of Faith structure and lift it and say, *See how easy it is for Me to lift it?*

I thought my heart would burst from my body. In a trembling voice I said, "Jesus, You can really lift it, can't You?"

I SAW WITH MY SPIRITUAL EYES

This was Jesus Christ of Nazareth, the Son of the living God, that I saw before me lifting the entire giant structure of the City of Faith. It was a vision that I was seeing with my spiritual eyes. And He was letting me know how easy it was for Him to lift my greatest burden.

In sort of a strangled voice I cried, "Lord, we're running out of money again. The devil is trying to shut us down."

Jesus said in a voice that seemed to fill my head and my entire body, *BUT I AM NOT OUT OF MONEY. I OWN ALL THE SILVER AND GOLD IN THE EARTH. IT WAS I WHO MADE ABRAHAM RICH IN FAITH, IN LOVE, IN VISION, IN MONEY, SO HE WOULD BE THE FATHER OF ALL WHO HAVE FAITH. AND BECAUSE ABRAHAM HAD FAITH, I STOPPED THE DEVIL FROM STEALING HIS MONEY.*

I thought suddenly of all the people of God who feel they are poor, and how sometimes all of us look at our WALLETS OR PURSES and wonder when they will ever fill up. As if Jesus was reading my thoughts, He said, *NEITHER YOU NOR ANY OF MY CHILDREN ARE POOR EXCEPT WHEN YOU FAIL TO KNOW WHO GOD IS, AND WHO YOU ARE, AND THEN FAIL TO GIVE TITHES OF ALL AS ABRAHAM DID. NOW WHEN YOU DO THIS AND GIVE TITHES OF ALL AS SEED-FAITH TO ME, MY RICHES WILL FLOW TO YOU TO*

SUPPLY ALL YOUR NEEDS. I WILL PUT BOTH THE RICHES OF HEAVEN AND EARTH AT THE DISPOSAL OF EACH OF YOU WHO BELIEVE AND OBEY ME.

I said, "But, Jesus, I've brought it as far as I can." (This was the first time I felt I had used *all* the faith I had. Is this the way you feel now about using up all *your* faith?)

As I kept looking at Jesus…thrilling at His magnificent presence before me…seeing how easy it was for Him to lift the City of Faith, He spoke again.

YES, THIS IS AS FAR AS YOU CAN BRING IT. I TOLD YOU WHEN I CHOSE YOU TO BUILD IT THAT YOU COULDN'T BUILD IT BY YOURSELF, BUT THAT I WOULD SPEAK TO YOUR FRIENDS AND PARTNERS AND THROUGH THEM I WOULD BUILD IT.

I began crying and could barely talk. I cried, "Jesus, You are my Savior; You are my Source. What do You want me to do?"

TELL THE PEOPLE! TELL YOUR PARTNERS. MAKE MY WORDS KNOWN TO THEM. TELL THEM YOU WANT TO BE THE BEST PARTNER THEY EVER HAD, THAT YOU ARE THE OTHER PART OF THE PARTNERSHIP. TELL THEM THEY ARE NOT ALONE WITH THEIR PROBLEMS AND NEEDS, BUT THAT I HAVE ANOINTED YOU TO BE THEIR BEST PARTNER.

GOD WANTED TO BLESS THE PEOPLE

And then He went on to say, *I HAVE SPOKEN TO BOTH OLD AND NEW PARTNERS. MANY ARE OBEYING, BUT SOME ARE IN DISOBEDIENCE. I DESIRE THEM TO OBEY SO I CAN BLESS THEM AND MAKE THEM A BLESSING. THEY MUST GET INTO FAITH AND OBEY ME. AND AS YOUR PARTNERS OBEY ME, I WILL SEND MY ANGELS TO STOP THE DEVIL FROM STEALING THEIR MONEY. ALSO, I WILL STOP THE*

DEVIL FROM STEALING THEIR SPIRITUAL POWER AND THEIR HEALTH. I WILL DO A GREAT SPIRITUAL, PHYSICAL, AND FINANCIAL WORK IN THEIR LIVES.

I felt all tingly inside and began to weep again. My whole being was trembling under the power of the Holy Spirit. Jesus, in the form I had seen Him, was no longer there. But I could feel His Spirit whipping through me like a wind, a fire, a glory, a great faith, a deep obedience.

As I raised my head and looked, the building structure still towered before my eyes and I knew it was like a giant empty shell inside, waiting to be finished and equipped. But inside me there was a light turned on to hold back the night that was now closing the day. It seemed I could see clear across the earth and beyond space into heaven itself. As I looked into heaven I saw a great calm that was opposite to the rushing and roaring I had been feeling in our world.

Then I saw men, women, children by the untold numbers appear before my vision as if they were cheering me on, and as if they were waiting for the doors of the City of Faith to open to them. They looked like they were straining to reach out and touch the glory of God. I saw them not in flesh, but in my spirit, but real nevertheless.

My mind raced to Malachi 3:10 in the Bible where God said, "Bring ye all the tithes and prove me, saith the Lord of hosts, if I will not open you the windows of heaven, and pour you out a blessing, that there shall not be room enough to receive it."

WHEN THE TRICKLE BECOMES A FLOOD

A blessing where there would not be room enough to contain it! Why, the only thing that cannot be contained is a FLOOD. It seemed God was saying, *I will give MY people NOT A TRICKLE, NOT A STREAM, NOT A RIVER, BUT A FLOOD of My blessings.*

But you say, "That's fine for you, Oral Roberts, but what does that have to do with me today?"

Friend, Jesus showed himself to me that day to let me know one simple fact that stands strong and true throughout the ages, and it is true for you right where you are today:

JESUS IS BIGGER
THAN ANY PROBLEM *YOU* HAVE

No matter what you are facing, Jesus can handle it. You may have done all you can do, and have used what seems to you like the last ounce of your energy and faith.

WHEN YOU REACH THE END
OF YOUR RESOURCES, JESUS HAS *MORE*
RESOURCES WAITING ON YOUR BEHALF

Do all that you can do. Then expect Jesus to do what only HE can do.

You're not in your problem alone.

JESUS IS THERE.

You don't have to carry the burden by yourself.

JESUS IS THERE.

You don't have to DO it all alone.

JESUS IS THERE.

Be encouraged! Jesus has a blessing in store for you that there will not be room enough to contain it!

If you are not planting your seeds of faith, if you are not giving to God, start giving as God tells you and then start expecting the windows of heaven to open up to you.

Start looking for miracles. Maybe just a trickle at

first, or a stream, or even a river. But keep expecting until a FLOOD of miracles fills and surrounds you for your deliverance!

You and Jesus are TOGETHER an unbeatable miracle team.

Remember, without you, Jesus will not. But without Jesus, you cannot.

The opposite is also true. *With* you, Jesus will! *With* Jesus, you can!

YOUR GOD-GIVEN KEY FOR TODAY

"God Is Bigger Than My Problem... He Is Greater Than My Need."

THURSDAY
Key: GOD IS A REWARDER

or How I Can Get Into Position To Receive The Rewards God Has For ME

For years — in fact, for all of my growing-up time — I never dreamed that God is a Rewarder.

I grew up under the kind of teaching that if we stepped aside the wrong way, we'd be slapped down by God or even cast into hell soon. Somehow I got all mixed up in my thinking. I'm still learning the truth about God — that He is a "rewarder of them that diligently seek him" (Hebrews 11:6).

I personally went for years with the wrong idea about God. Had I known that He is a REWARDER, I think I would have dreamed a different dream

139

when I was a teenager and I would have made God a part of that dream. I never would have run away from my mother and father and plunged my life into sin.

What are God's rewards?

If you think that God rewards you with sickness in your body…HE DOESN'T. If you think that He rewards you with poverty…or depression…or loneliness…or a long-faced religion that robs you of joy…HE DOESN'T!

God rewards you with a relationship with Him that puts joy in your soul, a shine on your face, a sparkle in your eyes, a lift to your shoulders, and a spring in your step. He rewards you with blessings…with health …with prosperity…with love…with a sense of purpose and fulfillment and meaning for your life. He is a REWARDER and His rewards are GOOD.

GOD REBUKES THE DEVOURERS

In Malachi 3:10,11, God says something about how He rewards us. He says, "Bring ye all the tithes into the storehouse, that there may be meat in mine house, and prove me now herewith, saith the Lord of hosts, if I will not open you the windows of heaven, and pour you out a blessing, that there shall not be room enough to receive it. *And I will rebuke the devourer for your sakes.*"

For YOUR sake.

Now let's look at this Scripture more closely. I want you to see three things about it that you can take with you and use today right where you are.

Number One. God says that there's something we must do. We must ACTIVATE His miracle flow toward us. It's like putting a key into a locked door. He says, "Bring ye all the tithes into the storehouse."

You may say, "Why does God need my giving…

my money?"

He doesn't need it for His sake. He has all the gold and the silver of this entire earth, for the earth is the Lord's and the FULLNESS thereof (Psalm 24:1). God wants you to give for YOUR SAKE. He says that your giving is for two reasons. First, that His work might go on in the entire earth. Missions teams might reach into the darkest nations with God's healing power. Television programs might span the nation with the message that "God is a good God." Churches might be planted. Souls might be saved. People might be delivered. Prayer and medicine might be combined. People might see the Word of God come alive before their eyes. God wants HIS WORK TO GO ON so that churches here on earth will be full and alive with miracles, signs, and wonders, and so that heaven will be populated.

TRIGGERING A RESPONSE

Second, God says your giving is going to trigger a response from God. He is going to PROVE HIMSELF to *you,* by pouring out a blessing on you.

I don't know how you feel about it, but that EXCITES me. I want to see God's work multiplied on this earth until every person has heard the gospel and has been touched by God's power! I want God's blessing pouring back into my own life! That's a twofold response that I WANT in my life!

Number Two. God says that His blessing back to you is bigger than you've thought it would be.

Hear that carefully. God has a greater blessing for you than you have imagined. He says that the windows of heaven will be opened to you and that He will pour out a blessing that you will not be able to contain! In Luke 6:38 we read about this type of receiving — this type of miracle, blessing, harvest — in similar words: "pressed down, shaken together, and RUNNING OVER." God has an abundance for you in all areas of your life that you haven't even thought about receiving yet!

What's the greatest miracle that you can imagine receiving from God today?

Well, think again, because the blessing God has in mind for you is even greater!

Number Three. God wants to REBUKE the devourer — the devil himself — who is trying to destroy you.

Write your name in the blank:

God desires to REBUKE THE DEVOURER

who is trying to destroy _Flo Diangara_!

(Write your name here.)

In Psalm 106:9 God is said to have "rebuked the Red Sea" and it dried up so the children of Israel could walk through on dry land. Today, God wants to REBUKE the trouble that has you covered up, so you can walk through to victory!

In Matthew 17:18 Jesus "rebuked the devil" from a child and the child was made whole. Today, God wants YOU to be made whole in spirit, mind, body, finances, relationships.

In Mark 4:39 Jesus "rebuked the wind and the sea" and calmed the waves threatening to swamp the disciples' boat. Are problems threatening to overwhelm you? Are you feeling like things are out of control? Jesus wants to REBUKE that force that's coming against you today!

In Luke 4:39 Jesus "rebuked the fever" from Peter's mother-in-law and she rose up out of the sickness. Jesus wants to REBUKE the trouble that has you down!

"STOP IT! THAT'S ENOUGH!"

What does *rebuke* really mean? In laymen's terms, it means God is saying, "Stop it! That's enough!"

Well, that's what Jesus is saying to whatever part of you today that is sick, discouraged, out of harmony, diseased, or painful. He's saying, "Stop it! That's enough!" Or in other words, "Devil, you take your hand off God's property, _Flo Dungan_!"

(Write your name here.)

God is in the business of rebuking our devourers because He wants us to have only GOOD REWARDS. He rebukes the devil's attacks. He rebukes demons. He rebukes disease. He rebukes trials and the storms of life. Now this doesn't mean God exempts us from problems. But it does mean He keeps the effects of those problems from destroying us.

I'm going to ask you to do two things today.

First, I want you to write down Malachi 3:10,11 on a piece of paper and carry it with you. I want you to pull it out at least seven times today and read it out loud to yourself:

> *"Bring ye all the tithes into the storehouse, that there may be meat in mine house, and prove me now herewith, saith the Lord of hosts, if I will not open you the windows of heaven, and pour you out a blessing, that there shall not be room enough to receive it. And I will rebuke the devourer for your sakes."*
>
> — Malachi 3:10,11

Next, I want you to say to yourself every time a problem starts to eat away at you or fill your mind — a

143

hundred times today if you need to…and say it like you *mean* it!…

YOUR GOD-GIVEN KEY FOR TODAY

"God Is My Rewarder And He Is Rebuking The Devourer For My Sake!"

FRIDAY Key: GOD WANTS TO HEAL ME!

or How I Can Know That It Is God's Desire To Heal ME!

A Roman centurion came to Jesus one day seeking healing for his servant. He told Jesus about how his servant was in bed paralyzed and in great agony. Jesus did not hesitate for a moment. He said immediately, "I *will* come and heal him" (Matthew 8:7).

In that one statement of absolute fact, Jesus was establishing something for you and me today, and for every human being who has ever lived:

THE NATURE OF GOD IS TO HEAL

It is God's will for you to be well. Never again believe that God wants you to be sick. That's a lie of the devil. God's nature is for you to be healed… whole in spirit, mind, and body…prosperous in your finances and your relationships.

In Exodus 15:26 we read, "I am the Lord that healeth thee."

God is not only your Source…your Rewarder… the rebuker of the devourer in your life. He is your HEALER.

Do you want to know what God is like? Look at the life of Jesus Christ. Jesus was constantly in motion — and if you read about His life carefully in the first four books of the New Testament, you'll find that He had either just come from healing someone or was on His way to heal someone ALL THE TIME. He was reaching out to people, touching them at the point of their need. Jesus today, in His unlimited form of the Holy Spirit, is in constant motion toward us. He is forever moving toward those in need with healing power and deliverance.

Now God uses many methods to bring us His healing power. One of His methods is prayer.

God encourages us to "lay hands on one another" and to pray for their healing. (See Mark 16:18, James 5:16.) I know this method works. I've laid my hands on more than a million people during my lifetime, praying and with faith believing for mighty miracles. I've seen the lame walk. I've watched as the blind begin to see. I've seen the deaf hear. I've watched goiters...tumors...abnormal growths disappear before my eyes. Yes, God heals through the method of prayer and nobody could ever convince me otherwise.

God also heals through medicine. He has allowed men and women of science to discover His healing chemicals that He placed in the earth, and to learn how to use them to help us get well. He's allowed physicians to develop great skills in surgery and therapy to restore us to wholeness.

God works through a balanced diet...through the loving words and concern of others...through Holy Communion...through climate.

God has unlimited methods for healing us.

And it's up to us not to limit God or to put a stop to God's many miracle methods coming into our lives.

YOU HAVE A PART IN YOUR HEALING

What is our part in getting healed?

It begins with *desire*.

Do you have a heart's desire? If you do, then you have a determination to see it happen in your life. It's not just a whim...not just a wish...it's a deep, motivating force that you think about day in, day out.

The Bible has many stories of people who were DETERMINED to get their miracle. And in their determination, they obeyed God, believed His Word, and they RECEIVED what they desired!

Abraham was determined. When God asked him to sacrifice his son Isaac, Abraham determined in his heart that he would obey God and trust the consequences to God. Although he loved his son more than he loved anything on the face of the earth, Abraham's highest desire was to love God and to obey Him. Abraham operated out of that desire when he prepared to sacrifice his son. God saw that his desire was pure and He provided a ram to be sacrificed in Isaac's place. Isaac was spared.

Are you determined today to seek God's highest will for your life? To obey Him fully? To believe God's Word?

Noah was determined. Noah kept building the ark even when everyone criticized him. He could easily have doubted God. No one had ever heard of rain before, or even thought about a flood that might destroy the earth.

Noah worked at building the ark for more than a hundred years. He could easily have given up along the way.

But Noah obeyed God and remained steady and kept on building, and building, and building.

Are you willing to ignore the criticism of others

today, or to stay steady in your faith no matter what the opposition might be or how long your miracle might take?

PUSHING YOUR WAY THROUGH TO JESUS

The woman with the issue of blood was determined. She pushed her way through the crowd until she could touch the hem of His garment for herself …and she received the healing that no one and nothing had been able to provide for her during twelve long years of illness. Are you willing to go after your miracle with all of your strength?

God has put determination — a deep desire for miracles — in each one of us. No matter what it takes …no matter what anyone may think…no matter what anybody may say…no matter what criticism we receive…we CAN BE DETERMINED to stand strong and to believe the fact of facts:

Jesus wants to heal ME!
In His timing.
In His method.
Jesus is my HEALER!

Say it to yourself over and over as you go about your work and life today!

YOUR GOD-GIVEN KEY FOR TODAY

**"I Know It Is God's Desire To Heal Me And For Me To Be Whole In Spirit, Mind, and Body.
I Will Trust Him To Be My Healer Today!"**

**Key:
YOU HAVE
SOMEONE WHO
LOVES AND
UNDERSTANDS
YOU**

SATURDAY

or
How You Can Respond
To The Love Strokings Of God

Do you feel an emptiness in your life? No meaning for your existence? Filled with boredom and monotony? Wondering if anyone or anything will ever cross your path to bring forth that something inside you that makes you very special? Does day after day roll on and real life keeps on passing you by?

I want to share with you today the story of a beautiful snow-white animal which was part wolf and part dog, named White Fang.

THE STORY OF WHITE FANG

When I was a little boy I loved to read Jack London's stories, "The Call of the Wild," "White Fang," and others. Jack London's story tells how White Fang was captured in the North woods by loggers who brought him to camp and penned him up. But he was so vicious and wild that he would tear into or kill whatever came across his path.

The first five years of his existence in the camp were spent in self-preservation. The whole of his experience was to learn how to survive alone. He could not be tamed. Finally the loggers decided to turn him loose to go back into the wilds. Then an event of special significance happened. That event was in the person of a man named Scott.

Mr. Scott loved animals and understood them. And when he saw White Fang, he understood his condition immediately and started toward him in the pen, putting out his hand and talking softly. When the loggers saw Mr. Scott approaching White Fang, they cried, "Mr. Scott! Mr. Scott! Don't get any closer to that dog. He'll tear you up."

But Mr. Scott continued gradually approaching the animal which had super intelligence yet was so wild and vicious in his nature. As he walked toward him, he kept his hand out and all the time he spoke in a low, soft voice. White Fang bristled, bared his fangs, and crouched to attack. Then suddenly the wild tension began to drain out of him and he slumped to the ground with his head between his paws. Slowly, carefully, Mr. Scott put his hand on his head, then on his neck and his sides and began to stroke him... stroke him and speak quietly in a low, calm voice.

Later he told the astonished loggers what he was doing. He said, "I was speaking not to the wild wolf nature of White Fang, but to the dog part... to the little dog that was hidden within the inner core of this animal's nature. And as I stroked, I was speaking to that little dog inside and saying,'Rise up, assert yourself, take command over your wolf nature.'"

THE DAY LOVE SHONE THROUGH

Day after day Mr. Scott would enter White Fang's pen to stroke him and speak to him in that low, calm voice, while the animal lay there quivering and moaning. Then one wonderful day White Fang looked up and when he did, there was a look of pure love in his eyes. He raised up his entire body and put his paws on the chest of Mr. Scott, who put his arms around him and hugged him. The loggers stood nearby watching with tears running down their cheeks.

Now the story of White Fang and Mr. Scott meant a lot to me as a little boy, and as I remember it today it has even more meaning to my life…and to yours… and especially in the way we react to that special *event* in our lives. The event in the form of a person named Jesus. In every human being, deep inside, is a wild, and often vicious, nature. This destructive attitude rises up inside us from time to time and too often it causes us to strike at others, also even to strike at God. But God, in His love for us, brought an event into our lives in the form of a Savior, His only begotten Son Jesus Christ of Nazareth, who reaches out with His powerful but gentle hand to stroke you, to stroke me, with love.

Oh, the love strokings of God!

As He strokes and speaks in that still, small voice inside you, He is speaking to the inner core of your being, to the God part of you, to that part that He created in His own spiritual and moral likeness. As Mr. Scott spoke to White Fang, so God speaks to that God-likeness in us to rise up and overcome the part of our nature that's untamable, that part that sends us into the wilds of human existence where we don't know who we are or where we are.

You can respond to those powerful, gentle love strokes of your Creator.

GROWING UP IN REBELLION

I remember growing up in rebellion, dreaming dreams that were not part of God's plan for my life, and when I felt those love strokes, I didn't know what they were. As God moved my Christian parents to reach out to me, I would not listen. The few times I read the Bible or heard a sermon or a song about Jesus' love for me, I was like White Fang in my striking out, in my vicious words that reflected the wild side of me. I didn't know God was trying to reawaken that part of Him that had always been in me as it is in every person. I didn't know that God was speaking quietly in my inner self and saying, *Oral, rise up, assert yourself, take command, be the master over your sinful nature through My grace. Become what I created you to be.*

Does the monotony of your daily existence make you feel: "Oh, what's the use? I'm a nobody. I'll never rise out of this. It'll all end and it'll be like I've never lived."

Then I say to you: Don't give up your dream, don't turn loose of your vision. There's a hand reaching out, and a voice speaking inside you. What is your response to that hand as it strokes that God part of you and tries to bring it forth?

There is meaning for you, more than you've ever dreamed and Jesus offers it to you in His Person. Hear His voice as He says to you, "The Spirit of the Lord is upon me, because he hath anointed me to preach the gospel to the poor; he hath sent me to heal the brokenhearted, to preach deliverance to the captives, and recovering of sight to the blind, to set at liberty them that are bruised" (Luke 4:18).

THE POWER OF THE VOICE

There's no question in my mind that while the strokings of White Fang by Mr. Scott did something very special so that he could be in position for the little dog to awaken within him, it was the *voice* of Mr. Scott that spoke to White Fang, and kept on speaking, in some mysterious way so that White

Fang heard it in the inner core of his being.

You say, "But that's the animal world; I'm a human being."

Yes, but it is God who made man, the animals, and all creation to respond to Him. And the Bible says, "Faith comes by hearing, and hearing by the word of God" (Romans 10:17). Look again at Jesus' words and as you read them OUT LOUD, listen to them as if they are coming directly from the lips of Jesus *to your inner self.*

Jesus says, "The Spirit of the Lord is upon Me and He has anointed Me to bring good news to those without the benefits of life as My Father designed it…to come to *you* at the *point of your need:* with your bills piling up, your not knowing how to get through the day, your wondering if you'll ever come out of this situation, your hurting inside and outside …and to say to you, 'I am here and I have good news!'" You have the faith in you to choose to hear Jesus saying this to you, so listen and hear.

Jesus said, "I have come to heal the broken in spirit, to mend the heart that is broken, to bring recovery of sight to the blind."

Helen Keller, who was born without sight or hearing or speech, was once asked through the sign language, "Miss Keller, isn't it awful to have eyes and still not see, to have ears and still not hear?" She replied, "Isn't it worse to have eyes and still not see and have ears and still not hear?" You see, Jesus Christ of Nazareth has come to return the sight and the hearing, to bring that intuitiveness to respond to God back into your existence, to give you the power, the inner strength, to make a major response to Him again!

152

JESUS IS YOUR YEAR OF JUBILEE

Then Jesus says, "I have come to proclaim the acceptable year of the Lord." Every Hebrew knew what that meant. That was the Year of Jubilee, the fiftieth year in Israel, when the land that had been sold in the previous 50 years automatically and legally reverted to its original owner. A person who was a slave was automatically freed on that year called the Year of Jubilee, and also all debts were canceled. Jesus is saying, "I AM THE YEAR OF JUBILEE! I am that Force and that Power. I have come to restore you to a full human being. I have come to reawaken that spiritual life force within you which is made in the image of God. I am saying to you, 'Rise up, assert yourself, take command of your life through My grace, My forgiveness, My presence. I will cancel all your sins. I will blot out all your past blunders. I will take away all the monotony, the meaninglessness. I will set you free. I will make you a NEW creature!'"

On the star-spangled night of Jesus' birth over the hills of Bethlehem, the angels put it in perspective when they shouted across the centuries, "Unto you a Savior is born, unto you a Savior is born this day in the city of David."

They're saying this Savior is born to you and He's born to you TODAY. The choice is yours.

Let's pray. *Our Heavenly Father, we come to You so grateful for the birth of Your Son Jesus to us… here …now. Remember us, O God, and give us miracles of deliverance. Amen and amen.*

And now, dear friend, I pray for you through the name of Jesus Christ your Redeemer. I pray that you will feel the love strokes of your Heavenly Father as His hand strokes your inner self, the core of your

153

being, and you hear His voice inside you telling you He and you belong together, you are to be one, and life is to explode in you until you know that you know God is in you and you are in Him forever. Through Jesus Christ of Nazareth I pray, I believe, and I expect many miracles to happen to you. Amen and amen.

YOUR GOD-GIVEN KEY FOR TODAY

"I Accept God's Love Strokes Of My Inner Being. I Choose To Listen For I Know He Is Speaking To Me."

FOURTH WEEK

SUNDAY   I AM CULTIVATING A LISTENING HEART . . . FOR I KNOW GOD IS SPEAKING TO ME

MONDAY   IN ALL MY "WHYS" I WILL LOOK TO GOD AS MY SOURCE OF DELIVERANCE!

TUESDAY   GOD KNOWS SOMETHING ABOUT MY LOSSES I DON'T KNOW

WEDNESDAY   GOD IS BIGGER THAN MY PROBLEM . . . HE IS GREATER THAN MY NEED

THURSDAY   GOD IS MY REWARDER AND HE IS REBUKING THE DEVOURER FOR MY SAKE!

FRIDAY   I KNOW IT IS GOD'S DESIRE TO HEAL ME AND FOR ME TO BE WHOLE IN SPIRIT, MIND, AND BODY. I WILL TRUST HIM TO BE MY HEALER TODAY!

SATURDAY   I ACCEPT GOD'S LOVE STROKES OF MY INNER BEING. I CHOOSE TO LISTEN FOR I KNOW HE IS SPEAKING TO ME

FIFTH WEEK

My Faith Is The Most Powerful Thing I Have

By Richard Roberts

SUNDAY

or
The Lesson I Learned About Faith Through My Wife's Perfume

Did you know that, as a born-again Christian, you can have an "added dimension" for fighting life's problems? That's right. The "added dimension" is FAITH.

On the natural level we have five senses — the senses of taste, touch, smell, sight, and hearing. According to the dictionary, our senses are the avenues through which we perceive the world around us. *Faith* then, for all practical purposes, becomes our sixth — or our supernatural — sense. When we train ourselves to use the faith we've been given on a regular basis in our day-to-day life, you and I have an added dimension for coping with our struggles.

Now maybe you're thinking, *Richard Roberts, that's not fair. Only Christians have this added dimension — or sixth sense — of faith.*

No, I didn't say that. Don't misunderstand. *Everyone* has faith. The Bible says in Romans 12:3 that God has given to every man the measure of faith. It takes *faith* to get on an airplane and believe that it won't fall out of the sky. It takes *faith* to sit down in a chair and trust that the chair will hold you up. It takes *faith* to drive a car and trust that it won't unexpectedly swerve out of control into the oncoming traffic.

So whether you are a Christian or not, you *have* faith. In fact, you have all the faith you're ever going to need. It's a matter of *what you put your faith in and*

157

how you choose to use your faith.

As Christians, we have chosen to put our faith in Jesus Christ who, the Bible says, is "the author and finisher of our faith" (Hebrews 12:2) and who is completely worthy of our trust. We know that it is impossible to truly please God without using our faith to believe in Him and to believe that He is a rewarder of us when we seek Him. (See Hebrews 11:6.) And we know that once we've accepted Christ, "the just [or those reconciled to God through personal acceptance of His Son's death and resurrection] shall live by faith" (Romans 1:17).

God wants those who believe in Him to learn to "exercise" their sixth sense of faith in much the same way that we trust our five natural senses.

WHAT IS FAITH? AND HOW CAN I LEARN TO USE IT TO FIGHT MY PROBLEMS?

According to the Bible, "faith is the substance of things hoped for, the evidence of things not seen" (Hebrews 11:1). Let me put that in a little more modern wording. In other words, let me give you the Richard Roberts version of that verse. To me…

FAITH IS WHAT YOU HOLD ON TO UNTIL YOU RECEIVE WHAT YOU'RE BELIEVING FOR

In the spiritual sense, *faith* is somewhat like *money* is in the natural sense. When you go into a store to purchase an item, you have to use money to get it. And you have to have enough money to pay for what you want. But is having the money all you need to do to get what you want?

No. You must then *tell* the salesperson what you want and you must *wait* until they help you get it. All the while, you're holding on to your money, confident that you'll receive what you've asked for.

When the salesperson helps you find what you were looking for, then you let go of your money in order to receive what you've asked for.

Using your faith is somewhat like using your money. You may have all the money in the world, but until you let go of some of it, you'll never get what you want. And unless you use the faith you have to believe that God will do for you what you've asked Him to do, you probably will never receive much from God that will help you in this life.

The more you exercise your faith and learn to use it as you would your other five senses, the more you learn to trust God and the stronger your faith becomes.

My wife Lindsay has a particular perfume that I really like her to wear. When I come into the room where she is or stand next to her, I can tell that she has it on because I can smell it. One of my natural senses — my sense of smell — tells me that that's Lindsay's perfume.

What if one of my other senses said, "That's not perfume because I can't see it"? Or, "That's not perfume because I can't taste it…or hear it…or feel it." Would that change my mind about it being her perfume? Of course not. My sense of smell tells me that it is. That's how our natural senses work.

And in that regard, that's how our "sixth" sense of faith works too. When you ask God to do something in your life, even when all your natural senses tell you that nothing is going to happen, your *faith* tells you that it is. Based on the Word of God and on your past experience in using your faith to trust God, you *know* that something good is going to happen.

A woman who was healed in a crusade I conducted in Boise, Idaho, several years ago said, "I *knew* when I came that something good was going to happen to me; I was going to receive my healing." And she did. That was her faith in operation. Her other senses might have told her that there was no way she could receive her miracle, but her supernatural sense — her sense of faith, if you will — overruled her natural senses.

In other words, she held on to her belief that she would be healed *with her faith* until she received her healing!

USE THE FAITH YOU'VE BEEN GIVEN TO FIGHT WHATEVER PROBLEM YOU'RE FACING RIGHT NOW

Faith is for the tough things...the hard things... the things that you don't have but *need* in this life. Faith is for today. It's for this life on earth that is full of struggles and needs. Someday when we're in heaven, we won't need to use our faith because we'll be with Jesus and all of our needs will be met.

Faith is God's power inside you to bring healing to that inner conflict you're going through...to release you from anxiety...to whip the devil's power. Faith is God's weapon put in your heart to fight against the satanic attacks of sickness, sin, and fear.

God has given you all the faith you'll ever need to fight any problem you have. But it's up to you to use it.

YOUR GOD-GIVEN KEY FOR TODAY

"God Has Given Me The Faith To Fight Any Problem I Have!"

Then exercise that faith to come against your problem — whether it's spiritual, physical, financial, or in your family — in Jesus' name.

MONDAY

**Key:
I WILL USE A POINT
OF CONTACT FOR
RELEASING MY FAITH**

or
**How A Bad Case Of Warts
On My Hand As A Little Boy
Taught Me To Let My Faith Go Up To God**

When I talk to people about releasing their faith — or, exercising it, as I mentioned to you in the previous section — I always emphasize the importance of first getting *a point of contact*. What do I mean when I say point of contact? Well, a point of contact sets the time and the place for your healing to *begin*. It's something you do, and when you do it you let your faith go up to God for your needs to be met.

Maybe I can explain it best by sharing something my dad taught me about having a point of contact when I was just a little boy.

When I was about ten years old, I developed a bad case of warts on my left hand — 22 warts in all. One day my mother decided the time had come to do something about them. She said, "Richard, we're going to the doctor and have those warts burned off."

That frightened me, of course. That was almost 20 years before my dad built the City of Faith Health-Care Center where there are Spirit-filled doctors, nurses, and prayer partners and where they are merging medicine with prayer. Plus, I have always been left-handed and that was my throwing arm she was talking about! Having the warts burned off would have put me out of circulation for a while in the sports that I loved so much.

When my dad came home later on, I told him what

161

Mother had said. He said, "It's wonderful to be able to go to a doctor for help when you need it. But before we do, let's pray. I believe that if we pray and believe, Jesus will heal those warts."

I sure was in favor of that!

So Dad took me into my room and sat down with me on the bed. He took my hand and said, "Now, Richard, I'm going to pray for you. And when I do, I want you to release your faith."

Not really understanding, I asked, "How do you release your faith, Daddy?"

He pointed over to the wall and said, "Richard, do you see that light switch?"

"Yes."

"That light switch is a point of contact."

"What do you mean a point of contact, Daddy?"

He said, "A point of contact is something you do, Richard, and when you do it, you release your faith. You see, there is no power in the light switch itself. That light switch is hooked up to the power company. And the power is in the power company. So when you flip the light switch, it makes the lights come on."

He could see I was beginning to understand. He said, "Your faith is like that light switch. Your faith is hooked up to God's power. And when you release your faith and let it go up to God, it's just like flipping that light switch and having the lights come on...it's the moment your healing *begins.*

"Now, when I pray, Richard, you release the faith that you have in your heart and let it go up to God. Okay?"

"Yes, sir, Daddy!" I said, excited to see what would happen. After all, that was my *dad* talking. I knew I could trust him.

As Dad started to pray, I did something that I believe now was the Holy Spirit revealing something important to me. In complete trust and childlike faith, I held my hands to my chest and, with a sweeping motion, pushed them up toward heaven — as if I was pulling my faith out from inside me and pushing it up toward heaven. And as I did it, I said to my faith:

"FAITH, GO UP TO GOD!

"FAITH, GO UP TO GOD!"

And it took a little time, but in a matter of weeks, every one of those warts had disappeared. Jesus had healed them. My faith *had* gone up to God that day as my dad prayed, and it set the time for my healing to begin.

Wouldn't it be wonderful if all of our lives we would retain that same sense of childlike faith in God's ability to meet our needs.

"Faith, go up to God!" How those words spoken from the mouth of a ten-year-old boy must have moved the heart of God. And how you and I today can *still* move God's heart to work a miracle in our life when we release our faith for whatever need we have and let it go up to God.

Do you need a healing in some area of your life? Then release your faith as I pray. You may even want to do what I did as a boy — and what I sometimes still do — and say, "Faith, go up to God"…and motion with your arms as I described to you. You can use this prayer of Richard Roberts as your point of contact with God — the time when you release your faith for your healing to begin.

Let's pray:

Lord, I thank You that You say in Your Word that You want us to be in health — spiritually, physically, financially, and in our family relationships. I come to You now to help this, my friend, to receive the healing they need.

And, friend, I join my faith to yours for something

*good to happen in your life as you let go of the faith
you have in your heart and focus on God's answer
that is coming your way beginning today.*

*In Jesus' name I pray and I believe...and I say to
my faith, "Faith, go up to God for a miracle!"*

Amen and amen.

YOUR GOD-GIVEN KEY FOR TODAY

"I Will Use A Point Of Contact For Releasing My Faith!"

TUESDAY

**Key:
I WILL KEEP
HOLDING THE ROPE
FOR MY MIRACLE**

or
What I Can Do For
My Loved Ones Who Need A Miracle!

One of the most frequent prayer requests I receive
in this ministry — both from those who write to me
each month and from those who call in to my daily
TV program for prayer — is for problems in the
family. Sometimes it's for a husband or wife who
needs to know Christ, sometimes for a child who is
on drugs, or for a parent who is discouraged and
struggling financially.

Families are a gift from God. In God's goodness,
He has placed certain people in your life who are
closest and dearest to you. When those family
members hurt, you hurt. When they have needs, you
feel their lack. When they're suffering *in any way,*

their pain hits you right in the pit of your stomach. It's as if you hurt twice as much as you would if their problems were your own.

All of us know what it is to have needs in our family. We have loved ones who are sick, or who are in need financially, or who still don't know the Lord though we've prayed for them for years. I know I do. And sometimes when the problem seems that it will never end, you become discouraged. You want to do something for that person you love so much, but at times you find yourself wondering, "Is there anything I *can* do?"

I believe that there is something you can do. In spite of the heartache you feel, the frustration you experience...

YOU CAN HOLD ON TO THE ROPE THAT GOD HAS THRUST INTO YOUR HANDS

You can refuse to give up until a breakthrough comes. You can do what people have done through the centuries — what the Apostle Paul's loved ones did for him when he was in a dangerous situation and what Richard Roberts' loved ones did for him when he was not walking with God. For I above most people know what it is to need the help and support of your family.

But before I share with you how my loved ones helped me, let me share this Scripture about the Apostle Paul from the book of Acts.

"The Jews took counsel to kill [Paul]... And they [the Jewish synagogue leaders] watched the gates day and night to kill him. Then the disciples took him by night, and let him down by the wall in a basket" (Acts 9:23-25).

Paul might never have made it out of this situation

165

alive to become one of the greatest leaders the Church has ever known if he had not had loved ones who, literally, held the rope for him. And one important thing to note is that they held on to that rope until his basket touched the ground. In other words, they didn't give up and let go of the rope prematurely.

Someone had to buy the rope. Someone had to find a basket that was large and sturdy enough to hold Paul. Someone had to map out the timing and make the plans — the escape at night under cover of darkness.

It took time. And it took a willingness to risk their own personal safety. But they stuck with it. And finally, at the wall of the city that dark night, they held on to the rope until the basket with Paul in it touched the ground.

If you're like me, then sometime, somewhere, in your life someone has held the rope for you. I know how important it is to hold on to the rope that God has thrust into your hands for someone you love. Because had my dad and mother not held the rope for me as a young man, I would not be preaching the gospel today and praying for the sick.

Many a time my parents slipped out of bed in the middle of the night and walked the floor, praying for their youngest son. They refused to turn loose of the rope when, as a teenager, I rebelled against God and against my dad's ministry and wanted nothing to do with God in my life. And years later, as I was going through the deep heartache and struggle of a divorce, when on all sides people were saying, "Let go," they continued to hold on to the rope for me.

I believe that largely through my dad's and mother's prayers for me and through their loving support God finally got ahold of my life. He literally turned my life around and now He's using my testimony to give hope to others.

All because someone held the rope for me. When things looked darkest, when they felt like giving up, when they wondered if a miracle would ever come… still they held on.

REMEMBER THESE THREE THINGS AS YOU HOLD ON TO THE ROPE FOR A MIRACLE

Yes, you *can* do something that will help the one you love who is suffering or in need. As you hold the rope for a miracle to happen in their life, remember these three things from the story of the Apostle Paul:

1. *Your efforts may never be known by people… but God will reward your faithfulness.*

The men who held the rope for Paul are never mentioned by name in the Bible. *Your* prayers and your efforts to help the one you love may not be known by people either. Sometimes not even by the one you're holding on for. And that's something you and I need to remember.

But God knows. And He says in His Word that what He sees in secret, He will reward openly someday. (See Matthew 6:1-4.)

2. *You may be called on to hold the rope at night …when things seem the darkest.*

Have you ever noticed that things always seem the worst during the nighttime? That's when fear comes in the strongest and discouragement sometimes covers you like a blanket.

But when the fear and anxiety come against you the hardest, remember it may just be the time when your loved one most needs you to hold on to the rope. The devil may be fighting the hardest he's ever fought…but God may be about to do a miracle.

3. *You may be the only one holding the rope in that person's life. And their basket may be about to touch the ground.*

At times, you may be tempted to let go of the rope. You may feel your strength running out. *But don't let go.* You may be the only one who is holding on to the rope, and their basket may be about to touch the ground. I'm sure there came a point when Paul was close enough to the ground that it would have been easy to do just that. Perhaps he could have lived and survived the fall. But perhaps he couldn't have. So they held on to the rope and eventually Paul's basket touched the ground.

You may say, "Richard, I've held on for so long. I've prayed; I've cried. I don't know if I can hold on any longer." But I say to you, *don't let go of the rope.* You may be the only person God has to hold the rope… and your loved one's basket may be about to touch the ground.

MOST MIRACLES I'VE SEEN
DON'T COME OVERNIGHT…THEY TAKE TIME

Friend, God wants to work a miracle in your loved one's life. But most miracles I've seen don't come overnight; they take time. God needs time to work in a person's life.

And a miracle that seems a little long in coming often has the most lasting effect in our lives.

If you have a loved one today who is hurting, God is concerned about their need. And He's concerned for *you.* He sees your pain. But most importantly, He sees your faith in Him. He can do a mighty work in both your life and the life of the one you love, if you will do what He's called you to do and continue to hold the rope for your miracle.

YOUR GOD-GIVEN KEY FOR TODAY

"I Will Keep Holding The Rope For My Miracle!"

Then remember that the basket you are lowering may be about to touch the ground.

WEDNESDAY

**Key:
I WILL BE
FAITHFUL IN
THE SMALL
THINGS**

**or
How One Man Got
A Big Miracle From Doing Something
That Seemed Small And Insignificant**

Throughout my ministry, I've had the opportunity to minister around the world. I've ministered to all kinds of people — to the high, the low, the rich, the poor, the sick, the well, to those who love God and to those who have not made up their minds about Him.

And I've noticed that most people tend to concentrate their thoughts and efforts on the big things in their life, while the little things are often overlooked.

But, friend, I believe the Bible shows us over and over again that in our relationship with God...

It's the little things that will make the difference in your life! It's being faithful in the little things that

169

causes the big things to work in your life.

Often what God requires of us are simple things, things that may seem insignificant in man's eyes but to God they are very important. Through doing them we learn obedience to Him. And it's our *obedience* that God is most pleased with. (See 1 Samuel 15:22.) It is our obedience to God that will enable us to do the big things when they're required of us.

LET ME GIVE YOU AN EXAMPLE FROM THE BIBLE OF WHY THE LITTLE THINGS ARE SO IMPORTANT

In 2 Kings 5, we're told the story of Naaman, who was a commander of all the military forces in Syria at the time of the prophet Elisha. As a "general" in the army, Naaman must have been adept at doing the big things that it took to fight battles and win wars. But through a little servant girl sent to him by God, he came to understand the importance of being obedient in the little things.

You see, Naaman was a leper. Although he was not a believer, his wife's Jewish maidservant was and she told him about the prophet Elisha. Out of desperation, Naaman went to Israel to see him.

But when Naaman arrived at Elisha's house, rather than the prophet coming out to greet him and say what Naaman thought would be a "magical" prayer over his leprosy, Elisha sent a messenger out to him instead. The messenger instructed Naaman to go and dip himself in the river Jordan seven times and he would be healed.

It was just a simple thing…a silly thing, in Naaman's eyes. Surely there must be something grander that he must do to be healed. And had it not been for his military aides who understood the simplicity of God's power and who spoke great words of wisdom to Naaman, he would have missed his healing altogether.

Listen to the words they said to their leader because they are very important words for you and me today. They said: "General, if the prophet had told you to do some *great thing*, wouldn't you have done it? If so, then, why not even more so do this *simple* thing." (See 2 Kings 5:13.)

THOSE WHO WANT TO DO GREAT THINGS FOR GOD MUST FIRST BE WILLING TO DO THE SMALL THINGS

I believe that in all our hearts, when we are born-again Christians, we want to believe that we would be willing to take on any great task the Lord might call us to do. But what God really wants of us is our willingness to do the small things He asks of us — the little things that may not attract people's attention or guarantee recognition, but that are important to God. He wants us to do the little things that are a matter of our obedience to Him, so that He in turn can bless our lives to the fullest.

Don't get so sidetracked on the big things that you miss the little things in your life — little things such as...

• studying the Word of God...for it's sharper than any two-edged sword

• telling the devil to take his hands off God's property — you

• taking care of your body with proper food and rest — remember, it's the temple of the Holy Spirit

• spending time in prayer communicating with God

171

• letting your life be a witness wherever you are and whatever you do

• planting seeds of faith in good soil to help spread the message of the gospel to every creature

Do you want to do great things for God someday? If you do, then be faithful in the small things today. For, my friend, it's the small things — that will *add up* to the big things — that will make the difference in your life.

YOUR GOD-GIVEN KEY FOR TODAY

"I Will Be Faithful In The Small Things!"

THURSDAY

Key:
I KNOW THAT
"MIRACLE LIFE"
IS IN EVERY
SEED I PLANT

or
There's A Miracle Ending To The Story Of The Little Seed Planted In The Ground Versus The Big Clod Of Dirt On Top Of It

Have you ever wanted to give something to God — to plant precious seeds of faith into the work of the gospel — but you felt that you didn't have enough to give? Or that your seed was too small?

We in this ministry believe very deeply in the biblical principles of Seed-Faith — that in any situation you face, you look to God as your Source, plant a seed out of your need, and expect a miracle to happen. And we've seen those principles turn thousands of lives around.

But some of our Partners have never quite been able to understand that it's not the size of the seed you plant that matters. What *is* important is that you give to God out of your heart and look to Him to multiply that seed back to you in the way you need it most.

Not long ago, a woman who had been watching my daily TV program felt impressed to help me financially with a Seed-Faith project that I was raising money for. After the program one day, she sat down and wrote out a check as a seed of her faith that she wanted to plant in the project.

In a note that was enclosed with her check, she said something that many people have said to us at one time or another. She said: *"This seed is so small I'm almost ashamed to send it to you. I'm not sure if it will be much help, but it's the best I can do."*

Have you ever felt the way that woman felt? Have you ever made that same mistake of thinking that the seed of faith you are planting is too small — even though you're giving God your best?

I'll tell you, when a friend or Partner of ours plants a seed of faith in this ministry and yet they don't realize that it's not the size of their seed but the intent of their heart that counts with God, it hurts us in our hearts. For we realize that person has never grasped the truth that no matter how small the seeds are that we are planting, when we plant them *in faith* and *out of our need*…

THERE IS MIRACLE LIFE IN EVERY SEED YOU SOW!

God is going to grow that seed up and not only use

it to bless this ministry, but He will also multiply that seed back into the life of the person who planted it in whatever way they need it most.

The seed that we plant out of our need, as unto the Lord, the Bible calls "precious seed" (Psalm 126:6). And there is the miracle life of God in every seed, no matter how small.

THE STORY OF THE LITTLE SEED VERSUS THE BIG CLOD

You may be thinking right now, *Richard, I believe in planting a seed out of my need. But I have so many problems and needs right now I'm just covered over with them. The seed I could plant is so small in comparison to all my needs.*

Friend, any seed is small…but only in comparison to what it grows!

Let me share with you the story of the little seed planted in the ground and the big clod of dirt on top of it.

When a seed is sown in the ground, Jesus said, "It grows up." (See Mark 4:30-32.) Now you take a little seed and you put it in the ground and you cover it with three or four inches of dirt, and then you water it and stand back and watch.

The dirt on top of that seed says, "I've got you now, seed. You're tiny and I'm a big clod. I'm on top of you and you're not *ever* going to come up. I've got you buried forever."

But as the dirt sits there so smugly on top of the seed, the little seed begins to sing, "The life of God, the life of God, the miracle life of God is in me."

The dirt yells, "Shut up! I weigh a hundred times more than you, seed. You're *not* coming up."

But the little seed just keeps on singing!

And something about the miracle life of God in that seed causes it to grow. The tender little sprouts begin to shoot up. And they begin to come up through all that heavy dirt. I've even seen it where that sprout would push a rock or stone out of its way as it grows toward the sky.

And the dirt is just going crazy! It's crying out, "I don't understand. I'm so much bigger!"

But that little seed — because of the miracle life of God that's in it — just keeps growing...and growing...and GROWING until eventually it produces a harvest that's a hundred or a thousand or even a million times bigger than the tiny little seed ever thought of being!

And, friend, your "precious" seed is like that too. It's *never* too small for the needs you're facing... because the miracle life of God is in it.

Your seed, when planted in God's work, will grow even if you can't see it growing for a while. The size of the seed is not what's important. It's the act of your obedience in giving it as unto the Lord so that God can multiply it back to you in the way you need it most.

YOUR GOD-GIVEN KEY FOR TODAY

"I Know That 'Miracle Life' Is In Every Seed I Plant."

Then never again say, "This seed is too small." If it's your best, it's *big* to God.

FRIDAY
Key:
I WILL SPEAK
MY FAITH OUT LOUD

or
The Importance Of Speaking Out
Of Our Mouths What We Believe In Our Hearts

This week I'm talking to you about the most powerful thing you have in fighting your problems: your faith. Already we've discussed several aspects of actively *using* your faith to come against problems. One area I haven't touched on yet, but one I feel the Bible shows us is very important, is the area of *speaking* our faith.

Now I'm not talking about speaking out certain words as if they are a magic formula we can apply to make our problems disappear. What I'm talking about is speaking out of our mouths what we already believe deep down in our hearts. It doesn't take the place of heart-believing, as some people may think, but the Bible indicates that it *reveals* what you believe and *reinforces* it.

Let me share with you a Scripture that shows you that when you *speak* to the problem coming against your life, and that speaking lines up with what you believe in your heart, it can have a powerful effect. In Mark 11:22,23 Jesus says:

"Have faith in God. For verily I say unto you, That whosoever shall say unto this mountain, Be thou removed, and be thou cast into the sea; and shall not doubt in his heart, but shall believe that those things which he saith shall come to pass; he shall have whatsoever he saith."

Jesus is not talking about an actual mountain here, like Mount Everest, for example. He's talking about the mountains of problems that we all face in our lives. He's telling us that when we speak to those mountains out of the faith that is in our hearts — and when we have the power of God living inside of us — those problems are subject to what we tell them to do. In other words, we can cause them to move out of our life.

How can we know that this principle of applying our faith will work? Because it worked for Jesus.

JESUS NEVER TELLS US TO DO SOMETHING THAT HE DIDN'T DO

The Scripture I just shared with you in Mark 11:22,23 is a very popular Scripture today. Many people are familiar with the words, but not everyone is familiar with the story behind it. Let me set the stage to show you what had just happened when Jesus spoke those words.

Jesus and His disciples were on their way to the city of Jerusalem when they saw a fig tree in the distance. Jesus went over to it to get something to eat and found that it was not producing fruit. Then he cursed the tree, saying, "Fig tree, don't ever produce any more fruit. No man will eat of you again."

The next day they returned the same way they came, and the disciples noticed that the fig tree had withered up. They said, "Look, Jesus, this is the tree You cursed. It's dried up from the roots now." And that's when Jesus said, "Have faith in God." He was saying to the disciples — and He is saying to you and me today — "Have the God kind of faith." Or, "Look at the examples I have given you and do as I have done. Learn to solve your problems the same way I solve Mine."

As believers in Jesus, we have been given authority

177

over the devil's power…over the satanic problems that he brings into our lives to try and destroy us. Jesus wants us to *use* the authority that He has given us. Jesus didn't pray, "Oh, God, please dry up this fig tree," and then wait for God to do it. No. He spoke directly to the fig tree — or the problem — and told it what to do, believing that it would happen.

There are many examples in the Bible of Jesus speaking directly to the problem He was facing… then seeing the problem disappear:

He spoke to the raging winds and the roaring waves, and they were stilled (Matthew 8:23-27).

He spoke to the demons in a man known as Legion and the man was set free (Mark 5:1-20).

He spoke to blinded eyes and they were opened (Mark 10:46-52), crippled limbs and they were straightened (Luke 6:6-11).

We need to understand the importance of speaking out of our mouths what we already believe in our hearts. When we *speak* our faith and come against our problems, that builds up our own faith *and* the faith of those around us.

As you speak *and* believe in your heart, great things can happen. Our "mountains" can become as "molehills" and be blown into the sea by the force of our faith in God.

YOUR GOD-GIVEN KEY FOR TODAY

"I Will Speak My Faith Out Loud!"

**Key:
I KNOW THAT
GOD HAS PUT
THE WEAPONS
I NEED WITHIN
THE REACH
OF MY FAITH**

SATURDAY

**or
What We Can Learn From A Young Boy
Named David . . . And His Faith-Stones**

I believe one of the greatest faith stories in the Bible is the story in 1 Samuel 17 of a young man named David, who came against Goliath, champion of the godless Philistines. In this story, the great Goliath, who stood nearly nine feet tall — challenged the army of Israel day and night. King Saul and his soldiers had heard Goliath's roar. And each time they did, their hearts turned to jelly.

Now in your mind I want you to visualize yourself in the Israelites' position, to hear the giant's roar. For each one of us has a "giant" coming against us in much the same way that Goliath came against the army of Israel. Our giant is the devil, and he's roaring night and day. He's coming against you with his evil plans of sickness, fear, discouragement, and other things that are unlike God.

It's a frightening thing to be caught face to face with your enemy when you know that your enemy is ten times bigger and stronger than you are. But let's see what happens when David — a shepherd boy from the hills of Bethlehem — came down to face the giant's challenge. For the outcome of their battle is something that you and I can take heart in today.

WHEN YOU SEE THE TRUTH OF THE SITUATION, YOU KNOW THAT THE BATTLE IS REALLY THE LORD'S

Why was David willing to face the giant when no one else was? You see, *David knew the truth of the situation*. He said to his people, "My friends, Goliath hasn't just defied the army of Israel, he's defied the God I serve. He's defied the very One in whom I believe and put my trust."

He said to King Saul, "The God who delivered me from the lions and the bears in the fields will deliver me from the hand of this godless giant."

Then, though he was young and considered foolish by many, he went out to face Goliath. He knew that he would not be going alone or without the weapons he needed to fell the giant.

And, friend, when you and I see the truth of the devil's attack in our lives…when we realize that the battle we are in is really the Lord's battle and not our own…we'll have that same assurance that God is with us and that He has put within the reach of our faith the weapons we need to do battle.

GOD'S WEAPONS WILL GET THE JOB DONE

King Saul gave David his armor to wear, but the armor didn't fit. You see, the world will always try to arm you with something that won't fit and that won't get the job done. We must use the weapons that God has prepared for us. The Bible says, "For the weapons of our warfare are not carnal, but mighty through God to the pulling down of strong holds" (2 Corinthians 10:3).

God's weapons get the job done!

David had a slingshot and, though in the natural it was no match for Goliath, he knew how to use it. He went down to a brook and picked up five smooth stones. And all through history God had been smoothing those stones. He knew that someday a young shepherd named David would need them to take on the devil's roar, just as He knows that you and I need to fight the good fight of faith.

I believe those stones were miracle stones of faith! And I believe that David knew they were. He picked up those five faith-stones, put them in his shepherd's bag, and started off to kill the giant.

"I'll feed you to the birds of the air," Goliath roared. But as David took off running toward him, swirling his sling above his head, he shouted back, "Goliath, I come not in my own name or strength, but in the name of the Lord whom I serve. *He* will deliver me out of your hand."

GOD KNOWS THE DEVIL'S WEAK SPOTS WHERE YOUR "FAITH-STONES" WILL DO THE GREATEST GOOD

As David faced Goliath, there was only one spot on Goliath that was unprotected: his forehead. God knows where the devil's vulnerable spot is. He knows where your faith needs to "hit" to cause the thing that's coming against you to get out of your life.

David aimed his sling and shot. He watched as the stone sunk deep into the giant's forehead. And as Goliath slumped to the ground, David ran to cut off his head with his own sword.

When the Israelites saw what David had done, they took heart. They put the godless Philistines to flight.

And, friend, you and I can take heart from David too. We can know that in whatever battle we find ourselves, we are not alone; the battle is the Lord's.

No matter what giant comes against us — whether it's the giant of sickness, of loneliness, of fear — God has put the weapons we need to fight within the reach of our faith. They are miracle weapons. He has given us faith-stones. And nothing can be more powerful than miracle weapons and faith-stones in the hands of a people whose God is the Lord.

YOUR GOD-GIVEN KEY FOR TODAY

"I Can Know That God Has Put The Weapons I Need Within The Reach Of My Faith!"

FIFTH WEEK

SUNDAY GOD HAS GIVEN ME THE FAITH TO FIGHT ANY PROBLEM I HAVE!

MONDAY I WILL USE A POINT OF CONTACT FOR RELEASING MY FAITH!

TUESDAY I WILL KEEP HOLDING THE ROPE FOR MY MIRACLE!

WEDNESDAY I WILL BE FAITHFUL IN THE SMALL THINGS!

THURSDAY I KNOW THAT "MIRACLE LIFE" IS IN EVERY SEED I PLANT

FRIDAY I WILL SPEAK MY FAITH OUT LOUD!

SATURDAY I CAN KNOW THAT GOD HAS PUT THE WEAPONS I NEED WITHIN THE REACH OF MY FAITH!

SIXTH WEEK

God Is Alive In My Life And The Lives Of My Loved Ones

By Lindsay Roberts

SUNDAY

**Key:
I CAN HAVE A
SOURCE FOR MY LIFE**

**or
God Will Supply
All Of My Needs If I Will Make Him My Source**

While I was attending law school at Oral Roberts University, for the first time I began to realize fully the significance of the Bible as God's *testament*. This word in the legal profession means "will or act by which a person bequeaths or leaves something to another." The meaning is the same when it refers to the Bible. The Bible is God's testament — His will — whereby He has left us something GOOD by the shed blood of His Son Jesus.

There is not a word in the Bible that says, "I sent My Son so that you will receive an inheritance of poverty and disease." There's not a word in God's will that says anything bad for your life. All it says is that God loves you and that He wants you to prosper — spiritually, physically, financially, that He wants to supply all of your needs according to His riches in glory, and that all good and perfect things come from God.

But that's not what people kept telling my family about God when my father died when I was a child. Many told us that God was punishing us because we had done something wrong or He was testing us and all kinds of things that made it appear that God was anything but a good God.

I can't remember many people telling us about the devil being a bad devil — that it was the devil who kills, steals, and destroys — except Oral Roberts.

I watched him on television every time he was on

and he always let me know that not only was the devil always against me, but that God was always for me — that God was a good God.

I learned what God's love is all about. Jesus, who had been my Savior, now became much more. He became a real, living, helping, loving, caring Person to me.

I listened with particular interest when Oral preached about God being my Source. For at that time I needed something solid to sustain my life. Up to that time I had not felt a need for a Source for my life other than my parents. And suddenly my source had been shattered with the death of my father.

I began to read in God's Word such Scriptures as Philippians 4:19, "My God shall supply all your needs according to His riches in glory by Christ Jesus." And I began to understand that God was my Source, my total supply, and that *He* would supply my needs.

I began to see that the world changes, your circumstances change, your finances change, even your parents can change, but God will never change.

If you don't have a father to go to for the money you need, you have to turn somewhere, and I found that I had a Source to turn to who would supernaturally provide for my needs. His method was for us to give to Him and He would cause our giving to come back to us — multiplied.

I also learned that everybody has something to give — even a 12-year-old girl. A seed can be a gift of love, a show of your concern, a prayer for someone, a gift of money. It can be a smile or a kind word. It can be a meal fixed for a sick friend. Whatever you give, if you wrap it up in your faith and plant it in the life of another person, you can give that as unto God and expect God to multiply it back in the form of a miracle harvest.

Now I didn't have much money, but I had something to give. I could help Mother with the dishes and other things around the house or help my little brother or older sister in some way. And I began giving this way.

And I happen to have been good in math, so I gave my time as a tutor to other young children. And when I was about 14 years old I helped in a program for delinquent children. There was always some way I could find to plant seeds in the lives of other people.

I was learning firsthand what the Bible teaches on giving and receiving. Seedtime and harvest, sowing and reaping is God's very same eternal principle that works in every area of our lives — spiritual, physical, and financial.

I wasn't old enough to have a mental attitude, *Oh, we don't have this or we don't have that.* All I knew was that God said He'd provide for us. It didn't matter to me how He did it, whom He did it through, or what He was going to use. All I knew was that if I gave to God I could expect Him to bless me back. He was going to provide *all my needs.*

And He has.

Through the years I've come to see that if we look to any one thing or any one person as our source and it fails us, we will surely fall apart. Yet, if we trust God Almighty for our total supply, nothing can destroy us.

When our little Richard Oral went to be with the Lord when he was only 36 hours old, I realized, perhaps for the first time, what mighty strength we really have in God when He is our ONLY Source. During that time Richard and I saw how totally dependent we had to be on God. We were thrown into a position where there was absolutely nothing to hold on to except God.

Richard and I held onto each other, but we had no

real rock-solid foundation in our humanness. We had nothing else to trust but God, and He gave us that tremendous peace that passes all human understanding. I had a calmness and a peace of mind that I knew that I knew that I knew that my God was in control.

Although everything medically had fallen apart in our little son's life, I had the most miraculous knowing that my God was still on the throne. And Jesus was still King of kings and Lord of lords. And, no matter how my darling son's life turned out, my God was still Almighty. I never blamed God. I only trusted Him.

Although my precious firstborn son had died and left me, God had not died. And if my Source had not left me, there was a chance to try again.

I can't begin to describe in words what total dependency on God is like, except that it is miraculous. I discovered that when your hopes and dreams, even your children, die, you don't have to die with them. There is a chance for a new life. There is a new beginning. Out of the ashes of our total brokenness, Jesus is standing right there with outstretched arms saying, "Come on, My beloved, let's get to work at making a miracle out of this."

From the depths of my heart I want to assure you today that God will supply all of *your* needs if you will make Him your Source.

YOUR GOD-GIVEN KEY FOR TODAY

"God Is The Source For My Life And I Can Trust Him No Matter The Circumstances."

Key:
I CAN KNOW THE DEVIL
MONDAY **WILL BE PUT OUT**
AT HOME PLATE

or
It May Look Like The Devil Is Winning, But Jesus Lives In Me And Jesus Is Ultimately Victorious Over The Devil

God is real. He's in the now. He's in the middle of our problems along with us, and He's at work on the problem. But the devil is real also. His job is to oppose any person who tries to live for God.

I've experienced enough in my life to know how real the devil is. But I also know he's no match for our Savior.

When Richard and I lost our newborn son, Richard Oral, one of the things that helped me get through that heartbreaking time was some very unusual encouragement the Lord sent me through a friend.

Several weeks before I was supposed to give birth, a friend called and said the Lord had shown her some things in a dream about me. This woman had said some pretty incredible things to me before, and every time the Lord had dealt with her about me it had come to pass. So I trusted what she had to say.

She told me that the Lord had given her a dream about me in which she saw me in a baseball game with the devil. We were the only two players!

Now I relate to baseball because I grew up watching the Detroit Tigers play professional baseball and I have a fairly good understanding of the game. It's funny how God knows what we can relate to.

In the dream the devil was hitting the ball and running the bases. He flew past me at first base, and I wasn't even close to stopping him. Then he went on to second base and I was losing more ground. He sped on around to third base as I continued to lose more ground. I just couldn't begin to catch him.

As the devil rounded third base and sped on toward home plate, I could see that I was no match for him. But as he went to slide in to home plate, there was Jesus standing strong and firm at home plate with the ball in His hands shouting, "Don't worry, Lindsay, I will put him out at home!"

Oh, how I rejoiced when I heard this. I felt like no matter what the devil did to me I would be all right, because Jesus was at home plate and the devil could not get past my Savior. I would be safe and the devil would be defeated.

Although I didn't totally understand it at this time, it was an encouragement to me that I let it settle deep within the pit of my spirit. It was a good word to hold on to.

When little Richard Oral went to be with the Lord, throughout the memorial service the next day I kept seeing the vision of Satan running the bases as it was described to me in my friend's dream. I couldn't turn loose of the peace that was inside me each time I thought about it.

Then it all became clear to me. Satan had tried to destroy my son's life by chasing him with the final blow of death. But, praise God, when the ultimate blow was dealt by Satan and my son was struck by death, there stood Jesus waiting with open arms at the gates of heaven, ushering my little son into eternal life and telling Satan, "This is where I put you out. You are out of your league. This child is forever home with Me here in heaven. Never again can you touch him. Now, he is *safe at home.*"

Even though the grief and hurt was almost un-bearable at times, never once did we feel that God *caused* our son's death. Instead, we believed God would find a way to turn our pain around and make something good out of our brokenness. And out of this experience we have become two completely different people. The compassion of Jesus has so filled us that we will never be the same.

I believe the devil tried to destroy Richard and me with this one act of death of our firstborn son, but Jesus is making miracles out of it. And the miracles began to happen immediately.

One of the nurses at the hospital had touched me to my core by her coldness and bluntness. (The City of Faith Childbirth Center had not yet been opened.) She told me she had watched my every move through-out those 36 hours of my son's life, and asked me now that my son had died, how did I feel about God?

She looked me straight in the eye and said, "Are you a hypocrite or are you for real: Is God real to you in good times, or, now that your son is dead, is God still real? Do you only believe in God when things are perfect?"

I said to her, "My God is a good God and I will praise Him no matter what. Jesus is still my Lord, and only because of Him will I make it through this."

"You are real and so is your Jesus," she said. "Please show me how I can accept Him as my Lord and Savior."

Richard and I led her in a sinner's prayer to receive Christ.

Right there in the midst of death in somebody else's hospital, seeds had been planted that brought the harvest of a beautiful new soul written into the Lamb's Book of Life in the eternal kingdom of God.

When the devil attacks you, you may feel like

you're being run around and around and around and there's no way to stop. You may feel torn apart inside, and you think you have been defeated. But I can tell you from experience, in spite of all the hurt and heartache and how bad things seem to be, Jesus lives in you and Jesus is ultimately victorious over the devil just as 1 John 4:4 says: "Greater is he [God] that is in you, than he [the devil] that is in the world."

Now say: It may look like the devil is winning in my life, but Jesus lives in me and He is ultimately victorious over the devil.

YOUR GOD-GIVEN KEY FOR TODAY

"I Trust Jesus To Put The Devil Out At Home Plate!"

**Key:
I CAN ENCOURAGE
MY LOVED ONES TO
BELIEVE FOR THE
MIRACLE THEY NEED**

TUESDAY

**or
No Matter
What It Looks Like, God Can Make A Miracle**

When my father died of leukemia, my family had been told that he was medically incurable. We knew the physician was speaking from his professional knowledge, and we accepted it.

If only we had known then what we know today! Even though someone may be medically incurable in the natural, they are never without hope when we place our faith in the supernatural power of the God of miracles who works through prayer and medicine.

A few years ago I had a telephone call from my long-time friend, Suzanne, who lives in San Francisco. "The doctors here have just discovered that I have leukemia," she said, "and have given me about two weeks to live.

"Of course they're going to try chemotherapy and everything else they can," she went on to say.

In spite of what I was hearing from on the other end of the line, I can't begin to describe the perfect peace of God that came over me that God is a healing God.

I handed the phone to Richard and the first thing he said to her was, "Suzanne, have you ever met Jesus as your personal Lord and Savior?"

"No, but I want to," she said. She was ready to receive Jesus, and Richard led her in the sinner's prayer right there on the telephone and she received Jesus as her Savior and the Source of her life.

Then I got on the phone again, and the first thing I said to her was, "Get out your Bible, Suzanne, and go in the back to the concordance and find the word *healing*. Look up all the Scriptures that say healing or healed or heal, such as 'I am the Lord that healeth thee' and 'by His stripes you are healed'. (See Exodus 15:26, Isaiah 53:5.)

"You claim those Scriptures and then take whatever the doctors tell you and pray over it, but don't be afraid of it." I said, "Walk by faith and not by sight. You put your faith in the Word of God and not in what everybody keeps telling you. Accept every word in the Bible as a word from the Lord for you and you're going to see a miracle."

I flew to San Francisco to minister to her and took every one of Richard's and Oral's tapes that had

193

anything to do with healing and I said, "Saturate yourself with good news. Don't listen to bad news. When your friends and loved ones come to see you crying, 'You're going to die in two weeks,' turn them off. You've got to get in an atmosphere of faith.

"And when the doctors give you your report you say, 'Praise God, I am ready for a miracle.' Take what they say and praise God for them," I said (because they were doing everything in the natural they could do to help her).

And every day she told the doctors, "I'm going to be a miracle. I'm going to be a miracle, I'm a miracle!"

When her fever went up so high it looked like there was no way she was going to be healed, she kept saying, "But I'm a miracle!"

When the doctors in San Francisco had done all they knew to do, they decided to do a bone marrow transplant. Now at the time there were only two places in the United States performing these transplants. The decision was made for Suzanne to be moved to Seattle for treatment and surgery was done. Although the surgery appeared to be successful, Suzanne still needed a miracle to rid her body from cancer. As only God would divinely ordain, Richard was conducting a three-day crusade at that very time in of all places…Seattle. I contacted Suzanne to find out if the doctors would release her just long enough to attend one service. And as she told later on *Richard Roberts Live… "I was fresh out of the transplant unit of a hospital in Seattle, Washington, when Richard came there for a crusade one weekend. Richard and Lindsay were visiting with me and I said to them, 'I would love to be in the crusade. I want to be healed by God.'*

"Well, I did go to the crusade and was seated off in a separate section with a mask on because my immune system was so weak at that point. I was so far out in the wings I could hardly see Richard but I was thinking, *I would do anything to get down there to be prayed for.* So when he began to pray for cancer patients, I stood up where I was and Lindsay walked up to pray for me. All of a sudden I felt a warm sensation from the tip of my toes to the top of my head and I knew at that very moment I was totally free of cancer!

"After I left the crusade, I was scheduled to stay in Seattle another two weeks for treatment but everything went so well I left on the sixth day instead of the fourteenth day.

"And ever since then at all my checkups the doctor says, 'Suzanne, I know you think you're just fine, but we should check just to make sure'.

"And every time he has come back to report with a smile saying, 'You were right. There's nothing there.'"

Suzanne had set the time to release her faith for her miracle when she came to that crusade!

Perhaps you or a loved one right now are facing circumstances that seem hopeless. Doctors may have said that one of you has an illness that is terminal. Maybe there is some relationship you feel is irreconcilable. You may feel like your financial situation is hopeless. But remember, God is a God of miracles. No situation is without hope when He is in the picture.

God has an answer for your problem. He has a solution to your need. He has a way out of this thing that seems to have you trapped. He has a way for you to emerge on the other side of this difficulty — a way that is greater than anything you've ever known.

First, I would say to you today just what I said to my friend Suzanne, turn in the concordance of your Bible and find Scriptures that relate to what you're going through. If you need a healing in your body, read in your Bible about the miracles where Jesus healed the sick.

Read Matthew 8. In that one chapter we read how Jesus healed a leper with the touch of His hand… how Jesus spoke the word of healing for a centurion's servant… how Jesus touched the hand of Peter's wife's mother and her fever left… how Jesus ministered that same evening in Peter's home and "they brought to Him many who were demon-possessed. And He cast out the spirits with a word, and healed all who were sick"… and how Jesus cast out the demons in two men who lived in the country of the Gergesenes. This is one of the greatest healing chapters in all the Bible!

If you need a money miracle, read how Jesus commanded a fish to capture a coin in its mouth so that the fish could be caught when Peter threw his hook into the water and the money could be used to pay their taxes. (See Matthew 17:24-27.) Read about the miracle of a net-breaking, boat-sinking load of fish that Jesus enabled Peter, James, and John to catch after they had "planted their seed" of loaning Jesus their boat for preaching. (See Luke 5:1-10.)

Do you need a miracle of provision for your family? Read about how Jesus fed thousands of people from the lunch of just a few loaves and fishes that a little boy gave Jesus. (See Mark 6:32-42.)

Build up your faith by reading what God has done. And remember, He hasn't changed. He is the same God today to help you. God said that He doesn't change. That means that His personality doesn't change. If God ever healed anyone, He heals today. If God ever delivered anyone, He delivers today. If He ever met any need, He can still meet needs today.

YOUR GOD-GIVEN KEY FOR TODAY

"I Will Encourage My Loved Ones To Believe For The Miracle They Need."

WEDNESDAY

**Key:
I CAN TURN
ON MY FAITH
FOR THE
MIRACLE
I NEED**

**or
A Point Of Contact Sets The Time For The
Release Of My Faith For the Miracle I Need**

I know nothing about the mechanics of automobiles. I can put gas in the tank and that's about the extent of my knowledge about what it takes to keep a car running. When my car needs to be repaired, it does no good for me to try to figure out what's wrong. I simply go to a mechanic — someone who knows about the car — and he fixes it. Then everything is okay, because I do know how to turn the key in the ignition to start the engine. And that's all I need to know.

It's the same way with our faith. I don't know much about the mechanics of faith. But I do know that after we turn on our faith, and release it to God, we set a chain of miracles in motion.

Just like I place the key in the ignition to set the time to start the engine, there is something about faith that needs to be released to God for the miracle we need.

The problem is not that we don't have faith. The Bible says God has given to every person the "measure of faith" (Romans 12:3). You don't have to go out and get faith. It's lying deep within your spirit but you have to release it. That's where a point of contact is needed.

A point of contact does not set the time necessarily for the miracle we need to be *completed.* God knows the timetable for meeting our need. But a point of contact does set the time for releasing our faith, for *beginning* the miracle process.

Countless numbers of people have shared with me in person or through a letter or through our Abundant Life prayer partners what God has done in their lives. These people had a need and they did something with their faith as an act of reaching out and touching Jesus. And when they did, His power came into their lives…sometimes slowly, sometimes quickly…sometimes as a growing tide, sometimes as a flood…sometimes with dramatic, visible results, sometimes with a quiet knowing that became a fact days or even months later.

The woman in Luke 8 who had an issue of blood for twelve years — an uncontrollable hemorrhage that the doctors couldn't help her with — set out to find Jesus. Her life was literally draining from her body and she needed a miracle, and she knew she needed one soon.

She decided if she could just get to Jesus she could be healed. When Jesus was passing by she reached out and touched the hem of His robe. It was the point of contact she chose to release her faith for her healing.

It takes more than just believing to receive a miracle. It takes believing WHAT THE LORD HAS SPOKEN TO US IN HIS WORD and then refusing to doubt in your heart. Mark 11:23 says, "Whosoever shall say unto this mountain, Be thou removed, and be thou cast into the sea; and shall not doubt in his heart, but shall believe that those things which he saith shall come to pass; he shall have whatsoever he saith."

I really discovered the power of God within this Scripture when the doctors at the City of Faith discovered a tumor on my right ovary. It was a very large tumor — larger than an orange — and they were concerned about what would happen to me if surgery didn't take place immediately. This was discovered on Friday and they wanted surgery Saturday morning. I felt a strong urgency to plant a seed out of my need and give to others so that God would multiply my seed back to me. I really felt like I needed to give something to activate my faith. I knew we were having a family seminar beginning that Friday night and continuing through Sunday. The entire faculty, staff, and student body were gathering together the weekend before school began to start the year out right. So I asked the doctor if I could wait until Monday and spend the weekend at the seminar laying hands on others and praying for them. I told him I needed to plant a seed of my prayers to receive a miracle harvest in return. He approved and I went to the services all weekend as planned.

Sunday night I was admitted to the City of Faith and surgery was scheduled for 7:00 Monday morning. That night the doctor explained something that could have been very frightening news, but God's hand was working all along. The doctor explained that the tumor was so large he would have had to remove whatever it had attached itself to, including my right ovary. Well, I said, "Wait a minute." We had already figured out that my left ovary, for all we knew, wasn't functioning at all and if my right ovary had to be removed, I was smart enough to know that meant I had no possible way of having children. I had already had two miscarriages and really wasn't prepared for the full extent of what this surgery meant. I asked him if he was sure and he said it was like a mountain squeezing the life out of a little molehill. The tumor was so large it was like a mountain compared to the other organs and it had to be removed — along with anything it had attached itself to. Well, it was like God lit a rocket inside of me and I began to praise Him. I just knew in spite of what the details were that I was in for a miracle. I knew it. I mean, I just knew it.

As I was getting ready to sleep, Richard prayed and agreed with me that God was in control and this would be our miracle. I went off to sleep and about 1:00 a.m. I was awakened and grabbed my Bible and turned to Mark 11:23,24. I knew the Lord had spoken to me to turn there, just as I knew my name. As I read, "Whosoever shall *say to this mountain,* Be thou removed, and be thou cast into the sea and shall not doubt in his heart, but shall believe that those things which he saith shall come to pass; he *shall* have whatsoever *he saith.*"

I started shouting and praising God at 1:00 a.m. in the hospital room. Because, you see, the night before the doctor had just explained that this tumor was like a mountain, destroying all the organs it attached itself to. And God had said I could speak to my mountain and tell it to be removed — all I had to do was speak to it, believe and not doubt, and it shall come to pass and I would have what I said. God showed me just exactly how to get my miracle. So I spoke to that mountain of tumor and said, "Be removed and cast into the sea (which meant out of my body)." I told God I believed in my heart, I didn't doubt, and I *expected* it to come to pass.

Well, the nurses and doctor woke me up very early the next morning and I couldn't help but tell them what took place during the night. They all were expecting a miracle with me, but the doctor said, "Okay, but let's check one more time." When he did, the tumor was still there and he said, "Well, maybe God will use surgery to remove the mountain."

At that point I could have lost the faith to believe for the miracle because the tumor was still there. But God immediately reminded me that we *walk by faith and not by sight.* Well, my faith kept saying: *I'm a miracle,* and I went to surgery. As soon as they made the incisions, the doctors began to buzz. Somewhere sometime from the time the doctor examined me to the time they did the surgery, God miraculously removed the tumor. My mountain was gone! I mean, completely gone. To the shock of the doctors and nurses, it was gone. No surgery was done — none was needed.

I remember waking up in the recovery room and the sweetest nurse said, "Honey, it's all gone." I began to cry thinking they removed everything and I'd never have children. She said, "You don't understand. When the doctors made the incisions to get to the tumor, the *tumor* was gone. It disappeared." She said, "They all stood there looking at the X rays and tests and ultrasound pictures taken earlier of the tumor and could hardly believe their eyes. When they cut you open, it was gone. They did *no* surgery. You're whole and can still have children."

This was a miracle from God. To this day I cannot describe the feeling inside of me when I learned that, as God promised in His Word, I received my miracle. I knew that I had received a miracle harvest from the seeds I had planted.

And remember this, God said in Acts 10:34 that He is no respecter of persons. That means it doesn't matter our age or who we are or where we're from, God has a miracle for us if we will do our part first and give to Him.

What about you? If you or a loved one has cancer or you have some other medical problem that doctors have called terminal or you are faced with a situation that seems hopeless in some other area of your life, will you get into the Word of God...will you hear the Word preached so your faith will become strong and active...will you select a point of contact that you feel good about...will you do something to release your faith?

It may be going to a specific meeting. It may be placing your hand on a particular Scripture in the Word of God. It may be having a certain person come to pray for you or your going to that person. It may be making a telephone call to a prayer group. It may be holding on to this book right now and, as you do, choosing to release your faith to God. A point of contact sets the time for you to release your faith for the miracle to begin.

Will you choose a point of contact? Will you release your faith? Will you expect the miracles to start? Don't just talk about it...do it.

Don't just plan it...act on it.

Don't just wish for it...believe it will happen!

YOUR GOD-GIVEN KEY FOR TODAY

"I Can Turn On My Faith For The Miracle I Need."

**Key:
I CAN KNOW
THAT GOD IS
FAITHFUL TO
MULTIPLY EVERY
SEED I PLANT**

THURSDAY

**or
When We Give Our Best To God,
He Will Bless Our Efforts
In "Full And Overflowing Measure"**

One Sunday our daughter Jordan was cutting teeth and was very fussy and she had kept me up all night. At 6:30 Monday morning when Richard said, "It's time to get up," I said, "Richard, I can't be on the television program today. I've been up all night with Jordan."

Sometimes when you're exhausted physically and mentally your whole attitude can hit rock bottom. Mine had. I was tired. I didn't feel good. And I began to get down on myself. I told Richard, "Nothing I can say today on the television program is going to make a difference anyway. Why don't you just let me sleep and I'll be okay tomorrow."

"You will be fine," he told me. "Get up and put yourself together and come on the show."

Still negative, I said reluctantly, "Okay," but I thought to myself, *But I'm not going to contribute anything!*

I got up and turned on a news program on television, as I always do in the morning to get an overview of what's going on in our country and in the world that day to see if it will spark anything for our program. On the channel I selected there was a woman telling about a call-in help service she provided. That day she was giving instructions on how to commit suicide!

Something struck me like a bolt of lightning and I said, "God, I may not be worth much to myself today, but I am going to do something for Your glory just to counteract this." So I got up and dressed and went to the television studio.

The first request I was handed from our phone prayer group was from someone who wanted to commit suicide. I began to talk about it on the air and I began to relate what I had just heard on the news program that very morning. I kept saying, "Suicide is not the answer. If you are in the act of suicide right now, stop it."

I found out by the end of our program we had received fifteen phone calls from people who were watching our program and who were going to commit suicide. The Lord spared their lives and a number of them prayed with our prayer partners to accept Jesus as their Savior.

I couldn't have received a gift that would have brought me greater joy than those fifteen phone calls. When you give your best to God, no matter how you feel and no matter how small it may seem, God is faithful to multiply the seed. He will bless your efforts and they will return to you "in full and overflowing measure," as we are told in Luke 6:38 *(TLB)*.

At that time Oral Roberts launched a plan to take God's medical presence to the world by providing scholarships for Oral Roberts University medical students. He made a statement that burned into my heart. "God healed me when I was a 17-year-old boy dying with tuberculosis, but why should I be privileged because I'm here in America? God cares about the people in every country of the world."

I realized that God does care about all of us around the world and we can't limit His healing power to the United States. The Lord touched my heart to sponsor a medical student. Of course, at first I thought, *You can't do that. You haven't got the money.* The Lord said to me, *Just be quiet and wait. If you have this desire in your heart, I will give seed to the sower.*

I said, "All right, I'll be quiet, but I ask that You tell Richard because it can't just come from me. He and I are one and we must agree on this."

That same day the Lord spoke to Richard and then He gave us both the desire to tell each other what we felt we should do. We committed it to the Lord and believed that He would give seed to the sower and, in turn, this desire of our heart.

We didn't have the money and we had no way of earning extra money above our salary because everything we make from records, tapes, and offerings goes to the ministry. But we had a desire in our hearts and we believed the Lord would grant it. And He did!

Richard's sister and brother-in-law, Rebecca and Marshall Nash, had owned a business and Richard had invested in it. In 1977 when Marshall and Rebecca died, the company was sold. Richard received most of the settlement over several years.

On that Saturday afternoon, as we committed our need to God and believed that He would supply it, I opened the mail and saw a letter from Marshall E. Nash, Inc.

Inside, there was a check for the balance of the settlement due to Richard for the exact amount it takes to give a scholarship to a medical student at ORU for one year! Now, friend, no one else but God could have done that.

Immediately we planted the seed. God kept His Word and gave seed to the sower. We know that God is also faithful to multiply every seed we plant and we will see the harvest as well.

YOUR GOD-GIVEN KEY FOR TODAY

"I Can Know That God Is Faithful To Multiply Every Seed I Plant."

FRIDAY
Key: I CAN HAVE MY TIME MULTIPLIED

or
Make What You Do With Your Time A Seed Of Faith You Plant, And God Will Bring You A Great Harvest Of The Thing You Need Most — Time

It's so difficult for most of us to determine what our priorities are. It has caused me frustration at times.

One day last year the reality of my busy workload hit me. I was trying to work every day on the *Richard Roberts Live* show, be a good wife, manage our home, cook, and take care of little Jordan. At about 11:30 that night, I couldn't sleep because I knew I had work that was not finished. I said, "Richard, my work isn't done. I've got to get up."

"No, you've got to get some sleep," he told me.

I said, "Richard, there aren't enough hours in the day. I'm not finishing all the work God has called me to do. I carry so much guilt because I can only spread myself so thin."

I felt guilty because I wanted to spend every single minute with Jordan but I couldn't. I had waited so long to have her and now I didn't ever want to be away from her. I also felt guilty because I have a husband who needs me and I wanted to be with him as much as I could be.

It seems to me that working mothers, in particular, are being torn and ripped and pulled. We know we have responsibilities in our family and job, and it takes a lot of time to meet those responsibilities. There is almost no time left for ourselves. It's a struggle just to get what *has* to be done accomplished.

Richard told me how to find peace that night when I felt such guilt. He reminded me of Philippians 4:6,7 which says, "Be anxious for nothing; but in every thing by prayer and supplication with thanksgiving let your requests be made known unto God. And the peace of God, which passeth all understanding, shall keep your hearts and minds through Christ Jesus."

Peace that goes beyond human understanding comes when you cast your care upon God who cares for you. If you are as much in need of time because of your workload as I was, I pray in the name of Jesus that you will find peace.

Richard reminded me also of Luke 6:38 which says, "Give, and it shall be given unto you; good measure, pressed down, and shaken together, and running over." Richard said to me, "If you will give your time to God, He will multiply that time back to you. And He will teach you how to use your time just right and to divide your time properly."

It sounded impossible when Richard said it to me, and it may sound impossible to you. But it works! I know, because I began to give God my time on the television program each day. I've learned that if you need time, *give* time. Make what you do with your time a seed of faith you plant and God will bring a great harvest from it.

One morning recently I overslept. Richard was already up preparing for the daily TV show. Jordan was awake but still in her crib playing with stuffed animals. I jumped out of bed thinking: *I've got to wash my hair.*

Now I usually wash my hair at night to save time in the morning, but I had been up working late the night before and had decided to let it go and get up early. Unfortunately, things didn't go as planned and I overslept. Now I could see that I'd never get to the studio on time. I made breakfast for Richard and Jordan and gave Jordan her bath and got her ready for the day. Every other minute I watched the clock and I could see I was getting further behind in my time. Still I couldn't neglect my duties as a wife and mother. You know, so often we work at all the little things that no one seems to notice and we can really feel sorry for ourselves. You know the feeling of "just once I wish someone would notice the extra time I took to make things right for my family." Then we think, *How come they seem to notice only when I goof and make mistakes.*

But this morning as I was hurrying, I felt God in the midst of all my rushing around. Then I was instantly reminded of Luke 6:38 when Jesus said, "Give, and it shall be given unto you." I remembered how Richard always applied that Scripture to everything — time, money, talent, prayers, friendship — and I knew right then that what I did for my family was a seed. And even if no one in the world saw it, God saw it. I thought of Galatians 6:7 which says, "Be not deceived; God is not mocked: *whatsoever* a man soweth, that shall he also reap."

I had sown time into my family and right then I asked God to multiply my seed into a harvest of more time for myself. Not just in the morning, but all day long so I could feel at the end of the day that there was enough of me to go around and not feel guilty over neglecting someone or something.

Now in the natural people say, "That's impossible." But I said, "No, God is going to multiply my time in the form of time."

I prayed, "Lord, I'm doing this unto You. You're going to have to help me through it."

I got in the shower and washed my hair and dried it and then started playing with Jordan. She always likes to play when I put on my makeup. I kept watching the time but it was like time slowed down — time was standing still.

This is absurd, I thought. *I've got all this extra time on my hands,* and I started to laugh because usually by 8:00 I'm in a panic. Here it was only 7:45 and everything was done and I was playing with Jordan and having a wonderful time. Then I thought, *No, it's not absurd. It's the Lord!*

Suddenly my time was multiplied. I got dressed quicker. My makeup was done quicker. My hair dried faster. There I was with an extra 15 minutes on my hands thinking, *What do I do with this time?*

Because I'd planted a seed of my time by helping somebody else that morning, God multiplied it back just as I had asked for it.

And that's how God is. If we give Him our day, our career, our time, our talent, our children, our husband, our marriage, our job, then it is no longer our responsibility. God takes care of it. Of course it's our responsibility to do our very best at the things we can do, but then we can confidently leave the results in God's hands. All the things we wish could happen and we couldn't make happen, somehow God makes happen.

Say as you go about your work today...

YOUR GOD-GIVEN KEY FOR TODAY

"I Can Have My Time Multiplied."

SATURDAY

**Key:
I CAN HAVE THE
DEEPEST DESIRES
OF MY HEART**

**or
God Will Give Us A Party**

One morning a very simple thing happened, yet the Lord revealed something very special to me through it. I was brushing my hair and I pulled out one of the hairs and something in my mind said, "Minus one." I thought, *That's funny. What does it mean?*

Then the Lord brought to my remembrance the verse of Scripture in Luke 12:7 that says, "Even the very hairs of your head are all numbered." I realized as never before that God notices even a little insignificant thing like that happening to you and me. *If God knows all about us,* I thought, *then He knows the very desires of our heart.* And I have found through the years that He not only knows the desires of our heart, He gives us the desires of our heart when we trust Him JUST AS Psalm 37:4 says. "Delight thyself also in the Lord, and he shall give thee the desires of thine heart."

One of the desires of my heart would sound silly to many people, but it was really important to me. It was to have birthday parties for *my* children. I wanted to see the look on the faces of my own little babies as they blew out their candles and opened their packages and put their tiny little fingers in the icing of a cake.

I had seen home movies of my brother, sister, and me as we grew up doing those same things and I couldn't wait to have children of my own to watch their little faces as they experienced their first birthdays.

I remember my little niece, Patricia, as she had her first birthday and the wonder in her eyes as she realized it was all for her.

After the death of our little Richard Oral I had a very, very difficult time attending birthday parties for the children of my close friends. I had friends that were pregnant every time I was and I watched in wrenching anguish as their children turned one, then two, and so on. The devil told me time after time, "You'd better enjoy their parties because you'll never have one of your own."

Well, I know the devil is a liar and the father of lies, but year after year of having no child of my own almost drained me of the dream. When I realized how I was letting the devil get to me, I began right away to give out of my hurt and plant seeds into the lives of my friends. I had baby showers and helped plan out birthday parties and buy presents. Every time I'd come home and cry out to God, "I know You'll honor this some day."

Then on April 23, 1985, our precious little daughter Jordan Lindsay was born, and one year later I began to realize that God was working a "heart's desire" miracle and it had my name on it.

Richard wanted to show little Jordan to our TV family on her first birthday. He asked if I would dress her up and take her to the program. I said, "Fine."

A dear friend, Geri Cochran, and I made her first birthday dress with ribbons for her hair and set the plans in motion for Jordan's big day.

I was curious about what we should do for a cake or decorations, if any, since this was the hour-long daily TV program. I didn't want to be ridiculous, so I asked Richard what I should do.

"Just leave it to me," he said. "I'll take care of it."

I wasn't sure what he meant, but I've learned that when Richard says he'll take care of something, he does.

The next morning, with butterflies in my stomach, I brought out little Jordan Lindsay into the studio, and there, before my eyes, were balloons and cards and decorations and even a pink and white birthday cake with "Happy 1st Birthday" written on it. I couldn't believe it.

As Richard asked me to describe my feelings of our little girl's first birthday party, I began to cry. I realized that, in all ways, my dream that had been shattered so many times before had become a reality. I saw the goodness of God and how He truly blesses His children for being faithful.

And if we just trust Him with everything, He will give us the desires of our heart — even if it is something that may sound silly to everyone but ourselves.

What is your greatest desire right now? You can be assured that if God knows the number of hairs on your head (see Matthew 10:30), He knows your heart's desire. As Psalm 139:1,2 says, "O Lord, thou hast searched me, and known me. Thou knowest my downsitting and my uprising, thou understandest my thought afar off."

Then Psalm 37:4 assures us, "Delight thyself also in the Lord; and he shall give thee the desires of thine heart."

After you have planted your seeds of faith, just trust Him and be faithful to Him in the waiting time to receive the desire of your heart.

YOUR GOD-GIVEN KEY FOR TODAY

"I Can Have
The Deepest Desires Of My Heart."

SIXTH WEEK

SUNDAY GOD IS THE SOURCE FOR MY LIFE AND I CAN TRUST HIM NO MATTER THE CIRCUMSTANCES

MONDAY I TRUST JESUS TO PUT THE DEVIL OUT AT HOME PLATE!

TUESDAY I WILL ENCOURAGE MY LOVED ONES TO BELIEVE FOR THE MIRACLE THEY NEED

WEDNESDAY I CAN TURN ON MY FAITH FOR THE MIRACLE I NEED

THURSDAY I CAN KNOW THAT GOD IS FAITHFUL TO MULTIPLY EVERY SEED I PLANT

FRIDAY I CAN HAVE MY TIME MULTIPLIED

SATURDAY I CAN HAVE THE DEEPEST DESIRES OF MY HEART

SEVENTH WEEK

Knowing The Name And Nature Of My Enemy Is Half The Battle!

By Oral Roberts

SUNDAY

Key:
YOU HAVE AN ENEMY
AND HE HAS A NAME:
THE DEVIL

or
How You Can Recognize
The Devil When You See Him At Work

In Genesis 2 and 3 we read the story of Adam and Eve and how they were deceived by the devil in the garden of Eden. The Bible describes the devil in this way:

> *"Now the serpent was more cunning than any beast of the field..."*

There's one characteristic attributed to the devil and that was his CUNNING. And, friend, that's the characteristic he displays today. The devil is real. He exists. And he's not dumb. He's cunning... scheming...always in pursuit of a new idea, a new way to destroy your life.

The Bible goes on to tell us how the devil *works:*

> *"And he said unto the woman, Yea, hath God said, Ye shall not eat of every tree in the garden?"*

Immediately the devil tried to take God's own words and twist them.

> *"And the woman said unto the serpent, We may eat of the fruit of the trees of the garden: But of the fruit of the tree which is in the midst of the garden, God has said, Ye shall not eat of it, neither shall ye touch it, lest ye die.*

"And the serpent said unto the woman, Ye shall not surely die."

SATAN SAYS, "MAYBE SO . . . MAYBE NOT"

Or, more literally, he said MAYBE SO, MAYBE NOT. Maybe you'll die, maybe you won't. Maybe God meant what He said, maybe He didn't. And with those four little words, MAYBE SO, MAYBE NOT, the devil introduced situational ethics to the human race.

Even though Eve and her husband Adam had walked with the Lord God in the cool of the day, and had always known a relationship with Him that was based on love for them...goodness to them... and absolute truth in their lives, they now began to entertain the devil's words against God, and to believe them.

Have you heard that voice in your mind? In your heart?

Maybe the Bible is true, maybe it isn't? Maybe God loves me, but maybe He doesn't? Maybe I can have a miracle, maybe I can't?

You'd better recognize who's doing that kind of talking!

The devil said, "For God doth know that in the day ye eat thereof, then your eyes shall be opened, and ye shall be as gods, knowing good and evil."

The devil started to promise Eve something better than what God had said. Or at least she thought it sounded like something better. And isn't that his trick today? "Go ahead and try drugs," he whispers to you. "It's better than not having them in you." Or "Go ahead and have this relationship with someone who isn't your husband — or who isn't your wife," he whispers inside you. "It's better than what you have."

HOW TO KNOW WHO THE DEVIL IS

Now see the devil for who he is and what he says.

First, he's a fallen angel. He rebelled against God and was cast out of heaven. And with him, a third of the angels. He was given power over this world for a season. And he's mad at God. He's trying to take all of God's creation down with him. He knows he's ultimately destroyed but he wants to take anything he can with him into hell and away from God.

Second, he's cunning. He knows human nature. He knows the laws of God and how God set things up. And he's going to do everything in his power to twist and warp God's perfection to destroy you. The devil knew Eve's weak point and he jumped on it. He knows yours.

Third, the devil knows the Bible. He knows God's words. And he loves to twist them too and try to twist them in your thinking and confuse you.

Fourth, the devil loves to introduce situational ethics into every circumstance he can. MAYBE SO. MAYBE NOT. He loves to cause doubt to spring up.

Now I'm not talking about the honest kind of doubt that begins to question and that leads to finding absolute answers and then turns to faith that has some JUSTIFICATION behind it. I'm talking about the destructive kind of doubt that leads to DISBELIEF.

And finally, the devil always tries to offer you something that he SAYS is better than God's way. And, friend, it sometimes *is*... but only for the moment. What the devil offers never LASTS.

You say, "What does this have to do with me today?"

You need to recognize that there is a devil and that he's out to destroy you. He's real. He's cunning. And he's out to do you in.

You have an enemy. His name is Satan…the serpent…the evil one…the devil.

Your enemies in life are not people…or things… or situations. Your enemy is the devil.

Next, you need to recognize that the devil is going to try to talk to you. He's going to come at you offering you more excitement, more happiness, more good feelings, than you have right now. He's going to say, "Maybe so, maybe not" about the things of God. He's going to come at your weakness. And he's even going to try to twist what you know about the Word of God to fit his own purposes.

Be on guard! Watch out for him! Don't give in to him! In fact, don't even give him the time of day! Don't listen to him!

Knowing the name of your enemy is half the battle. The other half is RESISTING him and overcoming him.

YOUR GOD-GIVEN KEY FOR TODAY

**"I Know The Name
Of My Enemy And It's The Devil.
I Also Know My Victor…
My Savior…My Deliverer…
And My Lord. His Name Is Jesus!"**

MONDAY

**Key:
THE DEVIL COMES AS
A ROARING LION AND I
HAVE THE POWER
TO ROAR RIGHT BACK!**

or
The Difference Between Fear And Faith

The Bible says that Satan comes to us "as a roaring lion, seeking whom he may devour" (1 Peter 5:8).

Notice that phrase, "as a roaring lion."

They say the way a lion devours his prey is to stalk it by going around it — round and round. And as he moves in a circle around his prey, he puts his mouth to the ground and roars. The sound seems to be coming from the north, the south, the east, and the west. It seems to come from all sides and it just envelops the animal he's trying to kill. And the animal doesn't know which way to go. He doesn't know the direction the lion is going to pounce from. The animal freezes in fear. The roar paralyzes him.

Now the Bible says that's the way the devil works. He comes "as a roaring lion." He's not a lion. Notice that especially. He just has a roar!

All of this sound that you hear in your inner spirit — all of the confusion and terror — so that you don't know which way to turn to escape the worry, the depression, the fear that grips you...that's not a lion that's able to destroy you. It's just a roar.

WHAT TO SAY IN THE FACE OF A ROAR

First, you say...and say it out loud..."The God I serve is able to deliver me." That's what the Hebrew children, Shadrach, Meshach, and Abednego, said in the face of a fiery furnace when the king Nebuchad-nezzar was roaring at them! (See Daniel 3:16-18.)

The God we serve can heal.

The God we serve can deliver.

The God we serve can save.

The God we serve can reward.

The God we serve *loves us!*

The God we serve WILL deliver us from destruction.

Second, you say…and say it out loud…"I will act on my faith, and not my fear, and move forward in my life."

Take action! Don't get paralyzed by your fear!

Time and time again the doctors at the City of Faith will ask a patient why he or she waited so long to come in for an appointment or to have a problem fixed, and they say, "I was afraid of what I might find out." Well, let me tell you, that kind of fear is a roar of the lion.

Fear never healed anybody. Fear never got a problem solved. Sitting down and waiting never got a need met.

PRAYER IS ONLY A PHONE CALL AWAY

Make a phone call to get prayer working on your behalf. You can always call the ABUNDANT LIFE PRAYER GROUP (918) 495-7777 in Tulsa, Oklahoma. They are on call 24 hours a day, 365 days a year. Right there in the Prayer Tower at the center of the Oral Roberts University campus, prayer is going up to God every minute, every hour of every day, every year. Call and agree with a prayer partner for your miracle.

If you need help with a physical need, call for an appointment with a physician. The City of Faith was built to help *you*. That's right, *you*. Don't delay. Men and women who are Spirit-filled and believe in the power of God are waiting to pray with you, to work with you, to find an answer to your problem until every humanly known avenue has been exhausted — and even beyond that point, to ask the Holy Spirit for divine revelational knowledge to help you. The City of Faith is a place of miracles.

If you need help getting out of debt, go see someone who can give you good quality advice.

If you need to get out of an evil situation…pack your bags and move! If you need to flee from something that is likely to cause your destruction…start taking action! If you need help getting rid of a problem with alcohol or drugs…make a call. Again, the City of Faith has an excellent "Set Free" clinic to help you overcome your addiction by the power of the Holy Spirit and the best of medical care.

Don't just sit by and let the devil stop you in your tracks. Don't listen to his roar.

Roar back!

Let him hear you clearly…

YOUR GOD-GIVEN KEY FOR TODAY

"When The Devil Roars At Me, I Will Roar Back With Faith In God!"

Key:
YES, SATAN ROARS
BUT GOD'S MIGHTY
TUESDAY **HEALING STREAM**
FLOWS ON

or
You Are Not Alone

Have you ever noticed when you get inspired to do something you know is from God, you know you're right, how you start thinking, "Wow! Everybody will be thrilled!"

Then suddenly all hell seems to break loose and you begin to say, "Hey, what's wrong? Why don't people understand? Why are they fighting me so hard when I'm only trying to do good?"

Our Savior knows all about that — for you know what happened to Him, also to His apostles and followers back there, also all through the generations. It's just a shock to your system when something like that happens to you.

But there's also some terrifically good things that happen which, if you notice and seize with your spirit of faith, will cause roses to bloom again for you and you will make it.

FOUR DECADES OF INSPIRATION

When I began this ministry four decades ago this month, I was inspired of God and full of enthusiasm. It seemed to me because God had healed me and spoken to me to take His healing power to my generation EVERYONE WOULD BE AS THRILLED AS I WAS.

Little did I realize that any dead fish can float

223

downstream but it takes a live one to swim upstream. Nor did I have any way of comprehending how Satan would come against me because I was obeying God to preach and teach and heal as Jesus did. I knew Satan had come against Jesus' preaching, His teaching, and especially His healing the sick. But I didn't know how tough it is to do what I'm called to do, to do it with excellence, and to do it regardless of what happens.

In early 1987 we were attempting to obey God's mandate to give scholarships to all the ORU medical school students to go as medical missionaries. Satan rose up on every hand to bitterly oppose…to accuse…to confuse people as to our motives…and to stop us. Letters we received from friends and Partners told us that before they heard the news — and the opposition — the Lord had put a burden on their hearts to pray.

A PARTNER FELT OUR BURDENS

One letter is typical and it will mean a lot to you in this particular time in your life when you're wondering if anything is happening behind the scenes with God to help you.

"Oral, I'm writing because I've had a burden for you and Evelyn for over two weeks. I just don't know how to explain it. I'll sit down at the table with my husband and the children, we're all talking and eating, then it hits me. Big tears start rolling down my cheeks and I can hardly swallow my bite of food for the lump in my throat. I have to get up and go pray for Oral and Evelyn.

"The Lord wakes me up four or five times a night to pray.

"THEN…I received your letter about turning the

ORU medical school into a total medical missionary outreach and about the financial need you have to do it in a specific period of time or the Lord is going to be taking Oral home, and it's no longer a mystery why my burden for you all is so heavy.

"I was driving to our store talking to God and I asked Him, 'God, WHY? Why do You always give Oral such odd, hard things to do?' His answer was, *Do you think Noah had a hard time trying to convince the people it was going to rain? They didn't even know what rain was! How do you think the disciples felt about trying to convince the people who had killed Jesus that He was still alive? If I have a job for somebody to do — well, they have to do it!*

"'God, what is Your timetable for Oral to train those medical students for medical missions?' He said, *NOW!*"

HE HAD THE TROPHY

Then she added, "Oral, I wrote you a letter once about a young man standing at the end of the field in a football game, his hair was down in his eyes, his football suit was half torn off, and he was caked with mud because they had played in a driving rain that turned the field into a quagmire, but he had the trophy. That was several years ago when I wrote you that letter, another time you'd heard from God and you thought you'd gone as far as you could go. But God helped you to go, and on, and on, and *He'll help you again!*

"Oral and Evelyn, let me say one more thing. I love you. Oral, don't plan on going to heaven in March. You'll be so disappointed when you don't get to go, and you'll pout and make Evelyn's spring and summer so miserable. All right?"

When I read her letter at first I couldn't keep the tears back. That God was burdening her heart to pray before she knew the mandate for medical missions to open the nations for the gospel really touched me. It awakened me to the fact that I AM NOT ALONE. When God tells me to carry out a certain task for Him, He also lays a part of that burden on other people and they are faithful to pray, then write and be Partners with us.

However, I couldn't help but laugh when at the end of her letter she let me know her faith was so strong she knew God who had called me to do this would make a way, and I shouldn't be thinking of going to heaven in March and be so disappointed I didn't get to go that I'd pout and spend the rest of the spring and summer making Evelyn miserable. I thought, *How perceptive she is.* I take my ministry so seriously I need a word like the closing of her letter to get me to laugh.

SOMETIMES IT'S GOOD TO LAUGH AT OURSELVES

The point I want to make to you today is that life is serious...but we also need a few moments to laugh at ourselves.

We got another letter from a man who's been our Partner for 25 years. His letter was short but it is a classic.

"Dear Oral and Evelyn:

"Hang in there. If it were easy, everyone would be doing it. Remember...only the person carrying the ball gets tackled. Statues are never built to critics in the stands. The dog barks but the train rolls on."

I've read and reread these words a dozen times and each sentence continues to leap off the page to lift me up. Read them with me.

Hang in there! When you know you have to do something that's right and whose time has come and the going gets hard, it's so easy to turn loose, to give up. Don't do it. Stay in the fight.

If it were easy, everyone would be doing it. The really good and great things of life really go against the grain of most people. Most people want something easy, and want to do things that will be popular and that they will be praised for.

Remember…only the person carrying the ball gets tackled. That's obvious, isn't it, but how often we need to be reminded of it. Yes, we're being hit for a reason; we're carrying the ball for God!

Statues are never built to critics in the stands. This brought back the picture of the boy holding the trophy. He looked like he'd been through something terrible and he had — while the critic under the covered stands only yelled at him. But when the game was over and the victory won, it was not the critic holding the winner's trophy — it was the boy who had stayed in the game no matter how tough the conditions.

The dog barks but the train rolls on. I can just see this, can't you? For several weeks it seemed every newspaper I picked up or newscast I heard, I saw or heard my name held up to ridicule, mockery, and anger. How dare a man say he heard God speak to him, especially Oral Roberts? "It's just a money ploy," most of them said. They missed the main issue, which is God's concern for the nations that are closed to the gospel and that can only be opened by sending medical missionaries. The news media didn't mention the real thing I was told to do by the Lord. My friend put it so aptly when he reminded me, "The dog barks but the train rolls on!"

This brother will never know how his words lifted my spirit causing me to jump out of my chair, praising God and saying, "Yes, Satan roars but God's mighty healing stream flows on — and my Partners and I are right in the midst of the flow."

THREE THINGS YOU NEED TO KNOW

There are three things I want you to turn your attention to today — and each time you're doing the right thing and it seems all hell breaks loose against you:

One, God has someone praying for you before they ever know what you're going through. And you can count on God's faithfulness to have that person and others praying for you.

Two, you're doing something important for the kingdom of God or the devil would not be after you. If you weren't carrying the ball he would not try to tackle you. You're important to God, Satan knows it, and he's trying to stop you in order to stop God. But the devil will have to get God before he can get you — and Satan is a defeated foe!

Three, there is no easy way to do what God says, for the easy way would mean you would be going with the crowd. Jesus said, "Narrow is the gate that leads to life and few there be who enter it. But wide is the gate and broad is the way that leads to destruction and many there are who go in by it." (See Matthew 7:13,14.)

Although the way of the Lord is not easy according to the way this world treats you, Jesus has a special word for you on that: "Come unto me, all you that labor and are heavy burdened. Take my yoke upon you, and learn of me; for I am meek and lowly in heart. For my yoke is easy, and my burden is light"

(Matthew 11:28-30).

Jesus is the Master Carpenter. He knows your size and just how to build the yoke of His way to fit easily on your spirit. In comparison with the heavy and ill-fitting load of Satan, Jesus' burden is light indeed.

In other words, God said, "It is better to obey…for if you be willing and obedient, you shall eat the good of the land" (1 Samuel 15:22, Isaiah 1:19).

Now that I have gotten through March and I know deep in my spirit that we are turning around the medical school…with my Partners providing scholarships for our medical students so that for each year's scholarship they will spend a year on the mission field…it's a lot lighter load to face next year and the next to give scholarships to each year's graduates THAN IF I DROPPED THE BALL OUT OF FEAR OF BEING TACKLED.

Friend, I tell you today that *you* are going to make it through this trial, this hard situation, this thing that looks impossible! I stand in agreement with you, and I won't come out of the agreement!

YOUR GOD-GIVEN KEY FOR TODAY

"Whatever God Tells Me To Do I Will Do It, Knowing I Am Not Alone."

WEDNESDAY

Key: THE DEVIL IS THE MASTER OF COMPROMISE

or
When I Am Facing A Fiery Furnace, I Have The Power To Make A Choice To Obey Rather Than To Compromise

Like a diamond on a velvet couch, beautiful Jerusalem, the city of God, was situated in the Judean hills. Now it lay in ruins. The Babylonian army led by King Nebuchadnezzar had burned and sacked the city, taking captive its people. Three young Hebrew men, Shadrach, Meshach, and Abednego, were among them.

Shortly after these young men arrived in Babylon, they heard music and saw people kneeling before an image of gold, shouting, "Great is Nebuchadnezzar, our god." The young Hebrew men's blood froze in their veins, but they remained upright. For written in the law of God was His command, "Thou shalt have no other gods" (Exodus 20:3).

Shadrach, Meshach, and Abednego were brought to the king. He said, "I'll give you one more chance. When you hear the music, bow to my god and all will be well. And if you refuse, I'll thrust you into a burning fiery furnace."

Shadrach, Meshach, and Abednego looked at the great image that the king had made of himself — some sixty feet high standing there on the plains of Gora. They looked at the burning fiery furnace, so hot that it singed the hair of all who came close to it. And in their hearts they knew the Word of God.

Friend, isn't that the way the devil comes at you today? He puts up an image of something in your mind and heart and says, "This is the most important thing on the earth to you. Bow down to it. It will be good for you."

These young men came face to face with an inescapable principle of life: Your faith is going to be tried.

YOUR FAITH WILL BE TRIED

The devil isn't content to let you know Jesus Christ as your personal Savior and Lord. He doesn't give up just because you have established a faith-connection with almighty God. Whether you live in Jerusalem, New York, Los Angeles, Tulsa, or someplace that nobody's heard of, you will have the opportunity to prove the kind of material you are made of. You will either live by your faith, or you will compromise.

Now the *law of faith* will nurture you...always. On the other hand, the *law of compromise* will never nurture you or satisfy you. And whatever you compromise to get, you will ultimately lose. The law of compromise comes from that crowd in this world led by the devil that says, "If you don't follow us, if you don't do the things we do, if you don't bow down to our ways, you won't make it."

Your only real option as followers of Jesus Christ is to dig down to the bedrock of real heartfelt religion and anchor your soul forever on the Rock of Ages.

Shadrach, Meshach, and Abednego refused to bow to the golden image. Without a moment's hesitation, without the flicker of an eyelash, they said, "Our God, whom we serve, is able to deliver us."

He is able!

Thank God, our God is able!

These young men knew God was able. They were not just saying He was able in order to bolster their own courage. They were speaking out of knowledge and experience. The record of their God declared that He was able. The prophets declared it. The Psalmist sang it. The children of Israel danced on the sands of the Red Sea and shouted that He was able. They remembered His outstretched hand, and His Spirit told them He was able. They believed this so strongly that their God — invisible though He was — was more real to them than the visible Nebuchadnezzar standing before them.

GOD MUST BE YOUR GOD

Everyone who knows God as his or her Source can know Him in this same way. His presence is real. He is able! But in order for you to know this, God must be *your* God and you must serve Him.

This was the first time anyone ever had the courage and faith to tell old Nebuchadnezzar the truth about God. He was enraged and beside himself with anger. He recognized the seed of rebellion and knew that if it were not quenched, his kingdom would not last. Screaming for his most powerful soldiers, he commanded them to heat the furnace seven times hotter and then to bind Shadrach, Meshach, and Abednego and throw them into the furnace.

Now Shadrach, Meshach, and Abednego stood up to the king. They said, "We may burn, but we won't bow." They refused to compromise. They lived by their LAW OF FAITH.

And when they refused to bow, they found that they wouldn't burn.

When the soldiers who bowed came near the fire — just close enough to throw Shadrach, Meshach, and Abednego into it — they died from the heat. But Shadrach, Meshach, and Abednego lived to walk in the fire with Jesus himself!

What happened when these three young men were cast into the fire? Why, Jesus himself who was seated at the right hand of the Father...stood up. He hurled himself through space and in a moment's time was beside them going into the burning fiery furnace with them. By the time the door was shut, He had ripped off their bonds and clothed them with divine protection. And when the king looked in, all four of them were walking around in the fire, unhurt and untouched by the flames.

FOUR WAYS SATAN SEEKS TO GET YOU TO COMPROMISE

How will the devil try to get you to compromise today? I believe he comes at you on four key points today...

FIRST: The devil will try to get you to compromise about the Bible. The Bible stands for heart purity, clean living, separation from the world's systems, holiness of life. The word *holy* seems to have become an abomination to many people in our world today. They would rather fill their minds and hearts with trash — with drugs and alcohol and filthy magazines and books and television programs. They are ashamed to even hear the word *holiness* in their preaching and conversation. But the Bible is clear on this point. God loves holiness. He wants you to have the power and the miracle that come with a pure life.

SECOND: The devil will try to get you to compromise about the Holy Spirit.

One of the greatest needs of Christians is to have a

daily experience with the Holy Spirit…to pray in the Spirit and to interpret back to your mind…to be expecting the miracles, signs, and wonders that come from the Holy Spirit's work in our world.

No one knows the importance of the Holy Spirit more than God does. He *commanded* His disciples to "tarry" until they were endued with power from on high.

When the disciples received the Holy Spirit into their lives, it did three things for them. It gave them the inner courage and power to win souls. In other words, it gave them BOLDNESS to tell others about Jesus Christ. Next, it gave them power to stand persecution. Third, it gave them daily living access to Jesus Christ in His invisible form, His unlimited self.

Who is the Holy Spirit? He is the same Spirit that was in Christ Jesus only in unlimited, invisible form so that each one of us might be filled with that Spirit and be followers of Christ, to do the works He did, and to have fellowship with God our Father like He did.

The devil doesn't want you to have a relationship with the Holy Spirit and he'll do everything in his power to get you to compromise on this point. He'll whisper, "You don't need the Holy Spirit," "You can't have the Holy Spirit," "You can get along without the Holy Spirit." But, friend, you need the Holy Spirit, and God wants you to have the Holy Spirit inside you and working through you on a day-to-day basis, right where you live.

THIRD: The devil will try to get you to compromise about healing, miracles, signs, and wonders.

"I'LL GLADLY TAKE THEM"

One day I was talking with one of the leading

preachers in this generation — a man who is winning souls but who had no heart of healing compassion toward the sick and afflicted, a man who is not open to the flow of miracles, signs, and wonders to accompany his preaching and teaching of God's Word. I said to him, "My brother, what are you going to do about the healing of the sick?"

He said, "I'm leaving them to you, Oral Roberts."

I said, "Thank you. I gladly accept them."

Our Savior came into this world of sin and sickness and demon power saying, "The Spirit of the Lord is upon me, because he hath anointed me to preach the gospel to the poor; he hath sent me to heal the brokenhearted, to preach deliverance to the captives, and recovering of sight to the blind, to set at liberty them that are bruised" (Luke 4:18).

Well, if that was the ministry of Jesus Christ, then that's the ministry I want to have too!

The devil will try to say to you, "Miracles aren't for today. They ended thousands of years ago," or "You can't have a miracle," or "Miracles aren't important."

I tell you — because the Word of God says so — that miracles *are* for today. Jesus Christ is the same yesterday, today, forever! What He did in human form, He does today in His unlimited invisible form through the Holy Spirit. The Bible says that the preaching of the Word of God is *supposed* to be accompanied by miracles, signs, and wonders. It says that Jesus preached, taught, and *healed* the sick.

FOURTH: The devil will try to get you to compromise about Seed-Faith. He says, "You shouldn't give to God's work," or "You are giving too much," or "You can't expect any good to come back to you from your giving."

Those are lies from the author of lies!

The Bible says, "Give, and it shall be given to you, pressed down, shaken together, and running over" (Luke 6:38). It says, "Whatsoever a man soweth, that shall he also reap" (Galatians 6:7). It says, "God loveth a cheerful giver" (2 Corinthians 9:7). It says, "My God shall supply all of your needs according to His riches in Christ Jesus" (Philippians 4:19).

WHAT ABOUT COMPROMISE IN YOUR LIFE?

Let me ask you an important question:

What is the devil trying to get *you* to compromise? How is your faith being tried? Are you giving in to compromise?

Life's fiery furnaces are very real. A fiery furnace is anything that comes to destroy your life — sickness, unemployment, temptation to sin. When the fire rages, you have a decision to make. You can compromise by getting so discouraged you give up and throw aside your hope or give in to the devil's ways. Or you can believe that your God is able to deliver you and He has the power to help you.

This is your hour…this is your day…for choosing the law of faith, to stand tall for Him.

Say to yourself until the words begin to ring in your heart…

YOUR GOD-GIVEN KEY FOR TODAY

"I Will Not Compromise For My God Is Able To Deliver Me!"

**Key:
THE DEVIL
HATES
PROSPERITY —
AND, IN
PARTICULAR,
YOUR
PROSPERITY**

THURSDAY

**or
How I Can Know The Difference Between
God And The Devil When It Comes To My Money**

As a young preacher I tried to pastor churches in towns where there was a college. I was determined to pursue more education as well as pay the costs of my tuition. I had a wife and two children and had to support them too.

In one such church, Evelyn, the children, and I lived with a friend since the church had no parsonage. Two families in a small house create many problems — no matter how much they love each other. I saw a great need for a parsonage for us and also for pastors following me in that church.

When I could arouse no interest among the church people to pay down on a suitable house for a parsonage, I felt a direct guidance of God to stand one Sunday evening and to give my entire week's salary to get things started. I gave ALL the $55 during one service.

When others saw me give my entire week's salary, they also began to give and to pledge. One man pledged $1,000! Everybody was astounded because they had never seen him give *anything* before. Soon we had the full down payment.

That night after the service Evelyn said, "Oral, how

could you give your entire week's salary? What are we going to do about groceries this week?"

You see, in raising the down payment for the parsonage, my own gift hadn't been replaced. We were still without any money personally. I said, "Evelyn, God led me to do it. I know it's a great opportunity for us."

I don't think I had ever thought about giving being an *opportunity* before I heard myself say it. It just slipped out.

"I don't know what opportunity that might be," Evelyn said. "We've got children to feed this week."

I could see her point. But something in what I had just said about *opportunity* stuck in my mind. I began to believe God would intervene in our situation — otherwise, He wouldn't have directed me to give everything we had.

We went to bed. At about 4:00 a.m., a knock came on the front door. I went to the door and there stood a member of the church. He apologized for coming at that hour and then he said, "I was at the service tonight but I didn't give anything. I went home but I couldn't sleep. About an hour ago, I got up, went out into the yard where I had buried some money, and now I'm here to give it to you. The only way I can get some peace is to give you this."

And he handed me four $100 bills.

He went on to say, "As you know, I'm a wheat farmer and I know you can't have a harvest without planting a seed. This is a seed for the new parsonage, and also for you and your family."

And then he left.

"EVELYN, THIS IS
YOUR GOD-GIVEN OPPORTUNITY"

Evelyn was peering around the bedroom door. I walked over and waved the four $100 bills. "THIS is the great opportunity God had in mind for us! God is going to meet our financial needs when we obey Him and give to His work!"

That experience showed me for the first time in a personal way that God WANTS us to have the things we need. He WANTS to use our giving as a way to bless us. He has made our giving the safest way to invest. And He has put this eternal principle into this universe for us to use to get our needs met.

What is this eternal principle?

The Bible calls it the principle of SOWING and REAPING.

God established that principle with Noah after the great flood. He said there would be "seedtime and harvest" from then on, until Jesus returns to earth the second time (Genesis 8:22).

Paul wrote, "Whatsoever a man soweth, that shall he also reap" (Galatians 6:7). He wrote to another church "concerning giving and receiving" (Philippians 4:15).

Notice one thing about these Scriptures...the giving and the receiving are always linked. They are like two sides of a coin.

The devil will try to confuse us on this very point. He says, "If you give, you'll have less...you won't receive anything back," or "It's fine to give but don't expect anything back," or "To receive is what you want to do, *not* give." He tries to get you to emphasize one side or the other, but not see them together.

GET YOURSELF IN POSITION TO RECEIVE

The Bible teaches clearly that when you give, you are placed in a positive position to receive back from God:

> *"Give, and it shall be given unto you; pressed down, and running over, shall men give into your bosom"* (Luke 6:38).

Also:

> *"Bring ye all the tithes into the storehouse, that there may be meat in mine house, and prove me now herewith, saith the Lord of hosts, if I will not open the windows of heaven, and pour you out a blessing, that there shall not be room enough to receive it"* (Malachi 3:10).

Now this principle of sowing seeds of faith and reaping miracle harvests is like the principle of gravity. It applies to everybody. It isn't just something for a few of God's people. It's a universal principle for us as God's people.

GOD'S WORD FOR YOUR TITHES IS "INCREASE"

God made it very specific. He said we were to give the tithe, which means "tenth." Ten is the number meaning "increase" in the Bible. God desires you to give so that He can INCREASE YOU. He links the very act of giving with multiplying back!

God made it practical. Some people think Christians shouldn't be concerned about money and material things. But without money, what can you do? What can you do for your family…for yourself…or for

God? How can you buy groceries...pay rent or house payment...clothe yourself...or even HAVE a tithe to give to God for Him to INCREASE even more back to you?

God wants you to have a rhythm of GIVING and RECEIVING. GIVING and RECEIVING. GIVING and RECEIVING.

The devil doesn't want you to do either.

He doesn't want you to give, so God's work can go on and you can be blessed by receiving.

He sure doesn't want you to receive, to prosper, to feel good about yourself, to have enough for your family, and to be able to GIVE again.

As a young preacher and student, I developed a habit of reading a few verses from the Bible each morning before I left the house. One morning I forgot. I came running back into the house in a great hurry, trying to cram in a verse or two before the bus arrived outside. I opened my Bible and my eyes fell directly onto 3 John 2:

> *"Beloved, I wish above all things*
> *that thou mayest prosper and be in*
> *health, even as thy soul prospereth."*

That verse hit me with such divine force that I still feel it. God wanted ME to prosper...ME to be in health...and MY soul to prosper. He wanted me to BE WELL in all areas of my life, including my finances and material things! That verse changed my life and my thinking from a life of the poverty syndrome to that of having my needs met.

> Friend, God wants that for you today.
> Say it again and again...

YOUR GOD-GIVEN KEY FOR TODAY

"God Wants Me To Prosper Through Giving And Receiving."

FRIDAY

**Key:
THE DEVIL CAN'T STAND
TO LISTEN TO FAITH-TALK**

**or
How You Can Send The Devil
Fleeing From Your Life Every Time!**

I believe the way you talk can literally change your whole life. I want to help you realize today how important it is for you to use faith-talk instead of poor-talk or fear-talk or failure-talk or if-God-can-do-this-talk or any other kind of negative talk when life's emergencies come against you.

Where does faith come from? The Bible says that a *measure of faith* has been given to every person (Romans 12:3). That means that you already HAVE faith. You don't need to go out and get it somewhere.

The problem with faith is that it's either lying in you dormant and still, inactive and ineffective, or you are USING it to get the miracles you need.

How do you get your faith activated? The Bible says that "faith comes by hearing, and hearing by the word of God" (Romans 10:17).

It says faith COMES. That means that your faith is like oil in the ground. It's there…it's to be used and released…but you have to drill for it and cause it to COME FORTH.

YOU HEAR WHAT YOU YOURSELF SAY

It says faith comes by HEARING. Most of us think about hearing in relationship to other people. "Did you hear what the preacher said?" "Did you hear what he said…or she said…about a matter?" The fact is that you also hear what you YOURSELF say.

When it comes right down to it, people who have studied the way we learn tell us that we remember only about ten percent of what other people say to us. Only about that much lodges inside us and becomes a part of our memories. On the other hand, we remember about ninety percent of what we OURSELVES have to say!

What does that mean to you today?

It means that your own words are even more important to your faith than what you hear from other people.

Finally, that verse says our faith comes by hearing THE WORD OF GOD.

Now to speak the Word of God, you've got to know the Word of God. You've got to know what the entire Bible says, not just one or two isolated verses here and there. You've got to know more of what the Bible says as a WHOLE. You've got to get the thread of the Bible as God has woven it throughout His Word. Then you will see how God has repeatedly said things and done things. You'll see what Jesus said and did as a whole, and you'll begin to get the big picture of God's plan and purpose for all of mankind — and, in particular, for YOUR LIFE.

On the night that I was healed of tuberculosis, I heard God speak into my spirit, *I am going to heal you, and you are to take My healing power to your generation.*

I went for years without knowing exactly what that

meant or how to do it. I started preaching almost immediately after I was healed. I pastored small churches in several areas as I struggled to know HOW to take God's healing power to this generation. I didn't have any role models. I didn't know how to pray for the sick. All I knew to do was to read my Bible and fast and pray and ask God what to do.

One day while I was sitting in class at the university, I heard God speak again, "Don't be like other men. Be like Jesus."

HOW I GOT INTO FAITH-TALK

Friend, there's no role model for you anywhere on this earth like Jesus. Jesus became real to me as never before. And when Jesus becomes real to you, you find yourself attracted to Him. You want to know Him more…be more like Him…and do the things He did. You want to talk the way He talked, and Jesus used FAITH-TALK.

What exactly is FAITH-TALK?

It's almost easier to describe what it *isn't*.

You've heard sick-talk…

"Oh, I just don't think I can get out of bed today. My bursitis is acting up and my head hurts."

You've heard poor-talk…

"We just can't afford that. Times are tough. We have to be careful with what we give to God."

You've heard doubt-talk…

"Well, I'm just not sure that will work."

You've heard negative, down-in-the-dumps-talk…

"Things just aren't going well right now."

But hear the flip side of those same remarks.

FAITH-TALK SAYS:

"I'm getting out of bed this morning and doing everything I can to turn this bad situation around."

FAITH-TALK SAYS:

"I'm going to give to God and trust Him to multiply my giving into a harvest of miracles."

FAITH-TALK SAYS:

"I'll give it a try."

FAITH-TALK SAYS:

"We're on the verge of winning. We're about to have a turnaround breakthrough."

THE MOST IMPORTANT QUESTION JESUS ASKS YOU IS: "WHERE IS *YOUR* FAITH?"

One night Jesus decided that it was time to go to Gadara to command the demons to leave a man who was living outside the city, and outside himself. He was totally unable to take control over his thoughts and actions. Jesus said to His disciples, "Let us get in this boat and cross over the Sea of Galilee."

A storm struck, however, before they arrived. The wind came whipping down the mountain and within a matter of minutes that small lake was churning with whitecaps.

The disciples were in terror. Storms like this could capsize a boat in seconds. They rushed to awaken Jesus, crying, "Wake up! Don't You care what is happening? How can You sleep? We're about to go under!"

Jesus responded to them calmly, "Where is your faith?"

In other words, Jesus was saying, "What are YOU doing about it? Why aren't you using your faith?"

Then Jesus rose up and spoke, "Peace, be still!

Stop your ranting and raving, wind. That's enough. Calm down!"

And the winds and waves obeyed His voice and the Bible says, "They came to the other side of the sea" (Mark 4:35-5:1).

I want you to see three things here. First, Jesus spoke. There is power in SPOKEN WORDS.

Second, Jesus spoke against the problem. He rebuked the wind and waves. In today's terms, He said, "Stop it! That's enough!"

Third, Jesus spoke out the results He wanted. He said, "Peace. Be still now."

That's your role model for today!

Address your problem with your words.

Get it out. Speak it out. Don't let your problem ferment inside you.

Speak against your problem. Tell it to go.

And then speak out the result you want to have. Don't just think it. SAY IT.

Jesus said to His disciples, "If you SAY to this mountain, 'Be removed and be cast into the sea,' it *will* be done" (Matthew 21:21, italics added).

That's FAITH-TALK.

And the devil can't stand to hear it. He won't wait around to hear very much of it. He hates the Word of God because he has to obey it: he can't counteract it. That means FAITH-TALK is your best weapon to send the devil packing!

YOUR GOD-GIVEN KEY FOR TODAY

"My Faith-Talk Is My Best Weapon Against The Devil."

SATURDAY

**Key:
THE DEVIL BACKS
OFF WHEN YOU
START TO ATTACK**

or
When You Start To Attack
Your Lack, The Devil Starts To Back Away

The Bible tells in vivid detail about a time when the city of Samaria was surrounded on all sides by the powerful forces of the Syrian army. The people of the city were shut up inside the walls, slowly being starved to death by the soldiers encamped around them. They had given up in their spirits and were now even eating the flesh of their own children. No more hideous scene is described in the Bible. (See 2 Kings 6 and 7.)

But something happened in that story that is critical for you to know today as you face life's needs and troubles. Something happened that I call a FAITH-ATTACK.

Inside the city was a prophet, Elisha, who was sent there by God to sit where the people sat, to feel what they felt, and to give a word of revelational knowledge to the king and his court when all hope was gone. Elisha boldly said to the king, "In 24 hours God is going to send deliverance. Food that is now so scarce no amount of money can buy it will be so plentiful by this time tomorrow that you can buy all you need for pennies."

An aide of the king, full of doubt and totally rejecting the words of revelational knowledge by the man of God, sneered, "If God were to open windows in heaven, could this thing be done?"

247

IN 24 HOURS THINGS ARE GOING TO CHANGE

The prophet replied, "You doubter! In 24 hours you will SEE the deliverance of the people with your own eyes but you won't get any of it."

Meanwhile...

Four lepers were sitting at the gate of the city. They were doomed to die. As lepers they were not allowed inside the city. They relied on those inside to toss out morsels of food. But now the people inside HAD no food. Nobody was going in or out of the city because of the armies camped outside the walls. Talk about being stuck between a rock and a hard place. These men were caught between a cruel enemy army and a starving city — with bodies riddled by disease and discouragement in their souls.

Finally one of them said, "Why sit we here until we die? If we sit here, we will die. Come, let us march to the enemy camps. If they save us, we will live. If they kill us, well, we're going to die anyway!"

YOU CAN GO ON A FAITH-ATTACK

The Bible tells us they "rose up" in the twilight hours to go against the army of the Syrians.

Now these men didn't know about the revelational knowledge of the prophet Elisha. They didn't even have the hope of his prophecy in their hearts. They knew they were no match for the 100,000 fighting men of the enemy army. They also knew that the twilight was not a good time to march — and that it would be difficult to see where they were going. But even facing all these negatives, they knew they must go on a FAITH-ATTACK. So by the sheer force of their will, they started out.

If you had been able to watch them from the top of the city walls you would probably have said, "Look at those crazy guys! They're going to get themselves killed."

They were hurting, but they marched on.

They were scared, but they marched.

They stumbled, fell, got up, fell again, but they marched.

It was twilight, but they marched.

They were like the bumblebee. Scientists tell us that the bumblebee cannot fly. Its wingspread is too small for the size of its body. But the bumblebee doesn't know it, so it goes ahead and flies anyway.

As these four gaunt, hungry, sick, weak men approached the tents of the Syrian army, the soldiers were asleep. They had no fear of attack from the city they had under siege.

But God, who never sleeps, saw the four faith-attackers coming against the army of Syria. God spoke to His angels to hook "horses of fire to chariots of fire" and pull them above the tents of the Syrian soldiers and make them sound like the noise of a mighty, conquering army.

The Syrians suddenly awakened and HEARD the sounds of the drumming hoofbeats of horses, the marching feet of soldiers, the rumbling roar of chariots, and in panic "every man fled in the night," leaving everything behind.

YOUR FAITH SCARES THE DEVIL

When the four faith-attackers came marching into the camp, they found the first row of tents empty. Yes, empty! I tell you…you never know what your faith sounds like to the devil…how it frightens him… how it puts him on the run. I'm talking now about YOUR faith.

There was plenty of food and gold and clothes and

everything the men needed. But they went to the next row of tents. Empty too! And the next and next and next. The entire camp was empty. After they had eaten and loaded themselves with gold and silver, they said, "Let's go back to the city and tell the people."

Elisha's 24-hour period was now at an end. Things were happening just as he had predicted. The people rushed out of the city and plundered what was left from the Syrian army. Food was suddenly so abundant that it was just as the prophet had said — pennies would buy all the food a person needed.

The king's aide, who had sneered at Elisha's word of revelational knowledge, tried to stop the rush of people out to the Syrian camp and was trampled underfoot and died. He had failed to be a faith-attacker because he refused to believe the Word of God from the mouth of the man of God…and to act on it.

What crisis are you facing today?

What does this mean to you?

I've got good news for you from the Word of God. You too can go on a FAITH-ATTACK.

YOUR BEST TIME TO START IS *NOW!*

You must START and start now. Read the story in 2 Kings 6 and 7 for yourself. Notice something critically important. These men STARTED to march BEFORE God caused the angels to act and the Syrian enemy to hear the sounds of soldiers, panic, and flee. These men did something with their faith before God moved in. As these men rose up, a miracle was put into motion in their personal behalf. When these men rose to their feet and set their face toward the Syrians, it was like the faucet being turned on…like the light switch being touched. God's delivering power began to flow toward removing their need and replacing it with a miracle.

When you turn all your faith loose and START TO GO ON A FAITH-ATTACK, a miracle of God is literally poured out to sweep the enemy forces away…to reveal plenty for you to receive…to provide what you need.

Say it today and every day…

YOUR GOD-GIVEN KEY FOR TODAY

"Today Is My Day To Go On A Faith-Attack Against My Need And For My Miracle!"

SEVENTH WEEK

SUNDAY I KNOW THE NAME OF MY ENEMY AND IT'S THE DEVIL. I ALSO KNOW MY VICTOR . . . MY SAVIOR . . . MY DELIVERER . . . AND MY LORD. HIS NAME IS JESUS!

MONDAY WHEN THE DEVIL ROARS AT ME, I WILL ROAR BACK WITH FAITH IN GOD!

TUESDAY WHATEVER GOD TELLS ME TO DO I WILL DO IT, KNOWING I AM NOT ALONE

WEDNESDAY I WILL NOT COMPROMISE FOR MY GOD IS ABLE TO DELIVER ME!

THURSDAY GOD WANTS ME TO PROSPER THROUGH GIVING AND RECEIVING

FRIDAY MY FAITH-TALK IS MY BEST WEAPON AGAINST THE DEVIL

SATURDAY TODAY IS MY DAY TO GO ON A FAITH-ATTACK AGAINST MY NEED AND FOR MY MIRACLE!

EIGHTH WEEK

The Seven Great Things I Can Do When I Need A Miracle

By Richard Roberts

SUNDAY

**Key:
I WILL MAKE JESUS
CHRIST THE MOST
IMPORTANT PERSON
IN MY LIFE**

**or
How Two Similar, Yet Different, Stories
In The Bible Show That We Can Receive God's
Forgiveness Or We Can Reject It ... It's Up To Us**

Friend, before I go any further in this book, I want to ask you a very important question. Listen to it carefully and answer it honestly for it's the most important question anyone will ever ask you.

Do you know Jesus Christ as your personal Lord and Savior? Have you asked Him to come into your heart and to be the master of your life?

I pray that you have. But if you haven't — if you've never been asked that question before or if you've never been given an opportunity to make a point-blank decision about making Jesus the Lord of your life — I pray that you will do it today. The Bible says that TODAY is the day of salvation. (See 2 Corinthians 6:2.)

Perhaps as you've been reading this book you've begun to see Jesus in a way you've never understood Him before. Perhaps you've begun to say, "I like the Jesus I'm seeing in this book." Or, more importantly, "I *need* the Jesus I see in this book."

Yet, for some reason, you feel that Jesus never could accept someone like you. "Not someone who has failed, or rejected Him, as many times as *I* have!" you say to yourself.

Friend, no one could have failed Jesus or rejected Him any worse than Richard Roberts did. Yet the very moment I truly repented of my sin and made the right decision about Jesus — the decision to make Him Lord of my life — He accepted me with open arms. He came into my heart and turned my whole life around. And I haven't been the same since.

And Jesus will accept you with open arms just as He did me when you ask Him to. The Bible says that *all* of us have sinned and come short of the glory of God. (See Romans 3:23.) We've all failed. We've all rejected Him. God sent His Son Jesus to die on the cross and to be raised from the dead so that He could forgive us and give us eternal life. You and I can accept that love and forgiveness and make a right decision about Jesus...or we can reject it. The choice is up to us.

Judas — the most tragic figure in the Bible — and Peter — one of the greatest — both rejected Jesus. Their next choice, however, made the difference in their final outcome.

Judas and Peter were both disciples of Jesus. Both rejected Him. Their stories happened within a 24-hour period of each other.

Judas had walked with Jesus as one of His closest followers for three years, yet he betrayed Jesus for 30 pieces of silver. In the garden of Gethsemane, he handed his beloved Master over to the authorities who came to take Jesus to His death.

Afterward, when Judas realized what he had done, he went out and hanged himself.

In Judas' mind, there was no hope left for himself.

But what if he had run to the cross and fallen at Jesus' feet and cried, "Lord, please forgive me"? Would Jesus have forgiven him? I believe that not only would Jesus have forgiven Judas and given him a second chance, but we might have had a fifth Gospel in the Bible — the Gospel of the second chance written by one who truly understood the power of forgiveness...Judas.

But Judas made the wrong decision about Jesus. He was almost saved, but lost.

Now let's look at what happened to Peter when he faced similar circumstances. On the night before Jesus was crucified, Peter was the disciple who said, "Lord, if everyone else forsakes You, I'll not forsake You. I'll stand by You through thick and thin." Yet Jesus knew better. He answered Peter, "Before the rooster crows, Peter, you'll deny Me not just once but three times."

Let's watch Peter now as he follows Jesus from afar as He was led away from the garden of Gethsemane. *Once,* outside the house of Caiaphas the high priest when confronted by a servant girl: *"I don't even know the man,"* he said of Jesus.

Twice, as another man identified him as being Jesus' follower: *"No, I am not one."* And *three times,* as someone else in the crowd recognized his Galilean accent: *"I don't know what you're talking about."*

Just then a rooster crowed. And the Bible says that Jesus turned from inside the house and *looked* at Peter...and their eyes met. Peter remembered what the Lord had said and he was devastated at what he had done. But what did he see in Jesus' eyes? Bitterness...distrust? A look that said, "Peter, I knew you were no good"?

No. In Jesus' eyes he beheld a look of genuine forgiveness, and the Bible says that Peter went out and wept bitter tears of repentance. He gave his failure to the Lord and received the sweetest forgiveness a human being can receive. He became Peter, the great apostle, the one who would walk down the street and, as he passed the sick, his shadow would touch people and they'd be healed.

Peter made the *right* decision about Jesus. He was almost lost, but saved.

IT'S TIME TO MAKE
YOUR DECISION ABOUT JESUS

Friend, we've all made the wrong choices at one time or another in our lives. We've all rejected Jesus in one way or another. We've all *failed,* just as Peter and Judas had failed. It's what we do with that failure that makes the difference in our life.

You can't undo what you've done wrong in your past. You can't run away from it. But Jesus can *forgive* you for your past. He can wipe the slate clean and give you a brand-new start. A second chance! For, as I've discovered in my life and millions of others have discovered as well, He's the God of a second chance.

Jesus has already made His decision about you: He loves you and wants to forgive you. Now it's time for you to make your decision about Jesus.

IF YOU WANT TO ASK
JESUS CHRIST INTO YOUR HEART,
PRAY THIS SIMPLE PRAYER WITH ME

Lord Jesus, today I make the right decision about You. I decide to make You my personal Lord and Savior…and I ask You to come into my heart now.

Lord, I've sinned and I know it. I've missed Your will for my life as I've tried to have my own way. Forgive me, Jesus, and give me a new heart that is tender toward You. I believe Your Word when it says in 1 John 1:9 that when I confess my sins, You are faithful and just to forgive my sins and to cleanse me from all unrighteousness.

Thank You, Lord, for forgiving me…for giving me a bright new future…for dying for me and rising

*from the dead to give me the miracle of a second
chance in You. Amen.*

Friend, if you prayed that prayer with me and truly
meant it in your heart, you were just born again into
the kingdom of God. You're a new person on the
inside! You'll never be the same again! Praise God!

YOUR GOD-GIVEN KEY FOR TODAY

"I Will Make
The Right Decision About Jesus."

Then, get your own personal copy of the Bible and
begin reading all the wonderful promises of God that
are now yours. Promises such as 2 Corinthians 5:17
which says, "Therefore if any man be in Christ, he is a
new creature: old things are passed away; behold, all
things are become new."

MONDAY

**Key:
I WILL CHANGE MY
THINKING AND MY
BELIEVING ABOUT GOD**

or
**Our Two Greatest Problems
Are Not What Most People Would Think**

If I were to ask you what the two greatest problems
are that plague our world today, what would you say?
Massive unemployment? The threat of nuclear war?
Hunger and starvation? Budget deficits? Cancer and
other "killer diseases"? If you're like most people,
those are problems you might think of.

But I believe that, even beyond problems such as those, the two *greatest* problems we have are: *our thinking* and *our believing*. For if our thinking is wrong, then our whole life is wrong. If our believing is wrong, then we have dealt God out of our lives. And in a time when we are facing crisis after crisis on a global scale, we need the power of God in our lives more than ever. We must change our thinking and our believing about God so that they are no longer our greatest problems, but our greatest blessings.

First, *we need to change our thinking and our believing about God.* Many times we have the wrong idea about the nature of God. We see Him as an angry God of judgment, ready to pour out His wrath upon us. But God's true nature is loving and giving. He is a *good* God who wants to bring healing and wholeness to His people.

In Exodus 15:26, He tells us, "I am the Lord that healeth thee." And that wasn't only for the Old Testament times, for God also says, "I am the Lord, I change not" (Malachi 3:6).

God has never changed. He's always been a good God. It is you and I who need to change our thinking and believing about Him. If we believe that sickness comes from God as a form of punishment, rather than from the devil, we will never ask God to heal us. We need to begin to recognize God's true nature and stop blaming Him for bad things that come our way...and start thanking Him for the good things.

Next, *we need to change our thinking and our believing about Jesus Christ.* Many people think of Jesus as a man who lived 2,000 years ago, who only brought salvation and healing to the people back then. But if Jesus ever saved a sinner, He's still saving sinners today. And if Jesus ever healed people in their bodies or emotions, or ever helped someone with their finances or with family problems, He is still able to do the same today…and He *is* doing the same today.

Hebrews 13:8 says that Jesus Christ is the same yesterday, today, and forever. He hasn't changed. But we need to change our thinking about Him. If we don't believe that Jesus is alive and full of power today, we'll never turn our lives over to Him and see the life-changing miracles that can occur. We need to believe beyond the shadow of a doubt that Jesus is for us and not against us, and that He wants to meet every need.

Finally, we need to change our thinking about faith. Many people think faith is something they have to work to get. But you don't have to get something you've already got. Romans 12:3 says that God has already given every person *the* measure of faith. You and I don't have to get faith, we just have to act on the faith we already have.

Just think for a moment. If you needed to get somewhere in your car (which you already have), what good would it do you to go and stand by the car, hold your keys in your hand, and say out loud, "I believe I'm going to get there, I *believe* I'm going to get there, I BELIEVE I'm going to get there!" It wouldn't do you any good just to believe it, would it? No matter how long you stood there or how long you shouted it.

Until you put your belief into action and got into the car, turned your key in the ignition and stepped on the gas, your belief alone wouldn't take you across the street…let alone to where you were going.

In much the same way, your faith is like that. Until you put your faith into action by stepping out and putting it to the test, you'll never know how God can honor it when you do. We need to learn to use the faith we have, rather than waiting for God to give us more.

LOOK AT YOUR OWN LIFE

Let's look at your own life right now. Are there areas where you have a problem with your thinking and believing? Maybe it's in the area of your obedience to God. I know many people who at one time believed that if they ever completely "sold out" to God and sought His will for their life instead of their own, that God would make them go overseas somewhere as a missionary. Until...someone came along and helped them straighten out their thinking and believing and they realize that God wants to give us the "desires of our heart" (Psalm 37:4). That He would never call us to do something that is totally contrary to the way we are made up on the inside. So they ran from God for years without realizing that there was no need to.

Do you see how your thinking and believing rule your life and govern your actions? The Bible says that "as a man thinketh in his heart, so is he" (Proverbs 23:7).

Let's get our thinking and believing back "on track" with God. No matter what problems you're having, God is ready and waiting today to help you turn what may be your two greatest problems — your thinking and believing — into your two greatest blessings.

YOUR GOD-GIVEN KEY FOR TODAY

"I Will Change My Thinking And My Believing About God."

Then ask the Lord to help you make Romans 12:2 a reality in your life, "...be ye transformed by the renewing of your mind."

Key:
I WILL UNDERSTAND THAT GOD'S MESSAGE TO ME IS GREATER THAN THE MESSENGER WHO CARRIES IT

TUESDAY

or
There's An Important Lesson To Be Learned From The Little Widow Of Zarephath

Are you hurting in some serious way right now? Is there a physical problem that you can't get rid of and that you feel may eventually take your life? Are you down so low in your finances that you feel you may never get up again? Is there a broken relationship with someone you love that has put you in a state of despair?

Do you feel that, no matter what the situation is, you won't make it another day without a word from the Lord?

Then I want to talk to you today about the fact that God often speaks to us through the words of a man or a woman of God. And I want you to see that you can receive that message of deliverance from the Lord, no matter who he or she might be, because the message God sends you is always greater than the messenger who is carrying it.

There's a story in the Book of 1 Kings, chapter 17, about a widow who was literally at the end of the line…and who needed to hear from God like you do today. In her darkest hour of need, God spoke to her through one of His prophets and told her what she could do to save her life and the life of her son. But it was up to the woman to receive that message and understand that God's message to her was greater than the messenger who carried it.

When the prophet Elijah arrived in the city of Zarephath, where God had sent him to ask a widow for some food, he found the woman gathering sticks for a fire. He said to her, "Would you bring me a drink of water and a piece of bread to eat?" And that's when Elijah heard the story of the terrible situation she was in.

"Sir, I have no bread to eat," she said, "nor anything else to give you. I have only enough meal in the barrel and enough oil in the cruse to cook one last meal for my son and me…and after we eat it, then we're going to die. I was gathering wood to build the cooking fire when you stopped me."

I want you to see this woman. I want you to see the look of despair in her eyes as she speaks of eating her last meal…of watching her only child die of starvation…of her own life ending.

Elijah saw her pain. But he also knew that God had an answer for the woman. He knew that if she would give him something to eat — if she would plant a seed out of her own need — then God could do a miracle in her life.

It wasn't easy for Elijah to obey God and ask the woman to give him part of her very last meal, but he did it anyway. He said to her, "Ma'am, go ahead and cook that last meal. But before you do, bake me a little loaf of bread first. And when you do that, thus saith the Lord: 'Your flour will not diminish and your oil will not run dry. You will eat from it from this day until that time that the drought upon this land is ended and I send rain upon the earth once again.'"

Now isn't that just what you'd want to hear when you're facing your last meal and starvation for you and your child is only days away? Some preacher

263

telling you to give him some of what you have when you don't have enough to begin with? Well, that's just how this woman probably felt. She must have looked at Elijah with shock written all over her face. And she must have thought the same thing that people often think today about a man or a woman of God who brings a message to them that they don't understand: *Who is this man Elijah anyway? And why is he asking me to do this?*

Who is this man Oral Roberts anyway? And why is he telling me to plant a seed out of my need so that God can bring me out of the financial devastation I'm in? Who is this man Richard Roberts? And why is he asking me to begin moving my arm that's been stiff for 20 years with arthritis?

You know, you're never going to get the right answer until you ask the right question. The right question for the widow of Zarephath in her situation and the right question for you and me today is not who is this person, but *what is God trying to say to me through His servant?* Yes, we're human beings and yes, we make mistakes just like everyone else. But God can still use us to help you out of the situation you're in because...

The message God is sending you is greater than the messenger who carries it!

THE WIDOW RECEIVED GOD'S MESSAGE AND HER LIFE WAS TURNED AROUND

As the widow stood there looking at Elijah, she knew she had only two options. To ignore what the prophet was saying to her and die, or to believe that the message he was giving her was from God...to follow his instructions and to live. So she fixed the meal just as Elijah said and gave him a loaf of bread out of the little they had.

And the Bible records what happened next like this: "And she, and he, and her house, did eat many days. And the barrel of meal wasted not, neither did the cruse of oil fail, according to the word of the Lord, which he spake by Elijah."

Time and again I have seen people in desperate situations in their lives, who are crying out for God to speak to them and show them the way out of the mess they're in, and yet they won't receive a word of deliverance from a man or woman of God who is sent to help them.

I know that I, personally, do not have all the answers to the problem you are facing right now. I'm just a human being, like you are, who is trying to do what God has called me to do in this world. But I also know that as God's anointed servant sent to help you, God can speak those answers through me.

God said that *His* Word would never fail. If what I'm saying to you in this book — or on my daily TV program or in my letters to you — touches something deep inside you and you believe that God may be speaking a word of deliverance into your life through me, just receive it for what it is. Don't worry about who Richard Roberts is or what you may think about me as a human being. Remember that God's message to you is greater than the messenger who is carrying it, and let God work His miracle of healing and deliverance in your life today...just as He did so many years ago for the widow of Zarephath.

YOUR GOD-GIVEN KEY FOR TODAY

"I Will Understand That God's Message To Me Is Greater Than The Messenger Who Carries It."

Then, begin focusing on what that message is telling you to do and obey the Word of the Lord.

Key: I WILL PUT ON THE WHOLE ARMOR OF GOD TO STAND AGAINST THE TRICKS AND STRATEGIES OF THE DEVIL

WEDNESDAY

or
How God Showed Me I Could Stop The Devil's Attack On My Life

Several years ago I had a very unusual experience as I traveled to Jamaica to conduct a great healing crusade. I had been to Jamaica once before, but this time was different. Through that experience, God taught me something very valuable about how we can stop the devil's attack against our lives.

For days before I was to go to Jamaica, I had felt a churning deep inside my spirit. The night before I was to leave on the plane, I became very aware that the Lord was dealing with me. I knew something "heavy" was going on, so I got quiet before the Lord and He began speaking to me.

The Lord told me that, because of the many miracles, salvations, and healings during my last crusade in Jamaica, the devil would come against my ministry in a stronger way this time; he was planning a full-scale attack to shut down our services there.

As I continued listening, Jesus said, *The devil has selected his chief demon over that part of the world to hatch a plot to kill you while you are preaching. But this attack on your life can be stopped if you'll do exactly as I tell you to do.*

Every day you are ministering, you must rebuke in Jesus' name every demonic spirit that would attempt to hinder My work in Jamaica, but especially rebuke this chief demon. Then gather your wife and your crusade team together and instruct them to put on the whole armor of God as I've explained to you in Ephesians, chapter 6.

Suddenly I understood why I had felt so restless in my spirit. I quickly shared with Lindsay what the Lord had told me to do and, gratefully, we determined in our hearts to obey Him.

The next day, after arriving in Jamaica, I called everyone together and told them what had happened. Then I began to preach from Ephesians 6, verses 10 through 18, where Paul said, "Put on the whole armor of God, that we may stand against the wiles of the devil."

After preaching this message, Lindsay and I and our team anointed each other with oil and prayed a prayer of faith over the entire crusade, rebuking the devil and his demons who would try to impede God's work, especially the chief demon of murder and assassination in that area.

Immediately I felt a breakthrough in the spirit. I knew that God had done something in the spirit realm and was going to perform many mighty miracles in the crusade throughout that island nation.

We continued to do as God commanded us to do in the days ahead and the Jamaican crusade was a great success. During that time God gave me a greater understanding than ever before of what it really means to put on the "full armor of God." I want to share that with you today because I know what it can mean in your life…and what it can *do* when the devil brings his attack against you. For when we are serving Jesus and witnessing to others of the power of God in our lives, all of us are subject to the devil's attacks.

HERE ARE THE SEVEN PIECES OF GOD'S ARMOR YOU MUST PUT ON TO STAND AGAINST THE DEVIL'S ATTACK

You may want to get your Bible and read Ephesians 6:10-18 before (or after) I tell you about each piece.

FIRST, you must put on the truth, Jesus Christ, to gird your loins — your power to produce and to create new things. This speaks of preparing for soul-winning, for producing "new Christians." In other words, to reproduce ourselves in Christ, Christ must dwell in us. And when the Truth, Jesus Christ, is in us, we are set free (John 8:32) and ready to win others to Him.

SECOND, the breastplate of righteousness. The Bible says in Galatians 3:6, "Abraham believed God, and it was accounted to him for righteousness." He believed God and came into faith, for faith is acting on what you believe. The breastplate of righteousness will protect that part of you where God has put your "believer"…your heart.

THIRD, your feet covered in shoes of the gospel. The gospel is the power of God (Romans 1:16). That means your feet can walk over and through the devil's roughest territory.

FOURTH, above all, taking the shield of faith. When you live by faith the devil will still come against you, but his blows will bounce off the invisible shield of your faith. He'll do you no permanent harm.

FIFTH, the helmet of salvation. This means living with your mind in a constant state of repentance and submission to God so that He can deal with you by His Spirit.

SIXTH, the sword of the Spirit, which is the Word of God. Your most powerful offensive weapon against the devil is being grounded in and knowing what God says in His Word, the Holy Bible.

And SEVENTH, praying always in the Spirit, or in your prayer language. (See 1 Corinthians 14:2,14,15.) This is something I do every day of my life. Rather than praying words that originate from my mind, I pray words that originate from my spirit — in my prayer language, which is also called tongues — as the Holy Spirit gives me utterance. (See Acts 2:4.) Then, after praying in the Spirit, I pray again — this time in English — and God enlightens my understanding. And I know better what God wants me to do.

WHEN THE DEVIL ATTACKS
YOU MUST COUNTERATTACK

Friend, you might not be a healing evangelist as I am, traveling throughout the world with the message of the gospel. But if you are a born-again child of God, sharing Jesus with those around you in whatever way you feel God leading you to, you are subject to the devil's attacks. It may not be an attack on your very life as mine might have been in Jamaica, but as long as you're doing something for Jesus Christ in this world, Satan will seek to inhibit that work.

When the satanic attacks come, you must be ready. When the devil attacks, you must counterattack...by putting on the full armor of God — every piece — so you can stand up strong for the Lord and be the overcomer you were made to be.

YOUR GOD-GIVEN KEY FOR TODAY

"I Will Put On The Whole Armor Of God To Stand Against The Tricks And Strategies Of The Devil."

Then read Ephesians 6 again and let it sink deep into your spirit.

THURSDAY

**Key:
I WILL NOT
GIVE IN TO FEAR**

**or
Through The Power Of
Jesus Christ Inside You,
You Can Live Without Fear In Fearful Times**

Have you ever noticed in the Bible how often God says to us: "Fear not" or "Be not afraid"? Those words appear again and again because God knew that one of the weapons the devil uses against us most often is *fear*. For if Satan can paralyze us with fear, he can keep us from doing what we know God is calling us to do in this world.

MANY PEOPLE ARE LIVING IN FEAR

As I travel throughout this country ministering in churches and auditoriums, and through thousands of letters I exchange with our Partners, one of the most frequent prayer requests I receive from people is in the area of fear. Some have a fear about the welfare of loved ones. Some fear the lack of finances. Others are afraid for their health or another area of their lives.

I believe that as the time of Jesus' second coming draws near, the power of the enemy is becoming stronger and stronger throughout this earth to stop God's work. We *are* living in fearful times. But through the power of Jesus Christ living inside of us, we don't have to give in to that fear. Second Timothy 1:7 tells us: "For God hath not given us the spirit of fear; but of power, and of love, and of a sound mind." We can fight the fear that is coming against us, but it will take our faith to do it.

Now, don't misunderstand. I'm not talking about the kind of fear that is a normal, natural respect for danger — such as not letting a child play with matches. The kind of fear I'm talking about, and the kind the Bible talks about, is a wrong fear. It's the fear that the Bible says "hath torment" (1 John 4:18). It *torments our mind;* it tries to control us.

WE CAN BE DELIVERED FROM FEAR

Years ago there was a great thoroughbred race-horse named Gallant Man that had won many championship and stakes races. One night just before that year's Kentucky Derby, his owner had a dream. In the dream he saw the jockey ride Gallant Man down the stretch and then stand up in the saddle, thinking he had already crossed the finish line. Another horse passed him and Gallant Man lost by a nose.

That dream became a fear to the horse's owner. A few days later, during the actual Kentucky Derby, everything happened just as the owner had feared.

A scientist heard the story of the lost race and reported that according to his studies "people often do the thing they fear most." Job, in the Bible, proved that was true. He had lost everything he ever held dear and finally, in his crying out to God, he said, "That thing which I greatly feared is come upon me" (Job 3:25).

But there is a way we can keep fear from controlling us.

First, acknowledge that tormenting fear is not from God; it is from the devil.

Next, start believing that God has the power to help you overcome your fear, that He is concerned about you, and that His goodness is coming toward you every day. Rather than dwelling on what evil might befall you next, do what the Bible says in Philippians 4:8. "Whatsoever things are true, whatsoever things are honest...just...pure...lovely...of good report...think on these things."

Finally, learn how to exercise your faith by sowing a seed of faith. Get a good seed in the "good soil" of the gospel — and do it for the desired results of God's freeing you from a fear you have...or a state of fear Satan wants you to live in. What really is fear? I believe fear is faith in reverse. It's believing, all right, but it's believing the wrong thing. We must release our faith to God to believe that something *good* is going to happen. Because your faith will drive out your fear.

HERE'S WHAT I DO

When I feel like I may be getting into fear in some area of my life, I immediately take it to the Lord in prayer. I say, "Lord, Your Word says in Luke 1:74,75, that we can be delivered and serve You without fear all the days of our lives. And now, Lord, I come against this fear that's tormenting me and I cast it out in the authority of the name of Jesus. Amen and amen."

You might want to pray a prayer like that right now. Come against that fear that's been tormenting you, in Jesus' name. Be free of it once and for all.

You *can* be delivered from the fear that "hath torment" by coming against it with your faith. Stand strong in the power of the Lord...and refuse to let fear dictate what you're to do for the rest of your life.

YOUR GOD-GIVEN KEY FOR TODAY

"I Will Not Give In To Fear."

Then, the next time you feel a tormenting kind of fear coming upon you, rebuke it in Jesus' name. "Resist the devil, and he will flee from you" (James 4:7).

FRIDAY

**Key:
I WILL GET
THE WORD OF GOD
INTO MY LIFE DAILY**

**or
How To Be Ready For The
Emergencies Of Life Before They Happen**

When I was a boy, there was a toothpaste commercial that went like this: "Crest has been shown to be an effective decay-preventive dentifrice when used in a conscientiously applied program of oral hygiene and regular professional care." I like to turn that around a bit and use it to describe the Bible. *The Bible has been shown to be an effective decay-preventive when read in a consciously applied program of spiritual hygiene and regular professional care.*

What is the "decay" in your life? The decay is anything harmful or destructive the devil brings your way: temptation, lack, sickness. The Word of God fights that "decay" in your life when you regularly read it, listen to anointed people preach it, and *apply it* by acting on it.

DEVELOP A HABIT OF
SPENDING TIME IN GOD'S WORD EVERY DAY

Do you brush your teeth every day? Yes, I'm sure you do…*now.* But when you were just a baby you didn't. Someone had to help you learn to do those things and to develop a habit of doing them.

When I was just a baby, I didn't lie in my crib and look up at my mother and say, "The Lord just impressed me that I need a toothbrush." No, it didn't happen that way at all. I learned how to brush my teeth because my parents forced me to learn how. Every morning and again before I went to bed at night, they'd come in and say, "Richard, have you brushed your teeth yet? Let me see your toothbrush." And they checked me every day, every day, every day, until I developed a habit of brushing my teeth twice regularly. It was the same way with my learning to put on clothes.

When I was a baby I was just as comfortable without any clothes on as any infant is. But as time went by my parents taught me that I must put on clothes…because if I didn't, I'd go to jail! And today I wouldn't dream of leaving my home and walking onto the set of my daily TV program, or anywhere else, without putting on my clothes.

Neither would I dream of leaving my home each day without first putting on the Lord Jesus Christ and His Word in my heart. I've developed a good habit of having a daily relationship with God and His Word.

DON'T WAIT UNTIL
THE EMERGENCIES OF LIFE COME

You know, many people never think very much about God or what God's Word has to say about life until they find themselves in some kind of emergency.

And when the emergencies hit, as they do sometimes in life, those people don't have anything to fall back on that shows them how to handle the crisis. They open their Bible and think, *I'll pull one little Scripture out of here and it will solve everything for me.*

Well, that one Scripture will help certainly, but the time to be putting God's Word in your heart is when you *aren't* in an emergency. That way when you need it, it's already sown in your heart. If you will "hide" God's Word in your heart, as His Word itself tells you to do, then it will be there in times of emergency. It will be "an effective decay-preventive." Don't be like most people and wait until sickness comes or until you're in the middle of a financial jam or until there's trouble in your home before you make time to study God's Word. Sow it in the garden of your heart every single day.

YOUR GOD-GIVEN KEY FOR TODAY

"I Will Get The Word Of God Into My Life Daily...Starting Today!"

Then, watch this Scripture about the power of the Word of God come alive in your life: "For the Word that God speaks is *alive* and *full* of *power* — making it active, operative, energizing, and effective" (Hebrews 4:12, *Amplified*).

SATURDAY

or
How I Learned That "Good" Dreams May Still Be The Wrong Dreams

I have already shared with you about the most devastating experience that Lindsay and I have ever been through — the loss of our little son, Richard Oral — and how God helped us through that time. Through that experience, I learned many things that I know I will never forget. One of the most important, and one that I want to share specifically today, is the importance of keeping your priorities in life straight …of getting in touch with your *true* heart's desire.

MANY THINGS WILL TRY TO PULL YOU AWAY FROM YOUR TRUE HEART'S DESIRE…SOMETIMES *GOOD* THINGS

I've discovered through the years that when you set your heart on doing something for God in this life, many things will try to pull you away from that…and not all of those will be bad things. Some of them may be very *good* things. They may even be things that God wants to bless you with, but that He doesn't want you to focus on or to make the most important thing in your life.

Often when we make that mistake of focusing our desires on the wrong things and getting our priorities out of order, we don't even realize we're doing it. Then God speaks to us and reminds us that we are to

277

seek *Him* first and with our whole hearts...and that He will take care of all the other things in life.

HOW GOD SHOWED ME THROUGH THE LOSS OF MY SON THAT I WAS NOT IN TOUCH WITH MY TRUE HEART'S DESIRE

For a long time before Richard Oral was born, my heart's desire was to have a son. When that son died in the intensive care unit of the hospital just 36 hours after his birth, I thought my heart would break with sorrow.

I prayed and I cried until the tears wouldn't come any longer...and I reminded the Lord that this child had been the deepest desire of my heart.

Through my tears, I heard the still small voice of the Lord inside me. And He was speaking words that I couldn't even begin to comprehend. He said, *Richard, you've had the wrong heart's desire.*

I said, "Lord, what do You mean? I thought producing a healthy little boy was a great heart's desire."

But God said, *It is a great desire, but your true heart's desire is to win the lost to Jesus, to pray for the healing of the people, and to go to the nations of the earth.*

Then I understood what God was talking about. Immediately I remembered Matthew 6:33 which says, "Seek ye first the kingdom of God, and his righteousness; and all these things shall be added unto you."

God didn't mean that I shouldn't want a son or that Lindsay and I shouldn't want children of our own. For in the days to come we would receive words of prophecy that God had spoken to people around us that He was going to give us other children. He just didn't want me to make that the main priority in my life. He didn't want me to set my heart on that above what I was really called to do in this world, which is to win the lost to Jesus Christ and to pray for their healing.

After that night in the hospital, I can promise you that Richard Roberts began reexamining his priorities. And I've been careful ever since not to let any other desire of my heart come ahead of my *true* heart's desire of serving Jesus with all of my heart, soul, and strength.

WHAT IS *YOUR* TRUE HEART'S DESIRE?

Is the greatest desire of your heart to make your relationship with Jesus the best that it can be and to do whatever He's called you to do? If it is, friend, then you may need to do what I did and take a close hard look at what the priorities really are in your life.

Look at Psalm 37:4. It says, "Delight thyself in the Lord; and he shall give thee the desires of thine heart." God *wants* to give us the desires of our heart. He wants to make our dreams come true. But He tells us in this verse that there is a condition under which He will do that. And that is when our greatest desire is to love and serve Him — in other words, to "delight" in Him. For it's then that our priorities are straight and we can enjoy the blessings of God to the fullest.

YOUR GOD-GIVEN KEY FOR TODAY

"I Will Get In Touch With My Heart's Desire."

Then, put Jesus first place in your life and don't allow other dreams and desires you may have — even when they're good ones — to come ahead of your relationship with Him.

EIGHTH WEEK

SUNDAY   I WILL MAKE THE RIGHT DECISION ABOUT JESUS

MONDAY   I WILL CHANGE MY THINKING AND MY BELIEVING ABOUT GOD

TUESDAY   I WILL UNDERSTAND THAT GOD'S MESSAGE TO ME IS GREATER THAN THE MESSENGER WHO CARRIES IT

WEDNESDAY   I WILL PUT ON THE WHOLE ARMOR OF GOD TO STAND AGAINST THE TRICKS AND STRATEGIES OF THE DEVIL

THURSDAY   I WILL NOT GIVE IN TO FEAR

FRIDAY   I WILL GET THE WORD OF GOD INTO MY LIFE DAILY...STARTING TODAY!

SATURDAY   I WILL GET IN TOUCH WITH MY HEART'S DESIRE

NINTH WEEK

God Has A Special Plan For My Life!

By Evelyn Roberts

SUNDAY

Key:
I CAN KNOW
GOD DESIRES
GOOD THINGS FOR ME

or
I Will Put God First

I thank the Lord for Oral Roberts. I love that man. And if a person can say "I love you" after 48 years of marriage, it's real love. When Oral is home and the front door closes each night, a contentment comes over me that I can't explain. I'm suddenly at peace with myself and the whole world. But as much as I love that man, I love God more.

And it's the same with Oral. He loves God more than any person or any thing in this world.

Years ago in our crusade days we owned a farm where Oral relaxed when he came home. He was always exhausted after a crusade and he found that riding around the farm seeing the animals lifted his spirit.

He had bought a few cows and horses and then someone invited us to an auction. The auctioneer was so enthusiastic he made you feel like buying every animal there, and we thoroughly enjoyed watching him.

Soon after this, on one of Oral's trips home we went to Missouri to attend an auction. That was a big mistake. You see, Oral is the kind of person who goes all out at whatever he does, and at that auction he got carried away and bought a cow — an expensive cow — one that we didn't need nor could afford.

I didn't say much to him, but when we got back to our hotel room I could tell he was troubled. Soon he was on his knees crying out to God, "Oh, Lord, I've disappointed You. I've let this cattle business become too important to me and I always want You to be first in my life. I've let You down. Please forgive me, Jesus, and I promise never to let this happen again."

Now there's nothing wrong with cattle auctions. It was just that they didn't fit in with the plan God had for Oral's life.

I saw a new side of Oral that day — a tenderness in his heart toward Jesus. He truly wanted Jesus to be first in his life. We stopped going to auctions, we stopped buying cattle, and we concentrated our whole lives on the ministry to which God had called us.

One of the greatest challenges of this ministry has been the building of the City of Faith. When I drive by it now, I think back to the chapel service at Oral Roberts University when Oral announced to the students, faculty, and staff that we were starting our new graduate programs. I felt like that was such a big step, and at the time I didn't even know about the City of Faith.

What a day! The students all stood and clapped — but my thinking was in a little different vein. I thought, *Why couldn't I just sit down in a little house with a picket fence with roses growing on it and have a husband who goes to work at eight o'clock in the morning and comes home at five o'clock in the evening?*

Then Oral asked me to get up and say something. I said, "Well, you know at this time of my life I would like to sit in a rocking chair and enjoy my grandchildren. But God has given us something bigger to do than we've ever done before."

A rocking chair has no part in our lives if God still has something left for us to do! We've got to get up and do God's will. And I'm glad that He gives us the challenge to stand up on the inside and say, "Lord, I will lay aside anything that keeps me from doing the job You have for me to do. You are first in my life."

Jesus has been first in my life since I accepted Him as my Savior when I was a 12-year-old girl. I don't remember going through a rebellious stage like a lot of teenagers do. I'm grateful that I had something inside me that pricked me and let me know when I was even a little bit out of line.

I remember when I went away from home and was teaching school in Texas, I met a couple of young men and dated them and one of them wanted to marry me. I had been away from home for about a year and hadn't been going to church regularly. I felt like I was really backslidden, but when one of those young men asked me to marry him I said, "Well, no, I'm sorry. I appreciate the honor of your asking me, but some day I am going to do something for the Lord. And I have to get a husband who will help me do that."

He said, "Well, I'm glad you were honest with me."

At that time I really didn't know what I was saying, but I believe the Lord knew that even then it was my desire to put Him first in my life. I'm thankful that I have a husband who wants me to put the Lord first in my life, just as I want him to put the Lord first in his life.

An elderly minister on television told a story that makes us see how no one but Jesus could ever deserve first place in our lives. He said when he was a young preacher there was a family in his community that bought a dog for their little son. It was a big loving dog that he could romp and play with. One day the little child fell into the swimming pool and the parents didn't know it. The dog jumped in and pulled him out of the pool and began to bark. He kept barking until the parents heard him and came out and revived the child.

Never again did that dog sleep out in the cold or eat the crumbs from the table. From then on he had the best of everything. And when the old dog died, they buried him in the front yard and put up this inscription: "Oh, how we loved him, for he saved our child."

When we think of the great price Christ paid for us on Calvary, the only response any of us could possibly have is, "Oh, how I love Jesus because He gave His life to save me and I will put Him first in my life."

YOUR GOD-GIVEN KEY FOR TODAY

"I Will Put God First In My Life."

MONDAY Key: GOD WANTS MY OBEDIENCE

or
I Will Be An Obedient Vessel And Do What God Wants Me To Do

I used to read the Scripture, "To obey is better than sacrifice," and wonder how that could possibly be true (1 Samuel 15:22). Then one day during the Vietnam War I read about a young man who stood in front of a government building in Washington, D.C., and poured gasoline on himself and set himself on fire.

That young man sacrificed his life. But it didn't help him, and it didn't help anybody else. However, it did help me understand why being obedient to God *is* far better than sacrifice. It brought home to me the Scripture that says, "Though I give my body to be burned, and have not [love], it profiteth me nothing" (1 Corinthians 13:3).

Sacrifice, as noble as it sounds, can have an element of self-will, a seed of rebellion. Obedience is better because it sets aside self-will in order to do God's will.

The Bible tells about a woman who was obedient. Her name was Deborah and her story is found in the fourth chapter of Judges.

Deborah was a housewife, a mother, and a prophetess. She was also chosen to be a judge of her people. She judged them, not in a courtroom, but under a palm tree where she lived. The people came to her there, and she counseled them.

At this time in history, the Israelites were in disobedience to God and He had let them be conquered by the king of Canaan. They cried out unto the Lord because they were being cruelly oppressed. Deborah heard from God and called a man named Barak to her. She said, "God commands you to go with ten thousand men against the enemy army. The Lord will go before you, and you will have victory."

Barak was reluctant. He knew that King Jabin of Canaan had a mighty army with nine hundred chariots of iron. He said to Deborah, "I won't go by myself. I'll only go if you'll go with me."

Deborah went with him, staying in contact with God all the time. Finally one morning she said, "This is the day, Barak. GO! You're going to win!"

Barak went out with his men and started fighting the enemy army. Before the day was over, the enemy was defeated.

Do you know what Deborah did when the battle

ended? She and Barak sang. I can just see them dancing around, singing their songs of praise, giving glory to God. (See Judges 4 and 5.)

Deborah is a woman I want to be like. Now, I don't want to be a judge or a prophetess. I want to be a person who obeys God no matter how small the task that He wants me to do.

Not all of us are called to be right on the front lines, but there are many of us who are called to stand back and encourage those who *are* on the front lines.

Deborah was not a soldier. She sat under a tree and spoke God's message and then she gave a vote of confidence to help Barak do what God told him to do on the battlefield. That's where I feel my talent lies. Deborah supported Barak, and I try to support Oral, my husband. If God were to tell me always to stay at home on my knees and pray for Oral, for the ministry, for Oral Roberts University, for the City of Faith, or for the new Healing Outreach Center, I'd do it.

I believe the important thing for each one of us is to be an obedient vessel of the Lord and do what He wants us to do. Our task may seem little or insignificant to us, but it's big in God's eyes if it helps other people to win the battles they face. And when we see the results come, we aren't to get puffed up and say, "Look what I did." The Lord is the one who brings the victory. We give the *glory* to Him. That's what Deborah did, and that's what I want always to do too.

YOUR GOD-GIVEN KEY FOR TODAY

"I Will Obey God No Matter What He Asks Me To Do!"

TUESDAY

**Key:
GOD WANTS ME TO
PLANT SEEDS
TO OVERCOME LOSS**

**or
When In Need, I Will Plant A Seed**

Not long ago I was asked to speak to a group about dealing with the death of a loved one. One of the things I talked about was the struggle we all have with bitterness when we've suffered any kind of loss. And I shared with the group the motto Oral and I have when we suffer loss:

"When in need, plant a seed."

I told them the way we've found to get grief out of our hearts and keep bitterness from creeping in is to reach out and help somebody else.

When I'd finished my talk, one of the women said to me, "Oh, Mrs. Roberts, I wish my mother could have heard you." She went on to say that after her father died, her mother shut herself up in her home for two years and wouldn't let anybody in and she herself wouldn't go out.

"I know what you're talking about," the woman said. "You can become so self-centered and bitter that you're no good to yourself or anybody else."

One of the things I had shared with the group was the grief and anguish my husband Oral and I had experienced when we learned that our daughter Rebecca and her husband Marshall had been killed instantly when their plane exploded over a Kansas wheat field. It was the worst struggle we had ever experienced.

Telegrams began pouring in to us, many from people we didn't know. The grief of our other children was almost overwhelming, but together we stood as a close family in Christ.

On the fourth night I was getting ready for bed when suddenly my grief was just more than I could bear. I said to Oral, "Honey, I'm not going to make it tonight. This is the worst night of all. Would you take me in your arms and pray for me?"

After we'd prayed, Oral said to me, "The Lord is speaking these words to me:

"Go on television in your half-hour program next Sunday morning and, while you feel the hurt and loss, tell the people how you feel and give witness to My power and to the resurrection."

"I can't do it, Oral," I cried. "It's too soon. I'll break down and I won't be able to get through it."

Oral said, "Then I'll go on by myself. The Holy Spirit is compelling me. We've got to plant a seed out of our grief. If we don't plant our seed now, we'll never get the miracle we need to get over this hurt, and it will haunt us the rest of our life."

"Can't we wait a few months?" I pleaded.

Oral said, "This grief will tear us apart. It will destroy my ministry. Let's not wait until the storm has passed."

"I'll not let you do it alone," I said. "I'll do it with you. I'll plant my seed too."

The day of the broadcast we looked at the camera and, with tears streaming down our cheeks, we told how we felt when we lost our daughter and son-in-law. There were moments when the words wouldn't come and we fumbled for them. Oral shared how Rebecca and Marshall had come to Christ in their youth, how they had lived for Him.

And then what a blessed seed he planted in the life of people who were watching who had lost loved ones and they did not have the assurance they were

Christians. I pray that this will speak to you today if you have lost loved ones and you do not know if they were Christians.

"But if Rebecca and Marshall hadn't been Christians," Oral said, "I believe in the brief moments before the plane crashed a good God would have given them time to call on His name. And all of you who have lost loved ones and don't know if they are saved and are in heaven with our Lord, how do you know there wasn't that moment before their deaths that the Holy Spirit opened their hearts and they accepted Jesus Christ?

"None of us knows how far God's mercy extends," he said. "But we know it extends further than man's, for on the cross one of the men crucified with Jesus, a thief, had in the last moment cried, 'Lord, remember me when You come into Your kingdom,' and Jesus did."

By the time the half-hour taping was over, I began to feel that our miracle was already starting to come up out of the seed we were planting out of our need.

A few years later we lost our son Ronald in a very tragic death and again I went through a terrible struggle. Oral and I prayed and sought the Lord. Oral prayed, "Lord, what shall we do? What would You like us to do to plant a seed of faith that will reach out to help people?"

God spoke to Oral and said, *I want you to read the New Testament out loud on tape with your comments.* And that's exactly what he did, and I stayed right with him day after day working the tape recorder and helping to edit out the parts that were too long to fit on the tapes. (Oh, that was hard to do. I wanted to leave in every word of his teaching.)

It took us a year and a half to complete the project. But do you know what? Reading God's Word out loud every day, day after day, brought a healing on the inside of me.

Once again I had found that when we reach out to others with our lives, even in our hurt — and especially in our hurt — the harvest comes back to us in the form of our own need.

In the midst of your tragedy...your loss...your devastation...what seed has God placed in your life that you can plant?

Write it here:

_____

_____

_____

Plant it today. Make a decision that you will reap a harvest in return in your own life that is greater than the mistake you've made, or the tragedy that has struck you, or the loss you have suffered.

Start giving of yourself. Pour your time, your energy, your money, your love, your ideas into something or someone, and do it as unto the Lord. Give it as a seed of your faith which God will use to overcome your loss.

YOUR GOD-GIVEN KEY FOR TODAY

"I Will Plant A Seed To Overcome My Need."

WEDNESDAY

**Key:
GOD WANTS
MY SEEDS
OF FAITH**

**or
I Can Plant My Own
Seeds Of Faith For The Miracles I Need**

Years ago, at the time we were starting the School of Medicine at Oral Roberts University, I wrote a book called *His Darling Wife, Evelyn.* When I sent it to a publisher, he sent me quite a large advance. I had not worked since I'd been married, but I remembered what it was like to have my own money and to spend it on what I wanted. I thought, *I have some money now. I can do this with it and I can do that with it. This is going to be a good time for me.*

My husband Oral came to me one day and said, "Evelyn, I really feel like you should give that check from your book to the ORU School of Medicine."

I said, "Oral Roberts, you're not going to tell me what to do with my money. You know that this is the first money I've earned since we've been married, and I have some things in mind that I want to buy."

He said, "All right, honey. Just pray about it." That's all he said.

I prayed about it and the Lord didn't say a thing. I said, "See there, the Lord doesn't want me to do it."

Then one night I went to bed and began reading 2 Corinthians 9:5, which says in the Amplified version: "I thought it necessary to urge these brethren to go to you before I do, and make arrangements in advance for this bountiful, promised gift of yours; so that it may be ready, not as an extortion — wrung out of you — but as a generous and willing gift."

This is what it said to me: "Now I have sent my servant to ask you for this gift. I don't want to pull it out of you. I want you to give it gladly and willingly."

It was just like God was standing there, saying, *Evelyn, I sent My servant Oral to tell you to give this money. Give it with a glad heart.*

I ran to my husband and told him what I had read. He just smiled and said, "I knew if you prayed about it, God would tell you to give it."

Oral and I have a habit as a part of our giving when we write out a check and are waiting for the offering plate to pass by — or before we put the check in the mail — we each touch it and AGREE TOGETHER to expect God to send us the exact harvest we need. We start EXPECTING as soon as we give. We start releasing our faith to believe that God *will* supply our needs.

So when I gave the check to the School of Medicine, I decided to write down all the things God gave back to me as a result of my giving. And before I quit counting, I had received 28 miracles that I *knew* were the result of my giving that check!

Oh, how grateful I am for the truth I learned from that experience — that everybody needs to plant their own seeds of faith for the miracles they need. And then they need to expect back their own miracles. This is something we are teaching the students at Oral Roberts University.

A few years ago Oral was visiting a relative who was in a hospital in Tulsa when a man stopped him in the hall and asked if he would go to his mother's room and pray for her. After Oral had prayed for his mother, the man brought in a ten-year-old girl and introduced her to Oral.

"Brother Roberts, this is my daughter," he said. "We were in the chapel service at Oral Roberts

University the other day and we heard you preach. During the service when Richard received the offering, he told us to write our biggest need on a piece of paper and attach our biggest and best gift to God on top. My daughter gave her biggest gift, which was fifty cents. Now she wants to tell you something."

"Seed-Faith really works," she said to Oral. "I gave my best to God and I got what I wrote down — for Oral Roberts to come and pray for my grandmother!"

Oral didn't know that little girl's grandmother was in the hospital he was visiting. He didn't know her granddaughter had prayed for him to come!

The logic of the world says Seed-Faith is crazy — particularly planting seeds of faith for a desired harvest. But it makes good sense according to God.

And Seed-Faith does work. When we give our best to God as a seed we plant, the harvest of blessing God brings to us will meet the specific needs we have.

YOUR GOD-GIVEN KEY FOR TODAY

"I Will Plant My Seeds Of Faith And Expect My Miracles."

**Key:
GOD WANTS ME
TO PLANT GOOD
SEED IN GOOD
SOIL FOR THE
HARVEST I NEED**

THURSDAY

or
Good Seed Planted In Good Soil Is The Key To Receiving God's Blessing

Several years ago I was asked to speak to the children in my grandson's third-grade class. I was going to speak on Seed-Faith, but it is a pretty big subject for a third grader to understand. Then the Lord gave me an idea. Somebody had given me a plant that had been grown in a little basket. It had bloomed and then died. So I stirred up the dirt that was left in the basket and planted some seeds in it.

I took the basket to school and the children were very excited and curious. I told them that I had planted seeds in the basket.

"I brought this so I could talk to you about Seed-Faith," I said. "Seed-Faith is something you do and, when you do it, you do it as unto the Lord and you expect something to come back to you."

I explained, "When you go out on the playground and see a little girl or little boy off in a corner and they have nobody to play with, you can plant a seed of faith in their life by saying, 'I'll play with you. I'll be your friend.' And the Lord will bless you for that good seed you plant.

"But if you go over to a lonely little child and kick him, that is a seed too. It's a bad seed. When you plant good seeds, you'll get them multiplied back to you in the form of something good. When you plant bad seeds, you're going to get back something bad.

"I'll leave this basket here with you," I said. "If I planted good seeds, you will see them come up. If I planted bad seeds, nothing good will happen."

When I left, the teacher had each child write a sentence or two about what they had learned from my talk and she sent them to me. I shall never forget what one little boy wrote in big bold letters: "Down with bad seeds. Up with good seeds!"

And that's what I would like to say to you today. "Up with good seeds!" — such as being positive in your attitude, believing for the best to happen...

Such as seeing the good things in yourself, your loved ones, and others...

Such as keeping a good attitude which can lead to a promotion, or being able to keep your job, or even a new and better job or position...

Such as refusing the devil's suggestions to get mad and try to hurt someone... or refusing to listen to the devil's lies that you should destroy yourself.

These are all things you can do which are good seeds and which are multiplied back in good things.

Many people catch hold of this idea when they plant their vegetable gardens. Then they know they are planting good seeds and what they plant will be multiplied back to them in like kind. Yet they often find it more difficult to understand that the Word of God teaches that our love and our faith are seeds we are to sow. These faith-seeds can take the form of giving our money... our abilities... our time... our efforts. The eternal principle of sowing and reaping works in every area of our lives — spiritual, physical, financial.

Let me share with you some other important things I've learned about giving.

First, give out of your need. If you need money, give money. If you need love, give love. If you need a friendly smile, give a friendly smile. If you need a prayer, sow a prayer. You make something happen when you give the very thing you need. It opens you up inside to the way God works. You get in a position to receive back. I don't know all the mystery of it. I just know that it works that way.

Second, plant your seeds of faith in the best soil you can find. You know what that means in the natural world. It takes the right kind of soil to grow prize-winning tomatoes or any other fruit or vegetable. The same is true in the spiritual realm.

Find the places where your seeds have the greatest potential to do the most good. Don't just scatter your seeds of faith at random. Plant them, but select the place or the way to plant them.

Oral and I plant our seeds in many different places, including the local churches we have been part of. We've also planted to build Oral Roberts University, the City of Faith, and the Healing Outreach Center. Why? Because these are fertile soil. They are extending this healing ministry of Jesus beyond our own lifetime and into areas where we can never go.

It's up to you to decide where you will plant... where you will give... and which soil has the greatest potential for yielding a harvest. The important thing is to decide, then do it... and then expect a harvest from the seeds you have planted.

And it's up to you to decide what kind of seed to plant. Start believing that each good seed you plant will be multiplied and sent back in God's own way and time and in exactly the way you need your miracle from His hand.

YOUR GOD-GIVEN KEY FOR TODAY

"I Will Plant Good Seed In Good Soil For The Harvest I Need."

FRIDAY
Key:
**GOD WANTS ME
TO EXPECT MIRACLES**

**or
I Will Expect A New Miracle Every Day**

One of the things we explain to people we write to and minister to is that it is just as important to RECEIVE as it is to give. We try to help them understand that after we have planted good seed in good soil, then we can begin to expect to receive back from God. It's here that we find so many people having a difficult time. Yet it is the most natural thing in the world.

A farmer who wants wheat is going to plant wheat seeds and the minute he plants, he starts expecting that seed to grow…to shoot forth, to grow up, to bear more *wheat*. And we are to do the same with our seeds of faith.

Many people have been taught that it's wrong to receive anything back from God. They get confused by comparing receiving with getting. But when used in the scriptural sense, receiving and getting mean the same thing.

That's the message of perhaps the most widely known verse in the entire Bible: "For God so loved the world, that he gave his only begotten Son, that whosoever believeth in him should not perish, but have everlasting life" (John 3:16).

Notice the word *that*. He gave...*that* whosoever believes. In other words, He gave in order that, or in anticipation that, whosoever believes should have everlasting life.

God gave Jesus to get something...to get a desired result. It was to get man back. God had lost man in the garden of Eden when a man chose his own way over God's way, disobeyed, and separated himself from God. God had a burning desire to get man back. Jesus was the *seed*. In fact, early in the Bible, God referred to Jesus as the seed when He made a promise to Eve: "The seed of the woman shall bruise the heel of the serpent." (See Genesis 3:15.)

Yes, God planted Jesus into this earth. He planted His life at Calvary. They planted His body in the tomb owned by another man, Joseph of Arimathaea. And God did it for the most precious desired result: you...me...us! God did it to get us back into a right relationship with himself so that He might bless us.

Now if God planted Jesus and expected a desired result, why shouldn't we plant for a desired result?

When I open my post office box, I say, "Lord, is my miracle in here?" Or when the doorbell rings, I'll say, "Lord, is this my miracle?" That's the spirit of expectancy I'm talking about.

Once when Oral asked me how I would explain the feeling of expecting a miracle to our Partners, I told him the best way I know to explain it is to think of a woman about to have a baby. There's a special feeling a mother has the last few days before her baby comes. She is waiting every minute for the cue to go to the hospital. She is anxiously looking for that baby to be born, well and whole.

I said, "Oral, I know you won't understand this

completely, but every mother will understand."

I believe we should be so eager and ready to accept what God has for us that the moment we ask for something we should start looking for it.

Oral, more than any person I've ever known, dares to reach out his hand in faith to take what God has promised.

I remember back in the 1950's Oral and the children and I would drive out Lewis Avenue to the edge of Tulsa and park on the side of the road by a piece of land.

"Some day we're going to build a university on this land," Oral would say. At that time there were cattle and horses and oil wells on the land.

Oral tried and tried to purchase the land over a period of years. But the owner wouldn't sell. Time went by and finally one day in the early 1960's Oral was in California holding a crusade and he got an urgency in his spirit to call his lawyer in Tulsa. He said, "Go buy that land today."

His attorney said, "Oral, you know we've tried to buy that land for years. You're just wasting your time." But my husband wouldn't give up. He said, "No, the Holy Spirit told me to buy it today!"

The attorney went out to the ranch, knocked on the man's door, and offered again to buy the land. To his surprise, the man said, "I'm glad you're here. I decided to sell it last night."

Today that land is the location of Oral Roberts University.

You may have a dream God has put in your heart but it looks like there's no way for your dream to come to pass. Don't give up on your dream. Plant your seeds of faith and keep expecting it to become a reality. No matter what others are telling you, believe that it was God who put that dream in your heart and He will bring it to pass.

YOUR GOD-GIVEN KEY FOR TODAY

"I Will Expect A New Miracle Every Day... Including Today!"

SATURDAY

**Key:
GOD WANTS ME
TO PROSPER AND
BE IN HEALTH**

**or
God Wants Me To Have All Of My Needs Met**

Many of us have been taught that a Christian has to live in poverty. But that isn't true. The Lord wants us to prosper. He wants our needs to be met. The Bible says in 3 John 2: "Beloved, I wish above all things that thou mayest prosper and be in health, even as thy soul prospereth." That doesn't simply mean prospering in money. That means that God wants your needs met whether it is a mental need, a physical need, or a spiritual need, or whatever. God wants to meet that need because He is a good God.

Oh, I tell you, that Scripture has meant a lot to me and to a lot of other people through the years.

I knew God was a good God because He had healed Oral of tuberculosis and He had brought us together after I had prayed that He would. I knew He answered prayer. But I never heard anyone say, "God is a good God."

I grew up thinking that God was an old man with a white beard, sitting up in heaven and if you did the least little thing He would throw you into hell immediately. I didn't think about the mercy and the goodness of God.

In 1947 Oral was pastoring a small church. We were just barely getting by when he discovered 3 John 2. One morning he left the house to attend a college class he was taking, but he ran back into the house.

"Did you forget something?" I asked.

"Yes, I forgot to read my Bible," he said. (He usually read it every morning.)

And when he sat down and opened it, it was to 3 John 2.

He called me from the kitchen and said, "Evelyn, come here. I want you to hear this Scripture. It says, 'Beloved, I wish above all things that thou mayest prosper and be in health, even as thy soul prospereth.'"

"That's not in the Bible," I said. "You've read the New Testament a hundred times. Why haven't you found it before?"

"I don't know," he said. "It just leaped off the page to me this morning."

At the time we needed a new car badly. Oral told me he was going to believe God to give us a new car, but I told him I didn't believe it. I thought that in order to be a Christian you had to live without almost anything.

In a few days our neighbor, who was a car dealer but we didn't know it at the time, leaned over the fence to talk to my husband who was mowing the back lawn. He said, "I'm Mr. Guss. I have a car dealership and I notice you have an old rattletrap of a car out here."

"You can say that," Oral said.

"I want you to bring your car down to my dealership," Mr. Guss said. "I will help you get the highest price possible for your car, then I'll help you work out a payment plan so you can have a new car."

"I don't know if I can afford it," Oral said.

"You don't understand. I'm going to help you afford it," Mr. Guss said.

Oral ran into the house telling me, "Honey, the Lord has answered our prayer. We're going to get a new car."

I said, "I'll believe it when I see it."

In a very short time it happened just as the man said. He sold our car at a high price and sent us to Flint, Michigan, to buy a new Buick at his cost and drive it back to Oklahoma.

On the way home it suddenly hit me what God had done. I said, "Oral, stop the car."

"What's wrong?" he asked.

I said, "Just stop the car," and he pulled over to the side of the road.

I said, "I just now realized what has happened. Do you know this car is a miracle? This car is the answer to 3 John 2 you read to me. God wanted us to prosper. This is the first step. Now I know He will supply all our needs in life."

"Evelyn, I've told you that all the time," Oral said.

"Now *I* know it's a miracle!" I said. "We've got to pray over this car and dedicate it to the Lord before we go another mile."

We got out and dedicated the car to the Lord and had prayer together and something important happened to us that day.

That car wasn't just a car. It was a symbol of a man's faith — faith in God's Word that He really did want us to prosper and have all our needs met. We began to believe that God wanted us to have more in this life than even we wanted. He wanted to meet our needs and to meet them with abundance.

Oral and I came to realize that God doesn't want us to just barely make it through this life...to eke out a bare existence…to be always on the brink of want…to barely cope with life. No. God wants us to be on top of life. He wants us to have ALL our needs met. He wants us to have a great marriage, not just a good marriage. He wants us to have great joy, not just a little happiness now and then. He wants us to be in health, not just "pretty good" health.

That Buick was far more than a new car. It was one of the most important lessons we've ever learned in our lives. It was proof that God is a God of blessings.

And it was a symbol to us that if God would meet our needs He would meet the needs of people we were going to minister to. That helped us get to the point where we could tell people, "God will meet all of *your* needs because He is meeting *our* needs."

And if I could come to your house and sit down and talk to you, that's what I would like to say to YOU today: I know God will meet all of *your* needs because He is meeting all of *our* needs and the Bible says God is no respecter of persons.

YOUR GOD-GIVEN KEY FOR TODAY

"God Wants Me To Prosper And Be In Health And So Will I Be!"

NINTH WEEK

SUNDAY   I WILL PUT GOD FIRST IN MY LIFE

MONDAY   I WILL OBEY GOD NO MATTER WHAT HE ASKS ME TO DO!

TUESDAY   I WILL PLANT A SEED TO OVERCOME MY NEED

WEDNESDAY   I WILL PLANT MY SEEDS OF FAITH AND EXPECT MY MIRACLES

THURSDAY   I WILL PLANT GOOD SEED IN GOOD SOIL FOR THE HARVEST I NEED

FRIDAY   I WILL EXPECT A NEW MIRACLE EVERY DAY...INCLUDING TODAY!

SATURDAY   GOD WANTS ME TO PROSPER AND BE IN HEALTH AND SO WILL I BE!

TENTH WEEK

How I Discovered God Will Meet "All" Your Needs And The Way He Will Do It!

By Oral Roberts

**Key:
GOD IS TRYING TO
COMMUNICATE WITH
YOU ON MEETING
ALL YOUR NEEDS**

SUNDAY

or
How You Can
Start Receiving The Communication

Every day of my life two things happen: One, I face needs. Two, I hear from people who tell me of the needs they are facing.

And every day of my life I try to help people get their needs met — spiritually, physically, financially, and for their families — and I try to get my own needs met so I can continue helping them.

And there's one thing I've noticed until it has become a part of my being: When needs are not met on a fairly consistent basis, the joy goes out of life and Satan seizes the advantage to sow the seeds of doubt in our minds that God doesn't care. When we yield to doubt over a period of time and it takes root in our spirit and mind, it becomes the soil into which Satan sows further seeds of rejection of God, whether we are willing to admit it or not. And eventually our rejection of God robs us from having a living experience with God in which He is real to us and we feel He cares whether we live or die, or whether our needs are met or not. I'm being very frank here because this is what happens to the kind of people I minister to — people with real needs — and it is my experience also. I know God is leading me to address this issue with you.

I pray you will be open in your spirit and mind to believe that God is the Source of meeting your needs,

all of your needs, and that you will give close attention to the Scriptures I give you during these next
seven days. Don't just read what I write about these
Scriptures, but be open to discover for yourself what
they *mean* — that God WILL meet ALL your needs —
also HOW God will do it WHEN you work with Him
in active and intense cooperation.

Few men of God have faced needs as I, Oral
Roberts, have faced, do face, and will be forced
to face as long as I live. And I'm a person who
cannot fight a *losing* battle. With me something
has to give, to change, or I develop resentments and
frustrations — and eventually I'll get in or get out of
calling myself a Christian. If this sounds like a hard
statement, so be it because it's like I am.

"ORAL ROBERTS, PLEASE BE REAL TO ME"

Once when we were doing a prime-time television
special at NBC Studios in Burbank, California, a
famous television and movie star asked to see me.
When I walked into his dressing room down the hall
it was full of his friends. Suddenly he jumped up,
threw his arms around me and with tears in his eyes
said, "Oral Roberts, please be real to me. Please be
real to me."

I said, "What do you mean? I am real."

"Oh," he said, "I've watched you on television and
cried out for what you said to be true, to be real, to
really work. Now that I see you in person, I want to be
sure you're really real."

"Well," I replied, "as you've seen me here and
hugged me, am I real?"

He relaxed and said, "Yes! Yes! You're real."

I like for people to look at my life and ministry like
this because it's the way I look at myself. If it's not real

to me, I can't make it real to anyone else. One thing I know: God is real to me and I'm real as much as I know how to let God work in me.

Are you ready to hear? To listen? To be open? If so, spend this week studying the Scripture I use almost daily to deal successfully with my needs and the needs of those who listen to me or write me. It's in Philippians 4:10-19. Read all of it, then let's get into it during this next seven days.

> *"But I rejoiced in the Lord greatly, that now at the last your care of me hath flourished again; wherein ye were also careful, but ye lacked opportunity. Not that I speak in respect of want: for I have learned, in whatsoever state I am, therewith to be content. I know both how to be abased, and I know how to abound: every where and in all things I am instructed both to be full and to be hungry, both to abound and to suffer need. I can do all things through Christ which strengtheneth me. Notwithstanding ye have well done, that ye did communicate with my affliction. Now ye Philippians know also, that in the beginning of the gospel, when I departed from Macedonia, no church communicated with me as concerning giving and receiving, but ye only. For even in Thessalonica ye sent once and again unto my necessity. Not because I desire a gift: but I desire fruit that may abound to your account. But I have all, and*

> *abound: I am full, having received of Epaphroditus the things which were sent from you, an odour of a sweet smell, a sacrifice acceptable, well-pleasing to God. But my God shall supply all your need according to his riches in glory by Christ Jesus."*

KNOW THE BACKGROUND OF THIS SCRIPTURE

I want you to know the historical background of this Scripture God inspired Paul to write. Paul was an apostle/evangelist/missionary. He was writing from prison hundreds of miles from his fellow believers in the city of Philippi. Although he had led them to Christ, and planted them as a church, he could not stay with them. He had to go to nation after nation to open them to the gospel. Because of his preaching and teaching and the miracles God gave to confirm His Word, Paul was confronted with bitter opposition, and sometimes he was thrown into jail. People didn't believe God spoke, and certainly not to a fellow like Paul who dared to say and demonstrate that God is a living God, He is a Person and as a Person He speaks. As God He is involved with all human beings. It's in God that we live and move and have our being.

Paul preached, "God created you, but He lost you as a descendant of Adam who rejected God and brought the entire human race down into sin and rebellion against God.

"*But* God loved you so much He sent His only begotten Son to die for you on a bloody cross, He raised Him from the dead to forgive your sins, to give you life and give it to you more abundantly, He ascended to heaven from which He sent His Holy Spirit to deal with your heart, to convict you of your sins and to reveal your Savior, Jesus Christ of Nazareth, to you to save you, to heal you, to bring you into worship of the true God, to reveal His plans for your life, and to meet all your needs!"

So when Paul came into an area, he not only said all these things but he demonstrated them by confronting evil spirits in people and calling them out, by confronting sickness in their bodies and speaking the word of faith for their healing. He was accosted physically by satanically inspired unbelievers, suffered shipwrecks, earthquakes, beatings, betrayal by close friends, and false accusations. He went through times of hunger, lack of clothes and shelter in cold and heat, and he suffered prison sentences. But he believed so fiercely that he would win the battle that he wouldn't give up or quit or blame God or deny God or lose his faith — rather, he had reached a point in time in his life and ministry where he could say, "I can do all things through Christ which strengtheneth me," (verse 13) and, "But my God shall supply all your need according to his riches in glory by Christ Jesus" (verse 19).

IF YOU'LL DO AS I TELL YOU, YOU'LL NEVER BE THE SAME AGAIN

In my experience I hear more Christians saying these words of Paul than any other. I know how very important they are to each of us. BUT THE KEY IS KNOWING HOW TO APPLY THEM TO OUR PERSONAL LIVES. I intend to give you that key directly out of Philippians 4:14-19. If you'll do as I tell you in this, you'll never be the same again!

First, look again at verses 4 through 13. Then after you've done that, draw an imaginary line between what Paul says in them and what He says in verses 14 through 19. Why do I ask you to do this? Because most believers I know pay more attention to what Paul said in verses 4-13 than what he said in verses 14-19. Yet both passages are critically important to your right understanding on HOW TO GET YOUR NEEDS MET.

So first pay close attention to verses 4-13 where Paul starts by saying, "But I rejoiced in the Lord greatly, that now at the last your care of me hath flourished again" (verse 10). Let me tell you a story illustrating what Paul is saying here:

"PLEASE PASS THE BUTTER!"

A family was eating dinner with some guests in their home and they were all talking and having a nice time when all of a sudden their little eight-year-old boy climbed up in his chair and screamed at the top of his voice, "Please pass the butter!" And his father said, "Son, you get down off that chair and you go to your room. You're not going to have any dinner with us tonight." The little boy went and they all resumed eating. When the meal was over, one of the children said, "Daddy, I was recording our conversation at dinner tonight. Would you like for me to play it so we can see what happened and what was said? There are many interesting things we talked about." And as they played the tape, they noticed that they had offered thanks for the food, and the father and mother had said to the friends, "We're so glad you're here." And they began to talk about many subjects — their families, their children, their jobs, the news of the day — and then there was a tiny little voice, "Please pass the butter." And the conversation went on. A little later there was a voice that said a little louder, "Please pass the butter." And the conversation went on. And then again there was this little voice, "Please pass the butter." And the conversation went on. And all of a sudden, "PLEASE PASS THE BUTTER!"

Now what does this story mean to you and me right now? It means in our hearts we are crying, "God, pleeeeeeease help me get *my* needs met."

People say to me, "God is too busy with all the affairs of this huge universe to be concerned about some little thing like (and they mention something about a need they have)."

That's not how Paul felt, and neither do I, and certainly not the little boy who kept saying, "Please pass the butter" until he had to yell, then got sent to his room without food because his need interrupted a so-called important conversation by grownups.

If God doesn't care about any human being and his needs, little or big, then why serve Him? Also, if something is closing off the *communication* line between God and me, or between you, God, and me, concerning the things we face in this life that Satan is using to try to steal from us and kill and destroy us, then we've got to open up that communication — and NOT take NO for an answer.

Are you with me in opening up this communication?

LEARNING THE SECRET OF CONTENTMENT

Paul, in that smelly, damp, and cold Roman prison, was in need, I mean real need. However, he makes it clear in verses 4-13 he's learned the secret of contentment and trust in God in whatever conditions he faces. For he says, "I can do all things through Christ who strengthens me" (verse 13).

Now most Christians stop after saying this powerful faith statement of Paul's. They make the most serious mistake of their Christian walk concerning getting their needs met when they don't go on to read verses 14-19.

Notice, right after Paul said, "I can do all things through Christ who strengtheneth me," he refers to having received a substantial gift of money his partners in the church at Philippi had sent him by one of their members, a brother by the name of Epaphroditus, to meet his financial needs which eventually led to his getting out of prison to resume his ministry. *And he rejoiced greatly!* He thanked God over and over "that at last your care of me has begun again."

Now he'd just said he could suffer any degree of want and still serve God, that he could do all things through the strengthening of his inner man by God. But he said, "I rejoice greatly that your care of me has flourished again." He is talking about himself, Paul, their brother in Christ, the one who brought the gospel to them. The one who taught them to trust in God as their Source of total supply. The one who entered into agreement with them and vowed not to come out of the agreement. Paul. You care about *me*, Paul, again!

Paul talks about himself unashamedly. He rejoices in the act of their caring for him as shown by the *money* they personally sent as individuals and as a body of believers in Christ from the church in Philippi.

He said, "You have been careful to care for me (in the past) but (this time) you lacked the opportunity." What does Paul mean by that? Paul was always traveling to spread the gospel and in that century when the barbaric Roman Empire ruled the world, it was not easy to travel. It was slow and dangerous and often Paul's partners didn't know where they were to send him money and the other provisions he needed as he preached the gospel. They cared, but they lacked opportunity to show their care.

By this time Dr. Luke had become a Christian and he had joined Paul's company as a full member — as a medical doctor to serve with Paul in doing God's work. From Acts chapter 16, to the end of chapter 28, Dr. Luke was by his side. Paul's needs and the needs of all the team had to be met.

Communication in those days was very difficult. When Paul was with the believers at Philippi he took great pains to be sure he communicated with them, as he did with every group he ministered the gospel to. Then, as now, communication was difficult. But he stayed with it, even when he sent this inspired letter back to them by Epaphroditus to read and know through it God was speaking to them. And in this same Philippian letter, God is speaking through Paul to me, and to you, making sure we're communicated with.

Remember, communication is in the hearing of the person you're trying to get something across to. You can say it and think they understand it only to be shocked later to hear them say, "Well, why didn't you tell me this?" You say, "But I did tell you." They reply, "I didn't understand that that's what you said." So there's a breakdown in communication. We all experience this to our detriment.

GO FROM CHRIST STRENGTHENS
TO CHRIST SUPPLIES

Now before I go into tomorrow's further discovery on how to get your needs met, I want you to really grasp what Paul has just said in order to set up *verses 14-19* where you will see HOW God will meet ALL your needs.

First, Paul has said, "I've learned no matter what happens, money or not, food or not, sick or well, through Christ strengthening me in my inner man I'll be able to serve God." Then in verses 14-19 he tells the rest of the truth, not leaving anything out, the way too many preachers and other Christians do today. Paul wants his partners in Philippi to know the whole truth so nothing will break the agreement God has with us to meet all our needs.

YOUR GOD-GIVEN KEY FOR TODAY

"While I Know Christ Strengthens Me Within So I Can Do All Things, I Must Know He Will Also Meet All My Material Needs."

MONDAY

Key:
HOW TO DEAL WITH
GIVING IN TERMS
OF RECEIVING
BACK FROM GOD

or
How To Experience How Good God Is

When I began this healing ministry four decades ago this month, the Lord spoke in my heart, *I want you to live what you preach and preach what you live*, meaning the gospel must be real to me and I must be real to people when I preach the Word of God to them or pray for them or have any contact with them.

It's important to point out that communication, for

it to be real, is a two-way street. Paul had communicated with his partners regularly for months and years before this letter to them. The proof of his communicating was in their communicating back to him what they had learned from his letters. So he said, "You did well in that you communicated with me concerning *my* needs."

You see, Paul had carefully communicated God's concern about their needs and he had shared with them a way to meet all their needs. That way involved them in doing something — and doing it from their hearts. They were to carry out God's instruction from their hearts or it wouldn't work and their unmet needs would frustrate and torment them until they lost their joy in serving God.

Now Paul explains what the communication was. "You Philippians know that in the beginning of the gospel (when I first came to you and you received the Lord), and then when I departed from you and went into Macedonia (a part of present-day Greece), no church communicated with me (there's that word *communicated* again) concerning giving and receiving, but you only" (Philippians 4:15).

THE KEY IS GIVING *AND* RECEIVING

Notice carefully, Paul indicated everywhere he went to take the gospel and to plant churches he taught them "giving and receiving" — but that none of them received his communication as well as the Philippian believers had. He is saying, "I taught you all the key of giving AND receiving — of sowing AND reaping — of seedtime AND harvest. I taught you first to give, to sow your seed. Then I taught you to expect to receive back from God from your giving, from your sowing. I taught you to give that you might receive and to receive that you might give, and to do this continuously in a cycle, a rhythm…to set up the conditions that will cause your needs to be met."

Giving and receiving.

Sowing and reaping.

Seedtime and harvest.

Then,

Receiving and giving.

Reaping and sowing.

Harvest and seedtime.

See, it's a cycle, a rhythm, a pattern, a harvest situation, planting new seeds, expecting a miracle, then receiving a miracle, then planting again, over and over and over.

In the natural realm you sow your seed in the ground and you get a harvest. From that harvest you put other seed in the ground to get another harvest, and you do this over and over. Sowing and reaping in the natural realm is a reflection of sowing and reaping in the spiritual realm of your life. It's your Christian lifestyle…your way of life in getting your needs met.

Right here is where you've likely been making the mistake of your life. As the church has taught you to give but failed to teach you to receive, you've allowed yourself to believe wrong; which in effect, is to deny the Word of God in receiving back. For example, do you resent us in the ministry of the gospel when we receive? Do you rejoice when all our needs are met, including our finances? Do you resent it if we drive a good car, live in decent and large enough houses, and have the money to do our job for God?

BE DELIGHTED OVER GOD'S SERVANTS HAVING THE MONEY THEY NEED

If you aren't delighted over this — if it's happening, and I say IF— then it's evident you have NOT been communicated with by Paul and the other writers of the Word of God on giving and receiving. Communication means you're giving AND you're receiving — you're sowing your seeds of faith AND you're reaping your miracle harvests.

The critics and unbelievers of the Word of God are always trying to harass me by saying, "All you want is money." I know they're either uninformed or misinformed or that they're lying. But let me reply out of what Paul is saying here, "Yes! I am trying to get the money out of the devil's hands into the hands of the people of God, including myself." I freely admit that. I'm trying to rescue the money because God said, "All the silver and gold in the earth is mine" (Haggai 2:8).

Of course, people who haven't been communicated with concerning "giving and receiving — sowing and reaping" as the Bible says, don't want any of us who are trying to save souls, heal the sick, send the gospel to the nations, and change the world, to have enough money. THEY WANT IT! And look what they do with it — they withhold from God what is His — the tithes and offerings. They deny that God is good and wants to heal and deliver His people by supplying all their needs. They want just enough "religion" to be outwardly religious but without the real Spirit of God ruling their lives. In fact, the literal truth is they don't believe in a living God, a God in the now. And they don't want you to. With their secular humanism — having their own way rather than God's way — they seek to dominate and rule the world! *And* cause the world to go to hell!

Well, Paul lived among the same kind of unbelievers. They got mad and threw him into jail. In fact, when Paul came to Philippi he cast a demon out of a girl who had been able by satanic power to tell people certain things. When the men who owned her and made charges for her services saw her healed and free from this demon, they were angry that their means of making money was destroyed. They weren't happy for the young woman. They were sorry for themselves. They had Paul and his associates thrown into the jail in Philippi. There as Paul and his companion Silas praised God at midnight, God shook the place by an earthquake and loosed their bonds. The jailer saw the miracle and he and his whole family believed on Jesus and with them Paul planted the church in Philippi.

ARE YOU RECEIVING THE COMMUNICATION?

Paul carefully taught all these new Christians at Philippi *"giving and receiving"* as a normal and required part of their walk with the Lord — and Paul's *communication* of it got through to them. They practiced it, giving out of their need and expecting God to multiply their seed sown and give back for their needs according to His immeasurable wealth in heaven.

The word *communication,* as used here between Paul and the believers, means that God's anointed servants actually go into AGREEMENT with God and with one another concerning giving and receiving — and they don't come out of the agreement.

Hear me. This is real Christianity, it's the way it began, it's the real thing today. And I for one am determined to do it exactly like I believe it was done in its original power.

It's not giving alone or receiving alone. It's both! And it's looking to God as your Source, not man. It's accepting the communication — the agreement — by giving your firstfruits. The tenth of every dollar you earn RIGHT OFF THE TOP as a seed you sow. Then it's accepting the communication — the agreement — to expect to receive RIGHT OFF THE TOP of God's "power to give you wealth" (Deuteronomy 8:18), and for God to meet needs in every area of your life.

Let me repeat:

What giving and receiving — sowing and reaping — really means in the biblical sense is this: "There is a God and He cares about you. You believe in God and you care about His gospel. And God and you enter into an agreement concerning giving and receiving — sowing and reaping — and you DON'T come out of the agreement!"

SEIZE THE
DIVINE PRINCIPLE OF GOD'S ABUNDANCE

To give and NOT receive is to deny a divine principle He laid down that He cares for you. On the other hand, to receive and NOT give is also to deny His principle laid down for you to live in His divinely planned abundance — and to usurp His authority by taking what you receive and fail to use it to plant new seeds.

GOD IS MORE RELIABLE THAN ANY MACHINE

How reliable is your God? Is your God as reliable as a Coke machine or any machine that dispenses Cokes or Pepsis or Dr. Peppers?

You put in your quarters and what do you do with your hand? You reach down to get the drink coming down in the machine. Yet you give to God and don't expect to receive anything. You say — either because you've been uninformed or misinformed or lied to by so-called religious leaders, "Well, I'm not supposed to receive anything back. That would be selfish." Rubbish! You simply believe more in the reliability of the Coke machine than you do in God. You believe in the reliability of the company which builds that machine and the company which supplies it, MORE than you do in heaven or God's kingdom on this earth — and more than in God who has a miracle waiting for you to receive from every seed of faith you sow.

Paul lived what *he preached* and preached what *he lived*. He was saying, "I give and receive — and I want you to enter into agreement with God and the ministers of His Word to give and receive."

You say, "Does this mean that every believer, including me, is to give TO receive?" Yes, it does!

Paul said this in his letter to the Galatian church which is to us in our generation, "Be not deceived; God is not mocked: for whatsoever a man soweth, that shall he also reap. For he that soweth to his flesh shall of the flesh reap corruption; but he that soweth to the Spirit shall of the Spirit reap life everlasting. And let us not be weary in well doing: for in due season we shall reap, if we faint not" (Galatians 6:7-9).

God says it's a mockery of Him to sow and not expect to reap from what we sow. He said that sowing to the Spirit causes you to reap back into your being eternal life. He also points out when you sow, don't give up on receiving because God has "a due season" for your seed sown in which you will reap, or receive.

He also says if you sow bad seeds, seeds to the flesh only, you'll reap that same kind of harvest — *and you will reap and receive it.*

The fact is that you have sown many seeds of your love and faith from which you've NOT YET reaped your miracle harvests. Don't you think since you've passed over many of God's "due seasons" for you to receive, today you should change your frustrations into "expecting a miracle"... starting this very hour?

YOUR GOD-GIVEN KEY FOR TODAY

"I'm Determined To Let Paul's Words Communicate With Me So I'll Understand Giving And Receiving."

TUESDAY
Key: THE ACCOUNT YOU CAN HAVE WITH GOD

or
How To Come Into Agreement With God — And Not Come Out Of The Agreement

Every husband and wife who have had children have done so by the husband's *seed* going into the wife's body, causing her to conceive a new life far greater than the seed. No seed, no baby.

Evelyn and I have been blessed to have 4 children and 12 grandchildren, each of them coming through this seed principle. And one of the most beautiful expressions about mothers-to-be is, "She's expecting." Four times Evelyn said, "I'm expecting a baby!" She knew because all the evidences were in her body that a new life was growing in her and she was expecting to receive a new life — our baby — in due season.

323

I remember the doctors of the Childbirth Center of the City of Faith asked me to come and help them with a woman who had come saying she was expecting a baby, but upon examination they had discovered she was not even pregnant. Somehow she had talked herself into believing she was pregnant without her husband's seed being implanted in her body and bringing her to conception.

She wouldn't leave unless she could talk with me and I told her she was not pregnant.

It may seem funny, but it was a serious matter. When the doctors showed me the evidence that she was not pregnant, and that this was a false pregnancy, I went into her room and told her the news.

She was quite put out with me at first. I asked, "Did you tell them you'd have to have my word?"

"Yes," she said.

"Now that I've gathered the evidence, will you receive what I tell you?"

"Yes, I will."

"You're not pregnant. Get up and go home to your husband."

"Well, all right," she said.

We prayed and she left.

YOU CAN'T REAP WHAT YOU'VE NOT SOWN

Now a person who wants to receive from God who has not followed His principles of giving *first,* is not pregnant with an expectancy that's real. Expectancy is based on a seed planted. You can't reap what you've not sown, you can't receive what you've not given. This is the gospel and it's good news because it gives you the truth…and the truth will set you free!

Now if you've missed everything I've said up to this point in Paul's letter to the Philippian believers, don't miss this. Paul told them, "No church communicated with me (communicated...came into agreement) concerning giving and receiving, but you only" (Philippians 4:15).

And what did that communication consist of? Acting on understanding of what God says, coming into agreement with it, and not coming out of the agreement. Paul added, "In Thessalonica you sent again and again to my need" (verse 16). In other words, what they had entered into by communication and agreement with God's man Paul in Philippi was to be acted on by them there AND WHEREVER Paul went to plant the gospel in other nations. It was not merely a local thing where some pastor came with a shortsightedness and small thinking and had them turn inward on themselves and NOT give to God's work beyond their local area. The believer or a group of believers in a church are to have a Christian world view and to enter into agreement with those God-ordained leaders over them to meet local needs AND those needs ordained of God so that we might "go into all the world" with the gospel.

Paul pointed out in 2 Corinthians 11:9 the Philippian believers were keeping their agreement and that they had sent money to him there to help spread the gospel in one of the most corrupt cities of the Roman Empire.

Now in faraway Rome he says, "I rejoice greatly that your care of me has flourished again" (Philippians 4:10).

UNDERSTAND WHAT COMMUNICATION IS

What was their *communication* with Paul as they showed their care of him again? It was money sent by them through different ones such as Epaphroditus.

Wherever Paul went, they communicated with him by sending the seed of their faith in the form of money. Why did they send money? First, so Paul's needs in doing God's work would be met. Second, to carry out their agreement with Paul to give. Third — and this is very important for you — for God to cause them to receive back so their own needs would be met.

The *communication* was full circle — when Paul got the money in his hands to do God's work and when they received back from their seed sown!

My Partners who are in communication with me and I with them have come into this same agreement of giving and receiving — of sowing and reaping — and getting our needs met from God our Source. I always give to them first before I ask for their communication back, and my real Partners respond to me as God's ministering servant in their part of the agreement. When I get their prayer requests, I realize it's like being face to face with them as an individual person. That letter — to me — *is* a person or a family with needs. When I write back after praying over them and their prayer requests which they have written in some detail, then give them a word of knowledge or a word of faith, and when they read it and take it inside their spirit, then we've *communicated* fully one to the other. This very same thing is to happen between a pastor and the people in the congregation of the church or in his ministry organization on a personal level. I as an evangelist am not called to do the work of a pastor, neither can he do my work. But we are to work together because we are both "set in the church" (Ephesians 4:11).

Now as I said before, communication really means that the other person gets the meaning of the message inside them, not merely reading with their eyes or hearing with their ears. It's a spiritual matter and the message must be received by the inner man, not just the mind.

GOD'S ANOINTED LEADERS
SEEK NO PERSONAL GIFT ONLY

As Paul held their seed of finances in his hands and knew as a man of God his desire was not just to get money, he very carefully said, "Not that I desire a gift" (Philippians 4:17).

No preacher worth his salt is out for money only. I know I've never been motivated personally by money. My motivation is God's call on my life to take His healing power to my generation — and that includes you and your family.

Listen carefully to what Paul's desire was. He said, "Not that I desire a gift: but that fruit may abound to your account" (verse 17). Hear it in your spirit: "That fruit may abound to your account." Now what is fruit? Something grown from a seed planted. Fruit is called what today? It's called *produce.* The seed is planted first, then nourished and tended to grow, *then to produce fruit!*

YOU CAN'T SURVIVE WITHOUT RECEIVING

Paul knew many of the believers in Philippi were struck hard financially from time to time because they had received Christ who was hated by the world they lived in. Some were discriminated against, some had lost their jobs or businesses, some faced people hostile to the gospel. They had to have their needs supplied or they couldn't survive. Therefore, Paul *communicated* with them the eternal principle of God concerning giving and receiving. *He knew they had to receive!* However, no matter how poor they were or how they were mistreated financially in their community, they were NOT to depend on those people as their source. They had a better Source of supply: the God they served. They needed to come into agreement to sow and reap in the gospel so that the God of the harvest would multiply their seed sown back for them to *receive* — which would supply what Satan and his crowd were trying to withhold from them. Paul knew they had an urgent need to give and to send their gifts to him as seeds of their faith. In turn, they would be given an "account" with God to draw upon. That's the real reason he wanted their gifts. He knew his God would multiply their gifts back to them and they would learn to trust Him as the Source of their total supply in their finances AND in every area of their lives.

Oh, I thank God for Paul and his courage to give us these eternal truths of our God. It gives me boldness to share these same principles with you, and for you to *know* I don't desire a personal gift but for you to have your own "personal" account with God from which He will supply your needs.

DON'T WRITE A CHECK THAT BOUNCES

If you write a check on a bank where you have an account, it will cash. If you don't have an account, your check will bounce. This is a serious matter and can lead to charges against you by the laws of the land.

Paul knew if the believers of his day did not get into giving and receiving, sowing and reaping, they would have no account with God to draw from in their needs. Yet he knew there was a danger of somebody accusing him of desiring a personal gift only.

And right here there's a big trouble in the church ...and with a cruel, uncaring, unbelieving secular bunch of people looking for an excuse to accuse God's servants. The Bible says one of the things the devil does is to "accuse the brethren" (Revelation 12:10).

Paul did not listen to the secular critics or to uninformed leaders and people in the church who falsely accused him of just wanting their money. (There's a Scripture where Paul was accused of preaching for gain.)

He knew God's eternal principle of giving and receiving, he knew it worked miracles — and he had the courage to say it and do it!

NOT A DEBT YOU OWE, BUT A SEED YOU SOW

I take the same stand. It distresses me when the pastor of a church doesn't *communicate* giving AND receiving to the people in that church, or when he doesn't teach them that giving is *not a debt they owe, but a seed they sow.* The very Bible he uses teaches giving and receiving so believers can have an account with God.

It hurts also when we who stand with Paul in "giving and receiving" get hit by some of those same preachers. But that's a small hurt compared to the hurt we feel concerning believers NOT being *communicated* with concerning giving and receiving. It hurts me to know that people aren't being taught in some churches to make God their Source of supply, and not man, and how to build an account with Him.

Paul plainly said, "Not because I desire a gift: but I desire fruit which may abound to your account" (Philippians 4:17).

And that's what I want for you. I'm committed to coming into agreement with you in giving and receiving — and not coming out of the agreement.

YOUR GOD-GIVEN KEY FOR TODAY

"I Can Have Fruit In My Account By Giving And Receiving."

**Key:
HOW GOD'S
ANOINTED
MINISTERS'
NEEDS
BEING MET
POSITIVELY
AFFECTS YOU**

WEDNESDAY

**or
How To Receive Your "Desired Result"
From God Through Giving And Receiving**

After Paul received the gift sent by the believers in Philippi for his needs in the gospel and he told them their giving and receiving had built an "account with God," he was in position to say what I and every God-called leader wants to be able to say, "But I have all, and abound: I am full, having received of Epaphroditus the things which were sent from you, an odour of a sweet smell, a sacrifice acceptable, well-pleasing to God" (Philippians 4:18).

This failure to be a partner in "giving and receiving" is the number-one problem I have to deal with. And often the very ministers who need to do this most oppose what the Word of God says and their people are full of unanswered questions about how to get their needs met.

GOD IS A GOOD GOD

If there's a point where God has enabled my ministry to make its greatest contribution, it's my belief and my boldness in preaching that GOD IS A GOOD GOD. In His goodness He has established the eternal principles of giving and receiving, sowing and reaping, seedtime and harvest. When we carry out these principles as individual believers, or as a church body, we will get our needs met according to the unlimited riches by our Savior in heaven.

I don't know of an anointed preacher who doesn't long to receive as Paul did and to be able to say, "All my needs are met, and therefore I can lick the circumstances hindering me and help even more people get all their needs met."

You see, if the spiritual leader can't say this as Paul did, he lacks the power to inspire others to believe God. No matter how well he preaches or teaches, if it's not in his spirit, he can't communicate it to people with needs and inspire their faith.

The heart of the problem in the ministry is the failure of ministers to understand these eternal principles of "giving and receiving," or of being afraid to teach them because they fear the Word of God won't work and they'll lose their people.

We ministers must preach the Word until it becomes part of our very lives, until we can live what we preach and preach what we live.

PARTNERING PRODUCES
AN ACCOUNT WITH GOD

Notice again what Paul said to those who were partners with him in giving and receiving. He said, "You have an account with God." This was an account created by the way they put their giving and receiving together. When they gave, they immediately went into expecting to receive back from God in "due season." That's the way having an account works: if you put something in, you can take something out. The only difference between a natural account in the bank and a supernatural account is that the natural account has no MULTIPLICATION potential. For in giving and receiving the way God says, what you give takes on a new nature, the nature of the *seed.* And a seed has MULTIPLICATION power.

Paul said this gift of money was not like regular money. As long as they had their giving money in their hands, it was just money, neither good nor bad, but neutral. If they used it apart from God's principles, it was "filthy lucre" (1 Timothy 3:3). But if they gave it in partnership agreement with the man of God for the gospel it had "an odour of a sweet smell, a sacrifice acceptable, well-pleasing to God" (Philippians 4:18).

THREE THINGS ABOUT YOUR GIVING

Paul tells you three things about your giving when you give expecting to receive:

First, your money picks up an odor from God that makes it "sweet-smelling money" — not filthy lucre.

When Evelyn and I give, we hold the check or the piece of money in our hands first, touching it and agreeing by our faith to plant this in "good soil." Then as we mail it or put it in the offering plate we AIM IT FOR A DESIRED RESULT to receive back from God in "due season."

This is an attitude we have. It is an act of our faith. It is a seed we sow which gives us an account with God, and from which we expect God our Source to multiply to spread the gospel and back to us for our needs to be met.

Some criticize us, but we believe this is precisely the spirit of what God is saying through Paul to all of us — so we boldly and expectantly do it.

Second, your money becomes a living sacrifice which God accepts. This is very important to you because the Bible tells of many gifts which were not acceptable to God, such as Cain's gift (Genesis 4:5) and the gifts of Ananias and Sapphira (Acts 5). Cain was rejected by God along with his gift, and Ananias and Sapphira died suddenly because they were totally insincere, actually lying to God by saying they had given when they hadn't.

It's time we understand the absolute seriousness of handling our money in the love of God and according to His partnership principle of giving and receiving.

Third, your money given in God's way makes you pleasing to God.

Do you realize the value of pleasing God? Of how He will bless and prosper you?

Think of when your child pleases you, how you love to do special things for that child. It's even more so with our Heavenly Father when we please Him in the way we are partners with Him in giving and receiving.

VERSE 19 IS THE KEY YOU MUST USE

This leads us to verse 19, the KEY that opens all heaven's resources to be applied directly to the point of every need you face day by day by day...

After Paul had said everything covered in verses 4-18, he comes to the DESIRED RESULT God has in mind for your giving and receiving — and what your giving and receiving is all about. And Paul says these incomparable words in verse 19 not only with his mouth and not only by his spirit, but by the authority of God himself: "But my God shall supply all your need according to his riches in glory by Christ Jesus."

Philippians 4:19, with these inspired words, is the verse I say more often than any other in the Bible. Why? First, I believe this promise — absolutely. Second, I live these words. Third, I deal with the largest number of hurting people more directly, perhaps, than any other man of God in the world. Fourth, I see the miracles happening in them and it causes my soul to soar, my faith to increase, and my love for God to grow more and more every day!

Now quickly go to chapter one of Philippians and look at these key statements of Paul to those who were "partnering" with him in the giving and receiving agreement and NOT coming out of it:

"I thank God every time God brings you to my mind" (verse 3).

"You are always in every prayer I pray" (verse 4).

"I have you in my heart" (verse 7).

"You are partakers (partners) of the grace of God in my life" (verse 7).

This is strong stuff. Paul was not a spectator watching what happened to his partners. He was in agreement with them in thought, in remembrance, in prayer, with his heart, and in making them a partaker with him in the grace — God's mercies — given to him.

DON'T BE A SPECTATOR, BE INVOLVED

Neither were they spectators merely watching Paul preach, heal the sick, cast out devils, spread the gospel in hostile areas, get thrown in prison for it, suffer for obeying God, being in giving and receiving with people in need. No! They were involved with him when he was personally present to minister to them or when he was far away doing God's work. They were never ashamed of him when the critics and opposers attacked him and accused him of being and doing terrible things.

What happened to them, Paul took on himself. What happened to Paul, they took on themselves. There was *communication*…there was *agreement*… there was *partnership*…there was God supplying *all* Paul's needs and their needs by a divine measurement: the riches of Jesus Christ applied to them on this earth!

I urge you prayerfully to consider doing what I have done as a high priority in my walk with Christ. When you say verse 13: "I can do all things through Christ which strengtheneth me," don't stop there. Go on and say verse 19, "But my God shall supply all your need according to his riches in glory by Christ Jesus."

Feel the strength of these inspired words of God said by the Apostle Paul as you allow them to sink into the very core of your being as His child.

YOUR GOD-GIVEN KEY FOR TODAY

"My Sacrifice Gift To God Has A Sweet Smell."

THURSDAY

**Key:
HOW A YOUNG
CHRISTIAN'S
INCOME WENT
FROM DECREASE
TO INCREASE**

or
How To Move In Your Giving From A Debt You Owe To A Seed You Sow For A Miracle Harvest

I heard of a young man who upon receiving Christ into his life got all excited about tithing his income to the Lord's work. He was on the bottom financially, really below bottom, since his salary was only $70 a week. Bills were piling up and his back was to the wall.

But he'd been *communicated* with on tithing, that the tenth is God's and that he owed it to Him. The communication stopped with that.

Whoever communicated with him made giving a one-way street. He didn't communicate that tithe means a tenth and in the Bible ten is the number that means "increase." No one told him the very reason God required the tithe from the earnings of His people was because He loved them so much He wanted His work carried on to meet all their needs — spiritual, physical, financial, family — *and* to take His Word of salvation to all nations.

INCREASE was not communicated to this young brother. Soon he realized the opposite was happening: decrease. When he got his $70 at the end of the week and gave $7 as the tithe to the Lord's work, it had decreased to $63 — $7 less than what he had.

GETTING UNDER
THE TEACHING OF SEED-FAITH

In desperation he cried out to God. Some way he found out about the teaching of Seed-Faith, either by hearing me or someone else.

RECEIVING hit him like a solar-plexus blow right in the joy center of his spirit. Every seed he sowed — that $7 each week — carried in it a miracle. The trouble was he didn't know that miracle after miracle had been coming toward him or past him each week. It shook him up that he had not been communicated with about receiving and about the miracles that had passed him by. Slowly, however, he began to change that hidden resentment into genuine expectancy about receiving from the hand of the Lord.

The next thing he knew, his $70 a week increased to $100 a week. Then $150, followed by $200. By the end of 18 months, his salary had increased to $700 a week!

At each level of salary he'd been faithful in giving his tenth, but with his new understanding of giving and receiving he'd stopped giving as a DEBT he OWED and gave as a SEED he SOWED! And each increase in salary had spurred him to "*give*" his tithe rather than "*pay*" it — to sow it as a seed of his gratitude that he belonged to God and was God's property, also to sow it as a seed of his faith for what he needed back from God. He discovered the joy of the Lord was bursting loose inside him as he got more and more involved with God's work in the spirit of sowing and reaping.

BE PREPARED FOR THE CRITICS

Then the critics came. "Do you realize how much money you're making?"

"I sure do — $700 a week, over $36,000 a year. I'm on top."

"You still giving a tenth?"

"Yes, sir, right off the top. I'm giving it as a seed, just like God said."

"We heard you used to make only $70 a week and you gave God $7 of that."

"That's right."

"And now you're earning $700 a week and giving God $70 a week."

"I certainly am."

"You know, you're crazy. You are giving $70 a week. That's as much as you used to make."

He made the mistake of listening to the critics, to people who don't know the way God works in His people. He got to thinking about it. Pretty soon he felt something was wrong about giving God *each* week as much as he used to make in one week. So he went to his pastor and poured out his heart about it, saying, "Pastor, I've got a problem. I need your help."

The pastor asked, "Do you really want me to help you?"

"I sure do."

"Please kneel," the pastor told him. Putting his hand on his head he prayed, "Lord, this young brother made $70 a week and while almost starving he gave You his tenth of $7 with joy in his heart. Then You began to bless and increase him. And all along the way, he gave with joy as a seed he was planting, expecting a harvest. Now he is earning $700 a week and is giving You $70 a week and suddenly it bothers him. He doesn't have the joy of giving anymore."

Pausing a moment, the pastor said, "Lord, reduce him back to where he was so he can be joyful about giving."

As he continued praying, the young brother began to pull his trouser leg, saying, "Pastor! Pastor!"

"Yes?"

"Pastor, I get the message. I get the message."

When this was shared with me, I really saw the hand of God in it. I heard again in my spirit Paul's words to the Philippian believers who were into giving and receiving with him in doing God's great work. Paul had received from them again and again. He told them their giving was fruit to their account. It was A SACRIFICE ACCEPTABLE, and pleasing to God.

WHAT GIVING OUT OF YOUR NEED MEANS

A *sacrifice acceptable* means giving out of your *need.* This is what this young brother had failed to understand when he was making only $70 a week and yet giving the tenth to the Lord: $7. He was "paying" his tithes rather than giving OUT OF HIS NEED and for the INCREASE that the tithe is intended to bring. But when he was "communicated with," he tied his giving to his receiving — his sowing to his reaping.

What you must learn is to give as God did. We're told in John 3:16 how God gave for a *desired result.* He gave His Son out of *His need* to get us back from Satan...so that we wouldn't perish, but have everlasting life. You say, "Does God really have a need?" Yes, more than we can ever know. He has a need to get back every lost son and daughter of the fallen Adam, which includes you and me, our families, and all human beings. Therefore, in John 3:16 and throughout the Word of God we see that giving and receiving is the principle God himself uses for a desired result. Man's way is to get and hold on to, and squeeze every dollar and any other thing he gets his hands on. And when he gets something and hasn't a thought of giving back, he becomes a *getter,* not a giver and receiver.

God's way is to give as a seed sown. He called Jesus "the seed of David" (Romans 1:3). When He "planted" His Son on the cross, giving Him as His best gift, and giving Him because of His need to redeem fallen mankind, He didn't just let Him hang there, forgotten. No! In three days He raised Him from the dead! He got His Son back. Only now, Jesus wasn't bound to a limited human body; He had a new body — a glorified body! God not only received back the Son He gave, but He began to get *us* back!

JESUS GOT INTO
AGREEMENT — AND DIDN'T COME OUT OF IT

It's important to understand Jesus was in agreement with His Father to give His life as a seed He sowed — and He didn't come out of the agreement. Also, Jesus gave *expecting* to receive something back, something far greater than what He gave. Jesus' desired result, along with that of His Father's, is our salvation and the salvation of the world. This desired result is still going on with every new soul saved.

Perhaps you and I can never fully grasp just exactly the power of sowing and reaping in terms of the way our Heavenly Father and His Son Jesus did it — and still are doing it in the spread of the gospel in each generation over the world. But there's one thing in Paul's communication concerning our giving and receiving, our sowing and reaping: it is in line with God's nature and with the way He does His mighty work of salvation and deliverance. We use the same principle God uses. Although we have no son like Jesus to give to the cross, we have SOMETHING representing the essence of our being to give…to sow…and to receive back from our Source in the form of the need we have in different areas of our life.

UNDERSTAND YOUR MONEY IS YOU

Concerning the money the Philippian believers gave to Paul in their giving and receiving, and the money we give to the gospel, the Bible looks on money as an extension of us. That's because money is the result of how we spend our time and how we use our talents and skills. Money is what we give of ourselves to get the things we need. It's the medium of exchange for goods and services. When we give money we're giving of ourselves, especially when we are *communicated* with in biblical giving and receiving.

Are you having a difficult time in receiving — in giving for a desired result? Is it hard for you to believe God is a good God? Are you open to this communication that when you give out of your good heart and into good soil God will put you in position to receive from His good heart a good result man can neither give nor take away?

You've got to have a spiritual breakthrough in this. Something is going to happen. There is a miracle, *many* miracles, involved. Spiritual miracles…physical miracles…financial miracles…family miracles are *supposed* to take place in your life. We're walking on holy ground in our giving and receiving.

I come into agreement with you in your giving and receiving — and I will not come out of the agreement. I'm expecting you to receive miracles and I will not stop expecting. Will you come into this same agreement with me?

YOUR GOD-GIVEN KEY FOR TODAY

"I Will Give For A Desired Result And I Will Expect A Miracle."

FRIDAY

**Key:
THE MIRACULOUS
RESULTS OF HAVING
A THANKFUL HEART**

**or
How Paul Teaches You To Praise God
NOT With Mere Words,
But With Your Heart For Meeting Your Needs**

God says, "Rejoice always" (1 Thessalonians 5:16).
Many times I've asked the Lord how can we rejoice always? With so many things coming at us to make us weep, and even to doubt God's existence or His goodness, how can we continually rejoice, that is, to have a thankful heart?

Again and again the Spirit brought me back to Paul as he told the Philippians, "I *rejoiced* in the Lord greatly, that now at the last your care of me has flourished again" (Philippians 4:10).

Paul was given a *reason* to rejoice. That reason had to do directly with what he had taught his partners about "giving and receiving" so that in their giving out of their need they expected to receive back from God's supply until all their needs were being met on a continuous basis.

Paul had taught them if they would come into agreement with him as God's servant concerning giving and receiving, he would come into agreement with them concerning receiving back from God their Source AND he would not come out of the agreement!

As I've told you, Paul's travels in the nations with his evangelistic and medical teams was slow and dangerous, and at times he was thrown into prison. It was often difficult for those in agreement with him concerning giving and receiving to locate him and sow out of their need into the "good soil" of his ministering the gospel to the nations.

But each time they discovered where he was, as they did this time in a Roman dungeon and sent Epaphroditus with the money Paul needed, Paul began rejoicing greatly. He was rejoicing because the care they had for him in the spreading of the gospel had a chance again to be expressed to him.

Now it's important to point out that Paul's rejoicing was fourfold. It's a good pattern for us to follow in learning to rejoice always.

First, Paul rejoiced in the Lord. You see, the reason he could teach them to trust in God their Source to meet all their needs is because he had made God *his* Source. God as Source was not just a word with Paul. He literally depended on God and trusted Him, instead of man, to supply all his needs. Therefore, when they located him and were able to sow into his need again, he knew it was God who had moved in their hearts to do it. He was deeply humbled over their remembrance of him, as expressed in their gift, but his rejoicing was in the Lord!

This is a very important key in giving thanks: You *appreciate* those who care about you and help you, but your *praise and worship* is to God. God is your Source, not those who give to you.

Second, Paul rejoiced in the Lord GREATLY. This means Paul didn't merely have words of praise, but his praise to God overflowed. He had a thankful heart. He didn't just say "thanks and God bless you." He didn't leave it at that. Paul had an ATTITUDE OF SPIRIT to praise and to magnify God.

So much is in your *attitude.* If your attitude is to use words only rather than spirit to rejoice in the

Lord, then that's what you have, words — not spirit. Words can be so empty, so meaningless, so soon forgotten. But attitude is an integral part of your spirit, your inner self, and it never ceases. It's amazing how other people know when our gratitude is mere words and when it is our heart speaking.

Third, Paul's rejoicing was based on his agreement with believers in their giving AND receiving, an agreement he never came out of.

Paul was praising God that their care of him was flourishing again. He was also rejoicing over what God was going to do for them in return. The seed they had planted into his ministry would become a miracle harvest for them to gather in. Soon they would be reaping far more than they had sown. Their giving put them into an attitude of receiving. Paul could see them rejoicing and praising God as their Source of total supply. He could see God touching them on earth with His supply from heaven itself. He saw them getting their needs met. And Paul knew what it meant for the Lord to meet a need that no one else could meet. He knew it would fill *them* with praise!

Fourth, Paul rejoiced because He knew that his partners — through their giving and receiving — had come to the place where they were trusting totally in God as their Source and they could say, "My God."

God meant everything to Paul. God was his life, his salvation, his healing and wholeness, his Source, his everything. And Paul meant something to God. God could depend on Paul. He could work His miracles through Paul. He could give His eternal principles through Paul. He could go into agreement with Paul and those who entered into agreement with Paul, His ministering servant.

Therefore Paul could say, *"My God."* God was a personal God to Paul. God was delighted for Paul to call Him "my God." God put His name on the line with Paul's agreement on giving and receiving — and God did not come out of the agreement. Paul knew as surely as day follows night God would honor his declaration of faith that *"My God* shall supply all your needs..."

So if you will come into agreement with God's Word today on giving and receiving, I — as a God-called man — can say to you, "My God shall supply all *your* needs!"

MY GOD-GIVEN KEY FOR TODAY

"I Will Receive Because I Know God Wants Me To Give And Receive."

SATURDAY
Key: HOW TO GET IN POSITION TO GET ALL YOUR NEEDS MET

or
What I Believe Happened Between Paul And Epaphroditus That Is For All Believers Today

The scene shifts. Paul has been in a desperate condition, but bravely standing on Christ's strengthening power that he can do all things. No matter how hard things get, he's determined to serve God and finish his course.

But Epaphroditus is there with the gift and the

memory. "You brought us the gospel," he's telling Paul, who is chained to the wall of the prison. "We're not ashamed of you, Paul, for being in prison because of the misunderstanding and persecution of the people."

Paul says, "Rome says I'm its prisoner, but I do not accept that. If I were Rome's prisoner I would have to be a criminal who broke their laws. But I've broken no law except to rise above all manmade laws, which attempt to stop the preaching of Jesus Christ who has risen from the dead. Jesus Christ is Savior and Lord and the only name given under heaven whereby men must be saved. I am not ashamed of the gospel because it is the power of God unto salvation by Jesus Christ. It is for Him I am here. *Therefore, I am a prisoner of the Lord!*"

Epaphroditus says, "Paul, we know that, and we're your partners no matter what you suffer for the Lord. We're in agreement with you and we won't come out of the agreement. As you know, I'm sent here in behalf of all the believers in Philippi concerning giving and receiving, the communication we received from the Lord through you. I have their message to you, also their gift. Here's the gift."

Paul looks at it, holds it in his hands, looks to the ends of the earth to those souls he'll reach through this seed. He says, "It's from the believers in Philippi. How I remember them. Daily, in every prayer I pray, I remember you as my partners. You're never out of my heart or mind. I receive this and smell the odor of a sweet smell on it. This is sweet-smelling money and not filthy lucre. Thank God for your gift and I receive it. What's the message?"

"Paul, the message is that all of us have great needs back in Philippi. Conditions are tough. Your communication on giving and receiving has given us something to hang on to. We know only that as we put our seed into God's work, we will be in position to reap our miracle harvests. Everybody back in Philippi is praying this seed gets into your hands because we've got to start receiving back from God real soon."

With shining eyes Paul says, "Epaphroditus, you tell them they've done well that their care of me has reached me again. But you tell them I receive this money not because I desire a gift. I don't desire a gift, but I desire that fruit may ABOUND to your account with God. I want you to be in position to receive and this is the way to keep your account abounding. You go back and tell them something very, very special is going to happen to them."

Now Epaphroditus is back in Philippi and they're all excitedly gathered around him.

"Did you see Paul?"

"Yes, I saw him."

"What did he say?"

"He said you have an account with God."

"Did Paul say that?"

"Yes, but he said to tell you he didn't want your money just as a gift for himself. He said he wants it understood he's really a man of God and he is not out for personal wealth. He only wants money for his needs and the needs of the gospel. He says when he is full and overflowing he can say what all believers have got to hear."

"What is it? Tell us."

"He said because of your care for him again he has all the money he needs to get the job done for the Lord and because of your giving and receiving he said to tell you, *For my God, my God … not somebody else's god, not some god I heard about … but my God, Paul's God, shall …*"

"Yes, go on …"

"Shall supply all your needs. All! Not half of them.

Not three fourths of them. All of them — spiritually, physically, financially, family, all your needs!"

"That sounds like the Paul we know. What else?"

"Paul said his God would supply all your needs according to His riches in heaven by His Son, Jesus Christ!"

"Oh, Epaphroditus, that means we don't have to depend only on earthly sources, but upon God himself and His heavenly riches, doesn't it?"

"That's right. Paul talked about heaven being full of riches and those riches are more than any needs we have. He talked about heaven bending low and touching our lives here on earth and causing a supply to come in ways we can't understand by our natural minds, but only by our faith."

"Paul said these things?"

"Yes, Paul himself."

One after another began to lift their voices.

"Paul told us this in his sermons, don't we remember?"

"But now he's put it in a letter to us and to all believers of all generations."

"I don't have to live hand-to-mouth as a child of God."

"My receiving time has come. My reaping time is here!"

"The God of Paul, the man who first told us about giving and receiving, that God is going to meet my needs."

"Yes, and by His riches, not man's."

The news spread all across the Roman Empire to the new churches Paul and his team had planted. "God is meeting all the needs of those who are into giving and receiving! The money they give is sweet-smelling money. Their gifts are acceptable to God and well-pleasing to Him. They have an account with

God. Paul's God is supplying all their needs according to God's riches by His Son Jesus Christ. The *partnering* between Paul and the believers at Philippi is really working, it's paying off, it's glorifying God, it's filling Paul and his team up so they can really spread the Word."

Now as I've told you how I think all this happened, let me remind you that these were new Christians. They didn't have to unlearn the bad teaching that giving has nothing to do with receiving. They understood that sowing is connected to reaping. They saw that having an account with God to draw from happens not only after getting to heaven, but happens to us NOW to get our daily needs met. They heard it from God's servant, Paul, under the inspiration of the Holy Spirit as the Word of God. They received it as a *direct communication* from God. They entered into partnership with Paul, in giving and receiving. And they kept on doing it, even to sending Paul gifts in a Roman jail, and they received directly from Paul the real truth: Christianity *works!* Receiving does follow giving! God does supply all our needs!

But make no mistake by presuming this will happen in your life if you don't know the eternal principle of giving and receiving and apply it diligently and joyfully in your daily walk with God. You don't get something for nothing nor will it happen automatically. God is involved with you in your needs to be met when you get involved with Him and His anointed servants as they preach…teach…and heal as Jesus did, as Paul did, and as all do who are God-ordained to be over you in the ministry.

I've never been so excited in serving God as the Source of our total supply as I am today. It's thrilling to know that "My God shall supply all your need according to His riches in heaven by Christ Jesus!"

YOUR GOD-GIVEN KEY FOR TODAY

"Through My Giving And Receiving I Will Establish An Account With God...Then I Will Know He WILL Supply All My Needs According To His Abundant Supply."

TENTH WEEK

SUNDAY WHILE I KNOW CHRIST STRENGTH-
ENS ME WITHIN SO I CAN DO ALL
THINGS, I MUST KNOW HE WILL ALSO
MEET ALL MY MATERIAL NEEDS

MONDAY I'M DETERMINED TO LET PAUL'S
WORDS COMMUNICATE WITH ME
SO I'LL UNDERSTAND GIVING AND
RECEIVING

TUESDAY I CAN HAVE FRUIT IN MY ACCOUNT
BY GIVING AND RECEIVING

WEDNESDAY MY SACRIFICE GIFT TO GOD HAS
A SWEET SMELL

THURSDAY I WILL GIVE FOR A DESIRED RESULT
AND I WILL EXPECT A MIRACLE

FRIDAY I WILL RECEIVE BECAUSE I KNOW
GOD WANTS ME TO GIVE AND
RECEIVE

SATURDAY THROUGH MY GIVING AND RECEIV-
ING I WILL ESTABLISH AN ACCOUNT
WITH GOD…THEN I WILL KNOW
HE WILL SUPPLY ALL MY NEEDS AC-
CORDING TO HIS ABUNDANT SUPPLY

ELEVENTH WEEK

There's Something I Must Do To Get From Where I Am To Where I Want To Be

By Richard Roberts

SUNDAY

Key:
I WILL GET A CLEAR
PICTURE OF MY SOURCE

or
How The Bible Can Give You A Different
Picture Of The Real Jesus, Which Is
Not The Picture That People Sometimes Have

Do you have a clear picture of who God — as revealed to us through His Son Jesus — really is? Do you have a picture of what Jesus is like in the Bible and how that relates to *your* life?

I know many people who have a false understanding about who Jesus is. They have a distorted picture of what Jesus is really like. They think of God as a God of judgment and wrath, rather than the God of love, mercy, and healing that the Bible shows us again and again that He is.

WILL THE REAL JESUS PLEASE STAND UP?

Back in the sixties there was a television program called *To Tell the Truth*. On each program, a panel of celebrity judges would question three different people who were all claiming to be the same person. By their questions they would try to determine which one of the three guests was the person they each claimed to be.

At the end of the questioning period, each judge would cast his vote for guest number one, number two, or number three. When the votes were cast, the moderator of the show — Garry Moore — would ask the now famous question, "Will the real John Doe (or whatever the guest's name was) please stand up?" And the real person would reveal his true identity.

353

I believe that is the heart's cry of many people today as they are bombarded on all sides with erroneous information about what God is like. Inside their hearts they cry, *Will the real JESUS please stand up?*

For a true picture of what God is like we can look at Jesus' life on this earth, for Jesus told us that when we've seen Him we've seen the Father. Matthew 14:14 says:

"And Jesus went forth, and saw a great multitude, and was moved with compassion toward them, and he healed their sick."

Friend, that's the Jesus I know, and that's the REAL Jesus. This Scripture tells us four different things that give us a clear picture of what Jesus is really like… and what we can be like when we pattern our life after His.

FIRST, JESUS "WENT FORTH"

During Jesus' life He was constantly moving forward; He was constantly making progress in those things that He knew He was sent to earth to do. And, friend, you and I must move forward as Jesus did, or we will stagnate right where we are. You can move ahead in what God has for you, or you can stop and dig your heels in the ground and stop the forward movement of God in your life. I believe that as a child of God, there is a going-forth time in your life…and that time is now.

SECOND, JESUS "*SAW A GREAT MULTITUDE*"

Jesus sees people differently than we do. First of all, when He looks at a crowd He doesn't see just a group of people. He sees them as *individuals*. He knows that every man, woman, and young person is sick in one way or another. And He wants to help us get out of that sickness, or whatever it is that is wrong.

How do I know? Let's look at the rest of the verse.

THIRD, JESUS "WAS MOVED WITH COMPASSION"

When you see people with needs, how do you react? Are you drawn toward them or are you drawn away from them? Often, as human beings, we are drawn away from one another in sickness, in pain, or in grief. We let each other down at those times when we need help the most.

But the Bible tells us that in our darkest hour of need, Jesus is right there with us. He is drawn *toward* us in our need; He is *moved* with compassion.

The Bible puts it this way: "But God commended his love toward us, in that, while we were yet sinners, Christ died for us" (Romans 5:8).

If you're in the midst of sickness or pain or any other form of need, don't make the mistake that many people make of thinking that you must somehow get your life in order before you can go to Jesus...or that He will be "turned off" by your situation, as human beings sometimes are.

Remember this Scripture in Matthew 14:14 and know that Jesus *wants* to meet you right in the middle of that need. He is moved with compassion *toward* you...not away from you. And He wants to help you out of the problem you're in.

FOURTH, JESUS "HEALED THEIR SICK"

Acts 10:38 says that "Jesus went about doing good, healing all who were oppressed of the devil; for God was with him." This is the Jesus I know...the

Jesus who comes to you with healing and with hope…who brings all of His miracle power to bear on the situation you're in the moment you ask Him to.

WHO CAN RESIST A JESUS LIKE THAT?

You know, for years and years in my life, I didn't have a clear picture of who Jesus was. As a teenager I ran from God and from my parents who represented God to me. But at the age of 19, I finally saw Jesus for who He really was. And when I saw Him as He really is, I couldn't resist giving my life to Him completely.

There are many people living in sin and in sickness today because they don't have a clear picture of Jesus. They don't believe that God cares about the situation they're in so they don't go to Him for help.

The *real* Jesus wants to turn around whatever negative situation you're in. Even now He's moving forward in your life. He sees you as an individual with individual needs. He is moved with compassion toward you and He wants to bring all of His healing, delivering power to bear on the situation.

See Him as He really is…and reach out to Him now as He is reaching out to you.

YOUR GOD-GIVEN KEY FOR TODAY

"I Will Get A Clear Picture Of Jesus Reaching Out To Me."

Then, begin studying the only Book that can give you that clear picture…God's Word.

Key:
I WILL BELIEVE
MONDAY
IN THE MAN,
NOT THE LEGEND

or
We Can Be Set Free Like
The Man At The Pool Of Bethesda
When We Know The Truth Of Jesus In Our Lives

I have known people who live their entire life based on hearsay, superstition, and legends, rather than on the truth. Jesus said that when we know the truth, "the truth shall make you free" (John 8:32).

Then Jesus made a startling statement. One that no man, before or since, has ever been able to make. He said, "I AM the truth" (John 14:6). He didn't just say, "I know the truth." He said, "I *am* the truth." And in order for us to have the truth that we need to base our lives upon, we must have the MAN, Jesus.

Let me share a story with you from the Bible about a man who didn't have the Truth to base his life on, only a legend.

A LEGEND WILL NEVER DO

In John 5:1-9 we see that one day as Jesus was walking through Jerusalem, He came to the pool of Bethesda where a great number of sick and disabled people were gathered. Jesus saw one man lying by the pool who had been lame for 38 years. He walked up to him and said, "Wilt thou be made whole?" In other words, "Do you want Me to heal you?"

It was the perfect opportunity for the man to be healed and to be set free of the infirmity that had kept him bound for 38 years. But because the man was living his life based on a legend, he almost missed out on a miracle.

The man misunderstood Jesus' question. He said to Jesus, "I have no man to put me in the pool. For when the angel comes to stir up the waters, someone always gets in before me." At that time there was a legend that at a certain season an angel came down to the pool of Bethesda. The angel would stir up the water and whoever could get into the pool first would be healed.

That was the legend this man believed in. But his belief did him no good. For he said, "I have no man to help me." And he was telling the truth — he didn't have a man. He only had a legend.

You see, a legend will never do. Hearsay will never do. Superstition will never do. Those things are not the answer…and they are not the Truth that will set you free. The Truth is a MAN, and His name is Jesus Christ of Nazareth, the Son of the living God. There are no legends and no magic formulas that will last for solving the problems you face in life. There is only a man, *the* Man named Jesus, who will bring His Word and His healing and delivering power to heal you and set you free.

IT'S GOOD TO BE SINCERE, BUT YOU CAN BE SINCERELY WRONG

The man believed that he might lie there by the pool until he could be the first one in after the angel troubled the waters. He was sincere in his beliefs… but he was also sincerely wrong. Jesus had the power to heal him merely by speaking the word.

He said to the man, "Rise, take up your bed and walk." The man obeyed Jesus' word and went away praising and worshiping God.

You know, it's wonderful to see people who are sincere in their beliefs. If you turn on the television any day of the week, you can hear people from every walk of life talking about their religious beliefs. Some people believe in tarot cards, some in Hare Krishna, some even believe practicing self-inflicted pain to try to atone for the sins they have committed. They are sincere in their beliefs, but like the man at the pool of Bethesda, they are sincerely wrong. They are basing their life on legends and manmade religions, not on Jesus Christ.

You see, it's not enough just to be sincere in what you believe. In order to have the power of God in your life you must believe the Truth…and that Truth is Jesus Christ.

ARE YOU LIKE THE MAN AT THE POOL OF BETHESDA?

If you are dealing with a problem in your life that has kept you bound for years, perhaps you should consider that — like the man at the pool of Bethesda — you may be relying on some human being to come and rescue you from your trouble. Or maybe you're trusting in what you've learned through superstition or tradition to help you solve your problems, rather than on Jesus Christ.

Turn to Jesus and ask Him to reveal His truth to you today. And just like the man at the pool of Bethesda, you can be set free.

YOUR GOD-GIVEN KEY FOR TODAY

"I Will Believe In The Man, Jesus Christ, Not A Legend."

Then don't be afraid to cast aside what you thought was true for Him who *is* the Truth.

**Key:
I WILL BE SPECIFIC
AND HONEST
WITH GOD
ABOUT WHAT I WANT**

TUESDAY

or
**Jesus Asked A Blind Man In The Bible,
"What Do You Want Me To Do For You?"
And He's Asking You And Me That Today**

In this busy, hustle-bustle society that we live in today, psychologists say that one of man's greatest problems is loneliness. People feel isolated and left out, as if they're sitting on the side of the road just watching life go by. In a world of high-tech communication tools, most of us have never really learned how to communicate with one another. We've never learned to open our hearts and be honest with other people about our feelings, our needs, and what we really want in this life. Often, we're not even completely honest with God.

Loneliness, pain, and feelings of rejection are not problems that only you and I have had to deal with. A blind beggar in the Bible named Bartimaeus had to deal with those feelings too. Mark 10:46 says, "As he [Jesus] went out of Jericho with his disciples and a great number of people, blind Bartimaeus...sat by the highway side begging."

I believe Bartimaeus represents many people today who are sitting on the side of the highway of life, alone, hurting, and rejected.

There are four things about his story that I want to share with you today. And I believe they're four things that, if you will remember them, can bring you out of the loneliness and isolation you feel in the midst of your problems.

#1: BARTIMAEUS WAS NOT SATISFIED WITH WHERE HE WAS

His dissatisfaction with his life made him cry out to Jesus as He passed by where Bartimaeus sat begging. The people told him to shut up, but the Bible says that only made Bartimaeus cry the louder, "Jesus, thou Son of David, have mercy on me."

You see, when you really begin to get honest with God about your problems and your needs, many people will try to stop you. They'll even say things to you like, "God doesn't care about the little things in your life, like feelings of loneliness or isolation, just the big things." When you try to rise above your circumstances, they may try to push you down and keep you in the state you're in because they're unhappy and they want you to be unhappy too. It's like the old expression, "Misery loves company."

Bartimaeus was down, but he decided not to let other people *keep* him down. Their persecution only made him more determined to be honest with God and to bring his problem to Jesus' attention.

#2: JESUS HEARD BARTIMAEUS' CRY

In the midst of your struggle, your loneliness, your pain, Jesus hears your cry. *For the cry of faith will always reach Jesus' ears.*

Jesus doesn't care about the words that we use in crying out to Him, but the attitude of our heart. When it's a cry of honesty about our condition and of faith in what He can do to change it, then our cry is like music to His ears.

When you and I finally get to that point, Jesus hears that cry of our heart…and His response to us is swift. The Bible says that Jesus stopped right where He was and commanded that Bartimaeus be brought to Him.

#3: BARTIMAEUS CAST ASIDE HIS BEGGAR'S ROBE

You see, his robe identified Bartimaeus with life's lowest station. When he heard that Jesus was calling him, he took it off and threw it aside, squared his shoulders, and came to where Jesus was.

God tells us again and again in His Word that we can come before Him boldly with our needs and requests. And when we really understand that, as Bartimaeus understood that he was *invited* to come before Jesus, I believe we will gladly share our deepest needs with the Lord. When you are a child of God, you don't need to approach God as a beggar approaches his master. God's Word tells you that you can approach Him as a son or daughter would approach their father, knowing that He is anxious to give you what you ask.

#4: BARTIMAEUS WAS SPECIFIC AND HONEST WITH JESUS ABOUT WHAT HE WANTED

When Bartimaeus was brought before Jesus, Jesus asked him a question. It was a very important question…and it's one that Jesus is asking you and me today. He said, "Bartimaeus, what do you want Me to do for you?"

I believe what Jesus was really saying was,

"Bartimaeus, unless you're honest and specific with Me about what you need, how can I help you?" It was a simple question, but a question that held the possibility of a miracle.

Now Bartimaeus could have just stood there and said something like, "Lord, I don't want to trouble You," or "You're probably not interested in *my* problem," or "Lord, bless me, a poor pitiful beggar." But Bartimaeus didn't do that! He knew that now was his chance and with all the honesty and faith and boldness he had in him he shouted out, "Lord, that I might receive my sight" (Mark 10:51).

And Jesus rewarded that honest cry of faith. He said to Bartimaeus, "Go thy way; thy faith hath made thee whole. And immediately he received his sight, and followed Jesus in the way" (Mark 10:52).

ARE YOU BEING SPECIFIC ABOUT WHAT YOU WANT FROM JESUS?

I believe that Jesus is asking you and me today: What do you want Me to do for you?

Bill, what do you want Me to do for you in your business?

Mary, what do you want Me to do for you in your family?

John, what do you want Me to do for you physically …spiritually…emotionally?

Jesus wants us to be honest and specific with Him. He's given us a free will and an ability to make our own choices in life. God doesn't just tell us what He's going to do in our life; much of the time He wants us to decide what we really want…and then ask Him to help us achieve it.

The next time you find yourself in the middle of a difficult situation, picture Jesus saying to you as He did to Bartimaeus, "My child, what do you want Me to do for you?" Decide what you want out of the situation, whether it's healing, or a restored relationship, or a financial breakthrough, and tell Jesus *very specifically* what you need from Him.

I believe that the more SPECIFIC you are in your prayers, the more you will see those prayers answered and the more you will know that those answers are a direct result of Jesus doing for you what you told Him you needed Him to do.

YOUR GOD-GIVEN KEY FOR TODAY

"I Will Be Specific And Honest With God About What I Need."

Now write your *specific* request here:

_____

_____

_____

_____

Then reread the story of Bartimaeus in Mark, chapter 10, and see how his miracle came to pass, in spite of the negative people around him, when he became honest and specific with God.

Key:
I WILL
REFUSE TO
PARK
BESIDE MY
FAILURES

WEDNESDAY

or
God Will Give Me
A Second Chance When I Ask Him To

Have you ever noticed how people are always parking their cars where they don't belong? We park in front of driveways, too close to a fire hydrant, and sometimes when there isn't room anywhere else we even double-park right in the middle of the street. In fact, we are so inclined to park where we don't belong that signs must be put along the streetside that loudly proclaim, DON'T PARK HERE.

But in addition to parking our *cars* where they don't belong, we sometimes have a way of parking our *lives* where they don't belong. As human beings, the greatest parking problem we have is *parking beside our failures.*

Jesus understands how devastating failure can be. He doesn't want us to sit in the middle of our defeats and failures, letting something that happened in the past prevent us from having a bright tomorrow. I like to think of God's Word to us and His promises of forgiveness and restoration as a sign He's posted by my failures that reads: NO PARKING ALLOWED!

ADMIT YOUR FAILURES
BUT DON'T LIVE IN THEM

You know, there have been times when I felt like

crawling into a hole and dying…times when I wanted to throw up my hands and quit…times when I felt like my life was over.

But in the midst of those feelings, I felt something else burning within me and I knew that God wasn't finished with me yet. I resisted the temptation to let those feelings of failure affect the rest of my life. I made up my mind that I wouldn't park beside my failures. I knew I couldn't bring back the past, but I made up my mind that I wouldn't park beside it.

Now, not parking beside your failures doesn't mean that you don't *admit* your mistakes and *failures*. The Bible says in 1 John 1:9, "If we confess our sins, he [God] is faithful and just to forgive us our sins, and to cleanse us from all unrighteousness." Notice that the first word of that verse is *IF.* That says to me that we can hold our failures inside of us — perhaps *never* admitting that we were wrong — and we can live in the past *if we want to.* God wants to forgive us and give us a second chance. But He can never do that until we've admitted that we were wrong.

When you've failed in some way in your life, it's very important that you admit your mistakes both to yourself and to God. When I went through a divorce, one of the first things I did was to get on my knees before God and admit that I had failed. I took my share of the blame and I told God that I was sorry for missing His ideal for my life. I asked Him to forgive me and to give me a second chance.

Then I discovered the good thing about making a mistake, or failing, is that you can learn from your mistakes. And when you are truly sorry and you ask God to give you a second chance, He always does.

God doesn't hang on to the sins you've confessed to Him and use them to hit you over the head every time you do something wrong from then on. When God forgives, He *forgets*. In Hebrews 8:12 God says, "Their sins and their iniquities will I remember no more."

God wants us to learn from our mistakes and our failures, but He doesn't want us to live in the shadow of them. He doesn't want us to "park" beside them because He still has something He wants us to do.

And when that dawns on you down on the inside as it did me, I believe you'll do as I did. You'll pick yourself up, dust yourself off and say, "God, whatever You have for my life, I'll do it." You'll put your life on GO again. You'll discover that some of God's greatest blessings come after our greatest failures and defeats …if we'll only give those failures and defeats to Jesus. It was only after my greatest failures that God called me to preach and to pray for the sick. If I'd given up and lain down in my failure, I never would have known the tremendous blessings God still had in store for *my* life, and *through* my life to the lives of many others.

DON'T BE AFRAID TO TRY AGAIN

You may be in the midst of a failure right now, a failure you'd like to sweep under the carpet, a failure that is keeping you from going on with what God has planned for your life. If so, Jesus is speaking to you today. He's saying, *"Don't park beside your failures. Don't give up. Put your faith in Me and try again."*

You know, it takes courage to try again. The devil would like to use your failures to paralyze you with fear. He tries to tell you that if you try again, you'll only fail again. But you don't have to make the same mistakes twice. Jesus tells you that "as far as the east is from the west, so far hath he [God] removed our transgressions from us" (Psalm 103:12). He can wipe the slate clean. He can change your heart.

Listen to these words from a song I often sing on my daily TV program, and take them to heart as God's word to you today: "People may judge you and you may even judge yourself, but this I know. God is *for* you...and He's saying to you, 'Try again.'"

Try again. Things won't turn out like before. Just try again.

YOUR GOD-GIVEN KEY FOR TODAY

"I Will Refuse To Park Beside My Failures."

THURSDAY

Key: I WILL STAY IN THE BOAT

or
When The Storms Of Life Come, There Are Four Anchors Of Faith I Can Hold On To

Did you know that being a Christian doesn't mean you're going to have a problem-free life? In fact, Jesus told us that in this world we *will* have tribulation... (John 16:33) and that we're not to be surprised or to think it strange or out of the ordinary when problem attacks come against us from the enemy (1 Peter 4:12). Being a Christian *does* mean, however, that there's Someone we can hold on to in the storms — Someone who will safely bring us through to the other side.

As I look back on my own life I see how God has

brought me through many storms over the years. Yes, I have problems just like you do. Being on television and being known by people don't exempt you from experiencing the storms of life that everyone faces. The Roberts family have seen their share of storms and problems. In fact, I don't know very many families who have experienced the number of storms that our family have.

But there's one thing I do know and it's this: When the storms of life come your way, God is there. He will never leave you nor forsake you. And *you* must not forsake your commitment to God or your commitment to those things He has called you to do, NO MATTER WHAT. No matter how the winds rage, no matter what people think or say or do, you must remain committed. For it is that very commitment that God can use to protect you and to preserve your spirit and your life.

FOUR ANCHORS OF FAITH YOU CAN HOLD ON TO

In the midst of my commitment to God, I have found four anchors of faith that have held me safe and strong throughout every storm. In the twenty-seventh chapter of the book of Acts, the Apostle Paul shows us from his own personal experience what those four anchors of faith are. Let's look at what happened to Paul and how it can help us today.

In obedience to God's call, Paul was in a boat on his way to Rome. For many days the wind blew against the boat and the sea washed over the deck, tossing the helpless vessel to and fro. In a frantic attempt to save themselves from drowning, the 276 passengers threw everything they could overboard. They cried out to God to save them. But still the storm raged and the very lives of the passengers were in jeopardy.

They seemed completely without hope when Paul finally stepped forward and said: *"There stood by me this night the angel of God, whose I am, and whom I serve, Saying, Fear not, Paul; thou must be brought before Caesar: and, lo, God hath given thee all them that sail with thee. Wherefore, sirs, be of good cheer: for I believe God, that it shall be even as it was told me"* (Acts 27:23-25).

And in those words, Paul gave those who sailed with him — and you and me today — four anchors of faith to hold on to.

ANCHOR 1: I BELIEVE GOD

In the darkest of moments, even when our very lives are threatened, we can stand with Paul and say, *"I believe God."*

There have been many times when I didn't understand the storm I was going through. But I BELIEVED GOD. I believed that God knew about my situation and that He cared.

You can be assured that God knows about the storm you're in right now. And He knows things about your situation that even you don't know.

ANCHOR 2: WHOSE I AM

You and I belong to God. We are *His* property and not the devil's property to do with as he wills.

Several years ago one of our women students at ORU was walking across campus one night. Suddenly she was accosted by a man who grabbed her and tried to rape her. As she struggled to escape his grip, the ORU student kept saying, "You can't do this to me. I'm God's property. Take your hands off me. I belong to God."

Suddenly the attacker let her go and ran away.

Later, after he was captured, the police asked the man why he let go of his victim without following through with his intentions. "I don't know," he said. "Something just came over me as she kept saying, 'I am God's property.'"

Paul said, WHOSE I AM. This young ORU student said, WHOSE I AM. And because of what Jesus did on the cross, you and I today can say, GOD, WHOSE I AM. We can say, "I'm God's property. I belong to God."

ANCHOR 3: WHOM I SERVE

Paul knew that he was serving God. He knew that just because he was in the midst of a storm it didn't mean that somehow he had gotten outside of God's will for his life. Paul also knew that even in the midst of possible tragedy, he was a coworker with God and he had a job to do.

You and I today are also coworkers with God. And *we* have something to do. We are a part of God's purpose for this world. Much of God's plan and purpose for humanity will never be accomplished unless you and I do our part. We must be as committed in our determination to serve God as Paul was committed, in spite of personal struggles or pain and even in spite of a threat on our very life.

ANCHOR 4: AND HE HATH GIVEN ME ALL WHO SAIL WITH ME

Paul knew that God had entrusted to him the lives of all 276 passengers who sailed with him. And God is entrusting into *your* hands the lives of many people — your family, your friends, your coworkers. Their destinies can be changed because of your acts, your words, the things you do and the way you do them.

371

When those around you know that you are a Christian, they're watching to see how you will handle the different situations that come into your life — particularly the hard and the negative situations. You may turn someone to Christ in the midst of your struggles, or you may turn them away from Him depending on what they see in *you*.

MAKE A FIRM DECISION TO STAY IN THE BOAT

There are times when you may feel like doing what the passengers on Paul's ship felt like doing: abandoning ship! They had even put down the lifeboat and were ready to take their chances in the stormy open sea. But Paul said, "Don't do it. The only way you can be saved is to stay in the boat!"

When times are tough, the answer is not found in running away, but in riding out the storm. No matter how terrible the circumstances…no matter what people say or think or do…when the storms of life come your way, hold fast to your commitment to Jesus.

Believe God.

Know that *you are His*.

Commit yourself to *serving Him*.

Be obedient to God with those *whose lives He has entrusted to you*.

And no matter how great the temptation becomes to abandon the ship, don't do it! Stay in the boat and Jesus will lead you through the storms and safely out to the other side.

YOUR GOD-GIVEN KEY FOR TODAY

"I Will Stay In The Boat With Jesus."

Then remember that Jesus is in the boat with you…
and with Him beside you, you'll never fail!

FRIDAY

**Key:
I WILL PLANT
MY SEED BEFORE
I EXPECT A HARVEST**

**or
How An ORU Student Discovered That When
We Give Our Best To God, No Matter How
Small The Seed, God Will Go To Great
Lengths To Bring Us The Miracle We Need**

Have you ever been in the position of needing a
great miracle in your life? You knew that you needed
to plant a seed out of your need in order for God to
bring you a miracle harvest…yet your need was so
great that you didn't feel you had any seed to plant.

Well, not long ago, I received a letter from one of
our ORU Seminary students who, not long before,
had found himself in exactly that spot. His family was
going through some hard times financially and were
at the point where they really needed a miracle. But
because he was a student at ORU, this young man
knew that before he could expect God to work a
miracle, he needed to plant a seed …even if there
was not much seed to plant.

At the time this was going on, I was preparing to go
overseas to preach a healing crusade. Because my

dad and I believe so strongly in the importance of Seed-Faith living — and that we must teach our students the importance of it for getting their own needs met — I often give the student body an opportunity to plant a seed of faith into my overseas healing crusades during one of our weekly chapel services. And I did exactly that as I prepared to leave for this crusade, not knowing that this young man was in chapel that day or anything about his particular situation.

Well, several months later, after I had returned from overseas, I received a letter from this young seminary student. In the letter, he told me about being in chapel that day and about what God had done for him and his family since he had made a decision that day to give God his best seed...even if that seed was very small.

Here is what he said to me in his letter.

"Dear Richard,

"Several months ago, when the student body was taking up a Seed-Faith offering during chapel for your overseas trip, we were really going through a rough time financially. Sensing in my spirit that God was going to work through you in a mighty way, I wanted to be a part of your ministry through my Seed-Faith offering. My only problem was that all the money I had in the world was 15 cents. And when I say all, I mean all. My billfold and our checking account were both empty.

"As I held the 15 cents in my hand, I thought to myself, *This is such a small seed to plant and I have such a big need.* Suddenly, the Lord impressed me also to plant, as a seed of my faith, my expensive Cross writing pen — one of my most prized possessions. At first I thought maybe that was silly. Then I realized that by doing that I would be giving some-thing of personal value to me, and that was more important to the Lord than the *amount* of what I gave. As I gave it, I was excited indeed to be a part of your ministry outreach. I knew that God could use even a Cross pen for His glory.

"You see, as a student I had come to understand that when we give out of our hearts, what we're really doing is releasing our faith to God and saying, 'Lord, as I give to further Your kingdom, I am expecting You to meet my needs by multiplying my seed back to me in the form of a miracle harvest' — whether it be finances or healing or some other need. And until we plant that seed, we have no right to expect a harvest.

"Well, the next morning was a Saturday and I rushed out of the house early to a nearby apartment complex where I had a job raking leaves. About 2:00 that afternoon, while I was working in the very back corner of the lot, my stomach began to growl. On top of having had no breakfast, there hadn't been any bread in our house that I could use to make a sandwich for my lunch.

"As I was thinking on these things, my thoughts were turned to praising God for all of the good things He had done for my family in the past. Suddenly I looked down and noticed a sack. I had not noticed it before, though I had been working in the same spot for about 15 minutes. When I noticed that the sack was perfectly dry, I was even more intrigued because there had been a tremendous downpour in the area only a few hours earlier.

"The thought flashed like lightning through my mind, *Could God actually be giving me a miracle lunch?* Hurriedly, I opened the sack to find a sand-wich and an apple. As I removed the sandwich to inspect it, I discovered that the bread was soft and fresh and the ham was fresh as well. To my great wonder, the sandwich was loaded with mayonnaise, exactly the way I like my sandwiches. I might also add that the apple was crisp and sweet, just the way I enjoy apples the most. After praising the Lord Jesus for this miracle lunch, I was so hungry that I sat down right there in the parking lot and ate it.

"Throughout the next several weeks, God continued His faithfulness to us through people blessing us with finances. Within six weeks after giving our last 15 cents and my Cross pen in chapel, God blessed us with $1,500 — ten thousand times the amount I had planted as a seed! And in addition to that, the Lord has also given me back *three* Cross pens! My family will never forget the faithfulness of God in response to our giving Him our best — even when our best wasn't very much."

Praise God for what this young man learned while he was at ORU! It's something that each one of us needs to understand on a personal basis in order to have our needs met.

Genesis 8:22 says: "While the earth remaineth, seedtime and harvest...shall not cease." Notice that it says seedtime and harvest, not harvest and seedtime. God says that seedtime comes *before* harvest. And before you and I can expect a harvest of the miracles we need in our lives, we must plant a seed of our faith — something that is valuable to us and that we give from the heart — into the good soil of the gospel. But we aren't to just throw our seed out without a thought about what will happen to it. We must PLANT it *knowing* that God is faithful and that He will grow that seed into a harvest and send the harvest back to us in the very form that we need it the most.

YOUR GOD-GIVEN KEY FOR TODAY

"I Will Plant My Seed Before I Expect A Harvest."

SATURDAY

**Key:
I WILL GO WHERE
MIRACLES
ARE HAPPENING**

**or
The Importance Of Determining
In Your Heart That Nothing Will Stop You
From Getting To Jesus And His Healing Power**

Do you need a miracle today? Do you need the power of God brought to bear upon some area of your life more than you've ever needed it before?

Then, my friend, *go where the miracles are happening.*

Go where the power of God is being demonstrated in signs and wonders.

Go where you can find other people who believe as you do in the miracle-working power of God and who will come into agreement with you for a miracle to happen in your life.

I believe that's why so many thousands of people have been drawn to the Oral Roberts Ministry since it began in 1947. People know that we obey God. And because we do, miracles happen in this ministry. Not just once in a while or on rare occasions, but on a daily basis. People know that when they link up their faith and obedience with ours, miracles will happen in *their* lives.

HOW FAR ARE YOU
WILLING TO GO TO RECEIVE YOUR MIRACLE?

As I've traveled throughout this country and in many foreign nations, I've noticed that when people are really hurting they will go to great lengths to get to where they know miracles are happening. Often people will travel hundreds of miles to get to the church or auditorium where they know I will be preaching and praying for the sick. Sometimes they are so ill they must even be brought to the service by other people because they cannot bring themselves.

In the second chapter of Mark we read about a paralyzed man who had heard of Jesus and the miracles He performed. Since he was unable to walk or travel on his own, four of his friends carried him to Capernaum where Jesus was.

The crowd around the house where Jesus was was so large that they could not even get near Him. In order to get their friend into the presence of Jesus — where they knew miracles were happening — they lifted him up on top of the house. And the Bible says, "They uncovered the roof where he was: and when they had broken it up, they let down the bed...When Jesus saw their faith, he said unto the sick of the palsy [the paralyzed man], Son, thy sins be forgiven thee...Arise, and take up thy bed, and go thy way into thine house. And immediately he arose, took up the bed, and went forth before them all." (See Mark 2:4-12.)

When they saw how large the crowd was, the paralytic man and his friends could have turned around and gone back home. The man could have lain on his bed of affliction for the rest of his life, waiting for the miracle to come to him.

But somehow he knew that wasn't the answer. He

knew that it was up to him to go where the miracles were happening. And that meant going as far as it took to get into the presence of Jesus where the power of God was being demonstrated…even if it meant raising the roof and being lowered down and through the ceiling.

IT TAKES DETERMINATION
TO RECEIVE YOUR MIRACLE

The paralyzed man and his four friends had determination; they knew it would take determination to get to Jesus.

I often see that same kind of holy determination in people today — the kind of determination that takes you *beyond* the obstacles and hurdles that will try to stop you in your way.

I remember a crusade in Omaha, Nebraska, where mothers and fathers began handing their crippled children over the balcony railings so they could be lowered to the floor where I was ministering to the sick. It was like the Bible story of the paralytic and his four friends happening all over again.

I remember a young man named Abdul who had to be carried to my crusade in Jos, Nigeria, because he was lame and could not walk. Everyone knew Abdul because he was a beggar and he sat in front of the post office each day to beg for his living.

At the crusade, Abdul was in the back of the crowd. He was unable to see me or even to come near. He could have been discouraged. But in his heart, Abdul was determined to reach for a better life than the one he had.

When I gave the altar call for people to receive Christ, someone helped him hold up his hand. Then as I began praying for the sick, a shout arose from the crowd as Abdul came walking — for the first time in his life — up to the platform where I was. He had determined to go where the miracles were happening. And when he did, a miracle happened to him.

DON'T WAIT
FOR THE MIRACLE TO COME TO YOU

Friend, we're living in a day when the power of God is being preached like never before and when miracles are happening everywhere. I personally know of many wonderful churches and ministries, like ours, who exist solely to help bring the power of God to bear on the problems and needs that you are facing.

Don't sit in the midst of your situation waiting for the miracles to come to you. *Go where the miracles are happening.* Pick up your telephone and call the Abundant Life Prayer Group at 1-918-495-7777. A caring man or woman of God will pray for you when you call and will pass your prayer requests on to me, also, and I will pray.

Or sit down and write me a letter and let me write you back a good word from the Bible that will encourage your faith. Many people have told me that my letter back to them ignited their faith to believe and they received the miracle they were needing!

Let me also strongly encourage you to get involved in a church in your community where the power of God is being demonstrated and where the sick are being prayed for... *where miracles are happening on a regular basis.*

When you actively pursue the healing power of God in your life and determine that you'll let nothing get in your way, I believe God will give you the miracle you need.

YOUR GOD-GIVEN KEY FOR TODAY

"I Will Go Where Miracles Are Happening."

Then be ready to do whatever it takes to get to a person or a place who is actively demonstrating the miracle-working power of God.

ELEVENTH WEEK

SUNDAY I WILL GET A CLEAR PICTURE OF JESUS REACHING OUT TO ME

MONDAY I WILL BELIEVE IN THE MAN, JESUS CHRIST, NOT A LEGEND

TUESDAY I WILL BE SPECIFIC AND HONEST WITH GOD ABOUT WHAT I NEED

WEDNESDAY I WILL REFUSE TO PARK BESIDE MY FAILURES

THURSDAY I WILL STAY IN THE BOAT WITH JESUS

FRIDAY I WILL PLANT MY SEED BEFORE I EXPECT A HARVEST

SATURDAY I WILL GO WHERE MIRACLES ARE HAPPENING

TWELFTH WEEK

I Can Be Loosed From The Things That The Devil Used To Try To Hold Me Down

By Lindsay Roberts

SUNDAY

**Key:
JESUS CAN LOOSE ME
FROM THE BONDAGE
OF SELF-IMAGE**

**or
I Can Be Freed From A Self-Image
That Keeps Me From Serving God
To My Fullest Potential
And Being All That He Wants Me To Be**

I grew up in Florida in a tennis community and I began to play tennis when I was young. I soon learned about a tennis player named Rod Laver. Rod was a small man who was slow on his feet and he lacked a very strong serve. But do you know what Rod's tennis coach called him? Rocket Rod!

What an unusual name that was for someone who needed to improve his serve. But his coach said, "Your serve is going to be like a rocket." And Rod began to see himself the way the coach saw him.

Now at that time Rod wasn't a rocket by any means. He was still a small man with a weak serve and slow on his feet, but the coach formed an image in his mind of what he could be…of his potential.

Today if you watch Rod Laver on television or see him play in person, you will see that his left arm, which is his serving arm, is the most muscular, developed part of his body, and his serve is so powerful the news media still call him Rocket Rod.

Rod Laver changed his self-image when he believed the man who believed in him.

A story in the New Testament has helped me understand how important it is to be loosed — to be freed — from things that tie us up and put us in bondage, including our self-image.

JESUS WANTS TO FREE US UP

One day Jesus told His disciples, "Go ye into the village over against you; in the which at your entering ye shall find a colt tied...loose him, and bring him hither. And if any man ask you, Why do ye loose him? thus shall ye say unto him, Because the Lord hath need of him" (Luke 19:30,31).

Notice what Jesus told the disciples to say. "The Lord has need of him." If the Lord had need of that little colt to ride in the streets of Jerusalem or wherever He wanted to go, how much more does He have need of you and me. We're God's creation. We are His children. We belong to the King of kings and Lord of lords. That means we exist to serve Him.

But in order to fully serve God, we have to be free to serve Him. That little colt was tied up. He was bound. He could do Jesus no good until he was freed, and it is the same with us.

There are things that tie us up and put us in bondage. Satan uses that bondage to keep us from serving the Lord to our fullest potential, but Jesus can loose us. He can set us free. He will give us power and authority to defeat Satan at his own game and become anointed servants of God.

You see, the colt had all the potential in the world to do the job he was called to do, but as long as he was tied up, he was not going to be of any use to Jesus.

I believe today we are like that colt. We have all the potential in the world to serve the Lord, but we're bound in many ways. The Lord has need of us, but there are many things in our lives we need to be loosed from before we can serve Him to the very best of our ability.

One of the main things that keeps us tied up is *our*

self-image — the way we see ourselves. I believe this is the most important because the things that keep us tied up revolve around it.

WE NEED TO
SEE OURSELVES AS JESUS SEES US

What we think of ourselves when we look in the mirror every morning is very vital to our service for God. If we see ourselves as impossibilities who can't do anything, who don't have the ability, who are too old or too young or not good enough, we are restricting ourselves in our service to God.

When we think like that, we put ourselves under the bondage of our self-image as Jacob in the Bible did.

In Genesis 32 we read about the time Jacob wrestled with an angel. Now Jacob was obviously a strong man — at least to everybody around him. But Jacob was not strong to Jacob. He had a problem with his own identity and self-worth. He was wrestling with the angel for one reason. He realized he wasn't being blessed and he said to the angel, "I'm not going to let you go until you bless me" (Genesis 32:26).

Instead of saying, "I bless you," as Jacob had requested, the angel asked him, "What is your name?"

Now that may seem like a simple question to answer, but Jacob wouldn't answer the angel. The angel asked again, "What is your name?" But Jacob still would not tell the angel, because he was in bondage to his name. Finally he called out, "My name is Jacob."

You see, the name Jacob meant "trickster, deceiver, conniver, schemer," and all of his life, Jacob had been bound by this name. He was too embarrassed even to call it out because that name represented his personality. It represented his life, and he was reluctant to speak his name to the angel.

The angel had recognized what Jacob's problem was, and he told him he was going to loose him from the bondage of that name, of that self-image. "From now on you are going to be called 'Israel' and that means 'contender with God'. You will have favor with God and man."

When Jacob began to see himself through God's eyes rather than his own, he began to see his potential.

I think what we call ourselves is very important, for words produce images. Words produce *self-image*. What we say about ourselves is what we are going to become.

Today we need to believe the man Jesus who believes in us, who tells us, "[We] can do all things through Christ who strengthens us" (Philippians 4:13). Our self-image is tremendously important. We need to begin to see ourselves through the eyes of one who believes in us — Jesus.

Say to yourself: Through the eyes of Jesus Christ I am somebody. I am made in God's image therefore and I have Christ's strength in me, therefore I will do something worthwhile for the kingdom of God.

Say: Jesus can loose me from the bondage of a poor self-image. He can set me free. "And if the Son therefore shall make [me] free, [I] shall be free indeed" (John 8:36).

YOUR GOD-GIVEN KEY FOR TODAY

"I Can Trust Jesus To Loose Me From The Bondage Of A Poor Self-Image...And He Will!"

MONDAY

**Key:
JESUS CAN LOOSE ME
FROM THE BONDAGE
OF FINANCES**

**or
I Can Be Freed From
Financial Bondage Which Keeps Me
From Serving God To My Fullest Potential**

A second thing we need to be loosed from is the bondage of finances and of feeling we are poor — poor in finances, poor in spirit, poor in attitude. For until someone shows us how we can be untied and set free in this area of our life, we will never serve God to our fullest potential.

Richard and I receive letters and telephone calls from many people who need to be delivered from the bondage of a "poverty syndrome." One 60-year-old man comes to mind. He said to me, "I've lost everything and I'm too old to start over again." I said, "Do you have breath in your body?" He answered, "Yes."

"Then you're not too old," I said.

He had a little piece of cardboard with three dimes taped on it. He said, "I'll tell you what. I want to give these three dimes to the Roberts' ministry. They're all I've got. Are they good enough for you to accept?"

I said, "I'm only going to accept these under one condition: that you promise to attach your faith to your giving and say, 'Lord, I give this with my faith, and I'm expecting a miracle.'"

He did just that, and do you know what? When he planted those three dimes in faith, the Lord gave him a creative idea to start a basket-weaving business. God showed him he wasn't too old to start over. Not long after that the man wrote to me and said, "I'm making so many baskets I've had to buy new buildings to expand. I can't keep up with the business, it's so great!"

God multiplied those little dimes because of the man's attitude of faith and his obedience.

His seed of faith has grown and grown and grown. The Lord had taken those three little dimes and made a miracle because that man had courage enough to trust God.

Gideon is a man in the Bible who was in bondage of finances. During a time when the Israelites were being harassed and enslaved by the Midianites, an angel of the Lord appeared to Gideon and said, "Oh, thou mighty man of fearless valor..."

What a statement of faith that is, for at the time this messenger of God spoke to Gideon, he was so afraid of the Midianites he was hiding in a winepress. But the angel said, "You mighty man of fearless valor."

In other words, the angel was saying, "You have leadership potential stored up in you if you will just turn it loose. I want to use you. I have need of you." (See Judges 6:12-17.)

Instead of accepting the word of the Lord, Gideon began to give the angel excuses. "God, you can't use me because I am poor. I come from a poor family. My clan is the poorest in the whole lot..."

Now the messenger from God hadn't asked Gideon how much money he had. He was talking about the skills Gideon had to lead his fellow tribesmen in overthrowing the Midianites and clearing the country of their idol gods, and Gideon was talking about his bank account.

Finally Gideon responded to the call of God and led his fellow tribesmen in delivering his country from the Midianites. He became a mighty man of fearless courage.

Whether you have 30 cents in the bank or 30 million dollars, God can use you to accomplish mighty things for Him. When you are loosed from the bondage of finances, of clinging too tightly to all that you have, God can bless you. As you start giving to Him, He will take that and multiply it back to you. He will bless you in ways you never dreamed possible.

YOUR GOD-GIVEN KEY FOR TODAY

"I Can Trust Jesus To Loose Me From The Bondage Of Poverty In My Finances And In My Attitude Toward Finances... And He Will!"

Key: JESUS CAN LOOSE ME FROM THE BONDAGE OF WRONG ATTITUDES

TUESDAY

or I Can Be Freed From A Wrong Attitude And Move Into An Attitude Of Faith

An attitude of faith draws the miracles we need. A wrong attitude keeps us from receiving miracles.

The good news is that we can be loosed from the bondage of a wrong attitude and move into an attitude of faith!

In the fifth chapter of Mark, we read about a man named Jairus who went to Jesus and asked Him to go quickly and heal his little daughter who was dying. Jesus said, "Yes, I will come."

On the way a woman who'd had an issue of blood for twelve years grabbed the hem of Jesus' garment and was made whole by her faith. Jesus took time to stop and speak to her. As Jairus stood by, one of his men arrived and said, "Don't bother Jesus now. Your daughter is already dead."

Jairus could have developed a bad attitude — becoming angry at the woman for taking Jesus' time when he needed Him. Or he could have let his own faith go out the window. But Jesus said, "Be not afraid, only believe" (Mark 5:36), and Jairus obeyed Him.

When Jesus walked into the home of Jairus where his daughter was, He said, "She's not dead; she's sleeping." Everyone laughed at Him. But Jairus *remained* in an attitude of faith and expectancy. He believed that a miracle was coming, in spite of what the situation looked like. And Jairus got his miracle. Jesus raised his daughter from the dead!

In the midst of the biggest disaster of Jairus' life, he never stopped believing. Can you think of the biggest disaster in your life? Did you stop believing in the middle of it? Did you think God had forgotten you? Or did you walk by faith and not by sight as the Bible teaches? If we keep our right faith-attitude, God can take care of what we need.

Jesus said, "Believe only and I'll handle all the rest, no matter what the circumstances look like."

YOUR GOD-GIVEN KEY FOR TODAY

"I Can Trust Jesus To Loose Me From The Bondage Of A Wrong Attitude...And He Will!"

Say to yourself:

1. A WRONG ATTITUDE KEEPS ME FROM OBEYING GOD AND RECEIVING MY MIRACLE.

2. AN ATTITUDE OF FAITH DRAWS MIRACLES.

3. I CAN BE LOOSED FROM THE BONDAGE OF A WRONG ATTITUDE AND MOVE INTO AN ATTITUDE OF FAITH BY REFUSING TO GIVE UP ON MY MIRACLE.

Key: JESUS CAN LOOSE ME FROM THE OPINIONS OF OTHERS

WEDNESDAY

or
I Can Be Freed From The Bondage Of Family, Friends, And Relatives That Keep Me From Being All That God Wants Me To Be

Sometimes those who know us best will hinder us from serving God to our fullest potential. They scoff if we talk about Jesus Christ. They say, "How can Jesus use YOU? You've been a failure all your life." They laugh if we give seeds of faith.

Maybe your family or friends are like this and say you will never amount to anything. Then you need to be freed from that bondage.

Not long after I married Richard I ran into the mother of a young man I'd known since I was a child. She said, "I told my son that you had married Richard and he started to laugh. He said, 'No, you've got the wrong person. You mean Richard married Stephanie,

Lindsay's older sister.'"

Stephanie was the one who could always speak and dress properly. She always did the right thing. I always sat in the background and wouldn't talk. I kept my hands folded and my mouth shut. I was very shy and inhibited. Fortunately I was blessed with parents who had the attitude of Jesus and told me I really could do all things if I let Christ be the one to strengthen me (Philippians 4:13).

But this young man wouldn't even believe his own mother! He still saw me as that little girl who supposedly couldn't come out of her shyness to do something with her life.

Sometimes we get bound by what our family wants us to do or by what our relatives or friends think about us. But we have to stand up on the inside and be ourselves, regardless of what our husband thinks, regardless of what our father thinks — or our mother, or children, or friends.

Even Jesus needed to be loosed from the bondage of family, relatives, and friends. In Nazareth Jesus was always called "Joseph's boy." They wouldn't see Him as the King of kings and Lord of lords, because they couldn't see beyond Joseph, the carpenter. And why should Joseph's boy have any respectability in Jerusalem, or Nazareth, or anywhere else?

We've got to be loosed from the bondage that our families or others put on us and just say, "I am Yours, Lord. Do whatever You want with me."

You need a Source that's never going to leave you or forsake you. And when you get your Source straightened out and you keep yourself right with God, don't worry about what others think. They will turn around when they see the change in your life. When they recognize what Jesus has done in your life, they will come looking for you to find how to have more of Jesus in their lives too.

Say:

I am a child of the King of kings and the Lord of lords.

I am somebody in God. I am special. God can use me! BELIEVE IT AND PROCLAIM IT.

YOUR GOD-GIVEN KEY FOR TODAY

"I Can Trust Jesus To Loose Me From The Bondage That Family, Relatives, And Friends Try To Put Me Under... And He Will!"

**Key:
JESUS CAN
LOOSE ME
FROM THE
BONDAGE
OF MY
CIRCUMSTANCES**

THURSDAY

or
**I Can Be Freed From Circumstances
In My Life That Keep Me
From Being All God Wants Me To Be**

When our precious little son, Richard Oral, lived only 36 hours and went to be with the Lord, the grief I felt was so great I honestly thought my heart was broken in half. There were days when I'd say to myself, "I'm really proud of how I'm overcoming these circumstances," then before I could breathe another breath, I would be overcome with grief again. Sometimes I cried until I was certain I had cried it all out and regained control. The next thing I knew I was crying all over again.

For someone who had been through as much tragedy and death as I had for 27 years and had remained in control, it was a frightening thing to feel out of control. If it had not been for the miraculous power of God to loose me from the bondage of grief and failure that I found myself in, I do not know what would have happened to me.

But God raised me up each day and gave me the strength I so desperately needed. The wonderful thing about it all was that God never expected me to get through the next week or month or year all at once — but to live just *one day at a time*.

In my mind I could not see my circumstances changing down the road. I wanted to, but I just couldn't see myself ever being happy again. So the Lord allowed me to handle all I could…one day at a time.

Some days it would seem that I was making progress, then something would happen to make me feel I was taking a giant step backward — like that first visit back to the doctor who delivered Richard Oral.

I knew deep inside that when I went back to the office where I'd had such joyful visits, filled with anticipation of a baby, I would fall apart. And I did.

The moment the doctor asked, "How are you?" it opened a door and a flood poured out. I felt ridiculous and out of control. I did the best I could to collect myself and go home. I felt like such a failure. I know what happened was totally separated from me or anything I did right or wrong during my pregnancy. I knew I had done my very best when I was pregnant, but nevertheless I felt like a failure.

And this is, perhaps, the most dangerous emotion to experience when you are caught up in tragic circumstances over which you have no control. When you are consumed with the fact you are a failure, suddenly you have a very warped perspective of your entire life. And most importantly, a very bad perspective of your future.

After that visit, I went home and called Richard at his office and told him I had to see him. When he got home, I looked him straight in the eye and said in a way I had never spoken to him before, "Don't you ever ask me to have another baby as long as I live!"

It was enough for Richard to suffer the heartbreak of losing a son, but now it seemed as if his wife was taking it out on him for the whole tragic circumstances simply because he was the father of her child who had died.

Richard was in a state of shock. But as hurtful as this was to Richard at the time, it turned out to be the best thing that ever happened. The minute I spoke those words it was as if the spirit of failure came right out of my mouth. Suddenly I heard with my own ears how I really felt about everything.

I apologized to Richard from the bottom of my heart. Then I told God how sorry I was for all the horrible things I had been feeling. It wasn't that I was mad at God or at Richard, or at anyone in particular, I was just upset because I didn't understand what was going on in my own emotions.

Once I had spoken that feeling from my heart, out of my mouth, I had a chance to be loosed from the bondage I was in. For the first time, I honestly felt like I could live through the grief of my baby's death and face the future. That was real progress. I released the fear of having another child and in my heart, I let God have all my children, no matter what…and something inside me was loosed.

The Bible says, "Death and life are in the power of the tongue" (Proverbs 18:21). Instead of allowing our circumstances to hold us in bondage, we need to speak life into our circumstances and expect the bondage to be broken. We need to speak power with our own words and expect a miracle from God to take place in our behalf.

God does not always miraculously lift us OUT of the circumstances we find ourselves in, but when we cry out to Him from the depth of our heart and tell Him exactly how we feel, we open the door for Him to begin a miraculous work of healing in us and to bring something *good* even out of tragic, heartbreaking circumstances.

YOUR GOD-GIVEN KEY FOR TODAY

"I Can Trust Jesus To Loose Me From The Bondage Of My Circumstances…And He Will!"

Key:

FRIDAY
JESUS CAN LOOSE ME FROM THE BONDAGE OF PRIDE AND REPUTATION

or

I Can Be Freed From The Bondage Of Pride And Reputation So That I Can Serve God To My Fullest Potential

One of the things that the devil tries to use to keep us from being all God wants us to be and doing all God wants us to do is our pride and reputation.

A few months ago someone printed an article about Richard and me in the newspaper. They made it sound like the stories were really facts. It sounded so accurate that I began to question, "What are people going to think of me? This isn't true about us, but will people believe that they took a few 'half truths' and mixed it up with the untruths? What will this do to our reputation?"

The Lord spoke to me and said, *I'll take care of your reputation. Don't waste your time defending yourself. You don't need to explain yourself to your relatives, your friends, or your enemies. You don't owe any of them an explanation. If you have a good reputation with Me, that's all that matters.*

In the forty-second chapter of Job we read about a man who tried to defend his reputation but got nowhere. This man, Job, had lost everything. He had been a wealthy man, and he lost it all and lost his family as well as his possessions.

Do you know what Job did? He tried to defend his reputation to those who were persecuting him — his friends who had turned on him. He tried to tell them what he did and why he did it, but he was wasting his time. Even though he had done nothing to bring about the trials he was going through, when he tried to defend his reputation, he got nowhere.

What turned the situation around? Job finally handed his reputation over to God and began to pray for his friends — for the people who were persecuting him — and the Bible says that Job was loosed from his "captivity." He was loosed from the bondage of Satan and his persecutors and the Lord restored his wealth and happiness. He gave Job twice as much as he had before his loss. (See Job 42:10.)

Don't worry about what people say about you, and, above all — as Richard says — "don't strike back." We don't have to defend our reputation. Jesus went to the cross and lost His reputation. We're in good company if the world tries to destroy our reputation as people who are following Jesus Christ.

God knows our reputation and He knows whether what people are saying is true or not. And the marvelous thing about God's grace is that even if it is true, He can still use us if we come to Him and ask forgiveness and submit ourselves to Him.

If people are lying about your past or even telling the truth but continue to bring up something to try to discredit you or destroy your reputation, get on your knees and pray, "Lord Jesus, I pray for them in Your name. Change their hearts. Now take the problem they've tried to put on me and turn it around for my good." Then go on your way and expect God to work a miracle in their hearts and a miracle for you.

YOUR GOD-GIVEN KEY FOR TODAY

"I Have A Good Reputation With The Lord. That's All That Matters."

**Key:
JESUS CAN
LOOSE ME FROM
THE BONDAGE
OF MY PAST**

SATURDAY

**or
I Can Be Set Free From Things In My Past That
Keep Me From Being All God Wants Me To Be**

Does something from your past have you in
bondage? The Lord wants to loose you from the
bondage today just as He did a man we read about
in the ninth chapter of Matthew. Verse 2 says, "They
brought to him a paralytic, lying on his bed: and
Jesus seeing their faith said unto the sick of the
palsy; Son, be of good cheer; thy sins be forgiven
thee."

The man was sick with palsy, but Jesus didn't say,
"Rise, and be healed of palsy." He said, "Thy sins are
forgiven." That must have seemed like a strange
statement to the four men who had let their sick
friend down through the roof of the house and to the
other people who were crowded around Jesus.

But Jesus had looked past the outward signs of
the man's problem and saw his real need — his need
to hear Jesus say, "I forgive you, son. Whatever you
did, your sins are forgiven." And that's what He said.

How would you like to hear the Master say to you,
"Your sins are forgiven"? Wouldn't that make you feel
good? That's exactly why Jesus went to Calvary — so
that the sins of your past, no matter what they were,
no matter how big or how little, are forgiven.

Jesus said, "For all have sinned, and come short of
the glory of God" (Romans 3:23). That's why Jesus
went to Calvary — so He could take your sins and my

sins and blot them out on the cross.

Some people will never let their past die. I like what Isaiah said in chapter 43, verse 25. "I, even I, am he that blotteth out thine transgressions for mine own sake, and I will remember not your sins..." That means God forgives us and forgets about it. When we remind God of the things in our past, He'll say, "What? I don't remember that."

God knew exactly what the man with the palsy needed to hear. And when he heard Jesus say, "Thy sins are forgiven," the man was healed of his physical problem also!

If we knew that our sins were forgiven, our soul was set free, a lot of other problems would be healed too. If we knew that after we have asked His forgiveness, Father God didn't even remember what we did, then we'd be loosed from bondage. And we CAN know that beyond any shadow of a doubt.

WE NEED TO BE LOOSED OF FEARS THAT COME OUT OF OUR PAST

There are things in our past other than our sins and transgressions that we also need to be loosed from before we can do all that God has called us to do. I mentioned earlier how I had to let go of my burden of losing my first child, Richard Oral. But the pain of that grief went back much further in my life than just Richard Oral's death.

You see, my father, who was so close to my heart, had died when I was a little girl. My grandfather died just before my little boy was born. And then my little boy died. The devil had a track record of taking the men in my life. I knew I needed to overcome that track record. I didn't need to forget my son, my father, or my grandfather, but I needed to erase the memory of the tremendous grief I felt and *most of all* I needed to overcome the tremendous fear of the devil striking my family again. I also had to overcome the fear of losing another family member, especially another child. You see, I had experienced two miscarriages and then I saw my son go to heaven. The devil did all he could to remind me of my past and make me believe it was bound to happen again.

I will never forget the night Satan attacked me with the greatest fear I have ever experienced in my life. Shortly after Richard Oral's death, I became pregnant again and about a month before I was to give birth, the most frightening experience of my life began to unfold. I began to shake all over. I mean, really tremble so uncontrollably that even as Richard held me I couldn't stop. Then we noticed my face was bright red and I was just burning up. I had this terrible fear come over me that our next baby would die when I gave birth and that this time I would die along with my baby. I began to cry uncontrollably and I told Richard I wanted to back out. I just couldn't go through with this delivery or I knew I would die and so would our baby. Well, when you're eight months pregnant you just don't back out. I needed an answer desperately. Richard recognized that this was an attack of the devil and I had to stand my ground and rebuke him in the name of Jesus. I suddenly realized just how right he was and called a meeting with the devil.

I said, "Devil, you've had a track record on the loved ones in my life. I won't take this! Devil, I want you to know this is a showdown! Either kill me right now or I'm going to serve God. And I'm going to forget what happened. I'm going to make it!"

No matter how much I loved God, until I could get past the memory of the tragedies, I was going backward and not forward. God knew that. At the time, a friend gave me a poster that I hung on my wall and a day didn't go by that I didn't look at it. It says: "Remember ye not the former things, neither consider the things of old. Behold, I will do a new thing…" (Isaiah 43:18,19).

I needed a lot of new things. I needed a new attitude. I needed new strength. I needed another baby. And the power of Calvary worked! There was nothing in my past that God couldn't make new again. The grief and fear from the past left and God did a new thing in my life. He enabled me to give birth to our beautiful daughter, Jordan Lindsay, and her little sister, Catherine Olivia, two years later.

If something from your past has you in bondage, trust in the Lord to free you. It doesn't matter what it is. Anything that keeps you from doing fully what God has called you to do and from living up to the potential He has placed in you can be loosed through the power of the resurrection. God will do a new thing in your life like He did in mine.

Say to yourself: I am tired of the bondage the devil has had me under because of my past. God will set me free from this bondage and will do a new thing in my life that will free me to live up to the potential He has placed in me.

YOUR GOD-GIVEN KEY FOR TODAY

"I Can Trust God To Loose Me From The Bondage Of My Past…And He Will!"

TWELFTH WEEK

SUNDAY
I CAN TRUST JESUS TO LOOSE ME FROM THE BONDAGE OF A POOR SELF-IMAGE…AND HE WILL!

MONDAY
I CAN TRUST JESUS TO LOOSE ME FROM THE BONDAGE OF POVERTY IN MY FINANCES AND IN MY ATTITUDE TOWARD FINANCES…AND HE WILL!

TUESDAY
I CAN TRUST JESUS TO LOOSE ME FROM THE BONDAGE OF A WRONG ATTITUDE…AND HE WILL!

WEDNESDAY
I CAN TRUST JESUS TO LOOSE ME FROM THE BONDAGE THAT FAMILY, RELATIVES, AND FRIENDS TRY TO PUT ME UNDER…AND HE WILL!

THURSDAY
I CAN TRUST JESUS TO LOOSE ME FROM THE BONDAGE OF MY CIRCUMSTANCES…AND HE WILL!

FRIDAY
I HAVE A GOOD REPUTATION WITH THE LORD. THAT'S ALL THAT MATTERS

SATURDAY
I CAN TRUST GOD TO LOOSE ME FROM THE BONDAGE OF MY PAST… AND HE WILL!

THIRTEENTH WEEK

God Has Something Good — No, Something Even *Better* — For Me!

By Oral Roberts

SUNDAY

**Key:
ROSES WILL BLOOM
AGAIN IN MY LIFE**

**or
How I Can Know That No Matter
What The Trouble, I CAN Recover!**

One day a pastor went to pray for a man who was suffering with a bad case of arthritis. His joints were badly swollen and he was in constant pain.

The sick man had a doctor friend who came each week to work with him. Despite the prayers of the minister and the medicine of the doctor, there came a day when the man began to BELIEVE he would NOT get well. His spirit fell. The smile vanished from his face. Soon a terrible bitterness came over him.

Neighbors who had brought food didn't come anymore because he didn't welcome them. The only person left was his nurse. And she didn't really want to be on the case because he had become so hard to deal with both in body and spirit.

The pastor said, "When I went to see him, I used my cheeriest voice. But he would just lie in the bed, all drawn up into a knot. He refused even to look at me. I wanted to reach him one more time."

While the pastor was still by the man's bedside one day, the doctor friend also came into the room.

After examining him he gave him a shot and then said, "You've been a very sick man. But I've been thinking of all the good things you've done in your life. And I've got good news today."

The sick man whispered, "Oh, yeah?"

"I have a new medicine that's going to turn your life around and you're going to be amazed by its results."

"Where is it? Do you have it with you today?"

"Yes."

"For God's sake, doctor, give it to me."

"Well, here it is. CHEER UP! ROSES WILL BLOOM AGAIN!"

Then he turned and walked out of the room.

The man lay there thinking over what the doctor said. Suddenly something took root in that man's spirit. He began to open his hands...to move his swollen joints...to inch his way over to the side of the bed.

The nurse came in. She had been crying, trying to get rid of her frustrations. She had asked the doctor to release her from the case but he had refused. Now she walked back into the room ready to announce she was quitting anyway, but then she saw this man sitting on the side of his bed.

In a few minutes he put his feet on the floor, then slowly and trembling, he stood to his feet.

He saw the nurse and smiled at her and said, "NURSE, CHEER UP! ROSES WILL BLOOM AGAIN!"

The pastor watched all this from the corner of the room. Deeply moved, he slipped out of the room.

Later, as he was driving downtown on business, a friend stopped him and said, "Preacher, do you have a moment?"

"Sure, what can I do for you?"

"Well, you know how bad business has been. I'm in the process of filing for bankruptcy. It hurts to have to let my people go when they need their jobs so much."

The pastor started to sympathize and then he remembered something. He said, "Listen, I've got good news."

"What is it? Tell me."

"CHEER UP! ROSES WILL BLOOM AGAIN!"

After this conversation, the pastor walked on down the street and he met his congressman. He said, "Hello, how are things in Washington?"

"Well, pastor, not so good. The deficit is soaring and the cold war continues and nothing we are doing seems to work."

"Haven't you forgotten something?" the pastor asked.

"What?"

"ROSES WILL BLOOM AGAIN!"

The pastor drove home, and on his way, he stopped to visit a young couple who had just buried a child a few days before.

The father said, "Pastor, do you believe in the resurrection of the dead?"

The pastor said, "Yes, in terms of the passing of your little child, I believe your child is ALIVE forever with Jesus. But more than that, there is a resurrection that happens again and again here on the earth. You're going to feel inspired, uplifted, strengthened in many ways in the days and years ahead."

And then the pastor said, "ROSES *WILL* BLOOM AGAIN!"

A few weeks later, the pastor was retracing his rounds. His sick friend was first on the list to visit. But he was no longer in bed. He was out in the yard doing some light work.

He saw his business friend who announced, "Pastor, I'm glad to see you. I've had a real turn-around. Orders seem to have come in from everywhere. I've even hired some new people and rehired all of my former employees too!"

The pastor stopped by the young couple's house and the young mother said, "Pastor, how do you think the people will feel if we come back to church on Sunday?"

He said, "They'll feel just great."

She said, "Look for us. ROSES ARE BLOOMING AGAIN!"

Friend, God is not through blessing you. When you think you've had your last miracle...you haven't. God has another one for you. When you think you've had your last blessing...you haven't. God isn't through!

Have you ever seen the desert rose?

I stopped my car in the desert one day to look at one close up. I stooped down and touched it, wondering how it could grow out of that hard-packed cracked earth. Isaiah 35:1 came pouring into my mind, "And the desert SHALL blossom like the rose."

Friend, it takes God to put the bloom on the rose. It takes God to make roses bloom again. But there's something for you to do too.

It's up to you not to give up.

It's up to you to "hope continually" (Psalm 71:14).

God is alive in the NOW of your life. He's at the point of your need right now.

Stir up that hope within you that says...

YOUR GOD-GIVEN KEY FOR TODAY

"Roses Will Bloom Again In My Life!"

MONDAY

**Key:
WITH GOD ON MY SIDE
... I CAN RUN FASTER
THAN I CAN RUN!**

**or
I Can Do More WITH God
Than I Can Ever Do On My Own**

Are you familiar with the story in the Bible of the man who outran the fastest horses in the country — the sleek, well-trained Arabian horses of King Ahab that pulled great chariots?

It is one of my favorite stories in the Word of God and I believe it relates to where you are today.

This is the story about the prophet Elijah who outran Ahab's horses — not one mile, not two miles, but a distance of at least 18 miles.

I have been in that area and have seen the terrain over which this race was run. It is not across smooth valleys but over twisting mountain trails. How could Elijah go over the hills and down the ravines so swiftly that he outran the chariots of Ahab?

A RACE THAT IS A SPIRITUAL BATTLE

It was more than a race between a man and a horse. It was a race with nature...a race against the mountains...a race that became a spiritual battle!

Ahab had led the people astray during his reign as king of Israel. He had been a bad leader, sowing bad seeds, and the people had followed him. Because of Ahab's example, bad seeds multiplied back into bad harvests, and eventually the land experienced a great drought.

On the other hand, Elijah had been sowing good

seeds. He had been proclaiming God's Word, and as a result, he was being hunted by Ahab. Attempts were being made on his life.

Now Elijah had come out of his hiding and had gone to the top of Mount Carmel where he called Ahab and the wicked queen Jezebel and their false prophets and had challenged them all.

Elijah said, "We have built our altars and we have put the animal sacrifices on them. NOW let's call upon our gods. I'll call upon the Lord God of Israel; you call on your gods. We'll ask them to send down fire. And whoever sends the first fire to consume the sacrifice will be God."

Elijah gave King Ahab's prophets the first chance. They called on their gods all day, even cutting themselves, but there was no answer. Then Elijah went so far as to pour WATER over his sacrifice. But in spite of that, the moment Elijah called out to the Lord God, God sent fire and consumed the sacrifice in a mighty show of divine power.

Still the famine wasn't broken. So Elijah cast himself upon the ground and put his head between his knees in deep prayer. Then he said to his servant, "Run and look toward the Mediterranean Sea." The servant did and returned saying, "I have seen nothing."

Elijah said, "Go seven times more" (which is the complete number of obedience). And on the seventh trip back, the servant said, "I see a cloud rising out of the sea like a man's hand."

THE SHAPE OF GOD'S PLAN

The shape of a man's hand! Elijah knew immediately that the shape of God's plan is the shape of a man's hand. He knew God was really going to work through him...a human being...and he felt in his

411

spirit that God was going to send rain. So he said to Ahab, "Get in your chariot and race to Jezreel. Get back to your capital city. It's going to rain."

Ahab jumped into his chariot and away he raced. I wish you could picture Ahab as he's in the chariot of iron and see him riding through the hills and valleys for those 18 miles. And then I wish you could see what Ahab saw. Just before he completed that 18-mile trip, there was a whizzzzz — and there was Elijah racing right past him! It must have been like a blur to Ahab's eyes.

One day as I sat at the foot of Mount Carmel, where this great race took place, I was reading this Bible story and these words stood out to me:

AND THE HAND OF THE LORD WAS ON ELIJAH AND HE OUTRAN THE HORSES OF AHAB.

The Lord gave me an image of my children when they were small and couldn't yet walk. Evelyn and I would take them by the hand and help them along as they took a little step, and then another little step. And when they'd start to fall, we'd pull them back up. Then as they got a little older we learned that we could put our hands under their armpits and we could let their feet just lightly touch the floor. And I mean they could run. Those little feet were just flying!

And the Lord said, *I want you to know that Elijah was not running this race. My hand was on him. My hands were under his armpits and he wasn't taking normal steps. His feet were just lightly touching the ground and when he was going down those hills he didn't have to worry about running too fast and stumbling and falling. I had him in My hands. And when he started up that mountain on the other side and his chest seemed almost to burst as he was*

*struggling to climb, I put My hands under him and up
that hill he went.*

And then the Lord gave me this phrase:

"YOU CAN RUN FASTER
THAN YOU CAN RUN WHEN
THE HAND OF THE LORD COMES UPON YOU."

What does that mean to your life today? It means
that as you go about your career or your job, you are
either doing it by your own ability and strength…
or…you are going beyond that and allowing God to
work His miracles through you. When you sow your
good seeds and obey God, He puts His hand under
your arms so you can run faster than you can run.

You can think faster than you can think.

You can do more than you can do.

Now, it's very important to understand that Elijah
had legs but he had to USE them. He had a chest and
he had to breathe through his lungs. He had to exert
his body. But he also had to BELIEVE that he could
make that trip in record time. He had to EXPECT A
MIRACLE to happen to him, to believe that God
intervenes…to believe in the supernatural…to believe
that God could touch him with His hands and that
the hand of the Lord could come upon him.

Do you believe today that it's possible for the hand
of God to come upon you?

What race are you facing today?

What challenges lie before you?

What is God asking you to do?

Reach up with your arms and say to God, "God,
I'm trusting You to put Your hands under my armpits
today and help me to run faster than I can run by
myself. I'll do everything I can do, but I'm trusting You
to do what only You can do. I'm trusting You to help

me get this job done in record time. I'm trusting You to help me do the best I can possibly do as a testimony to Your power. God, I'm expecting a miracle today."

Now lower your arms and start running! And expect God to run with you!

YOUR GOD-GIVEN KEY FOR TODAY

"I Can Run Faster Than I Can Run . . . With God's Help!"

**Key:
I CAN "TRACK"
WITH GOD TO GET**

TUESDAY

**HIS RESULTS
INTO MY LIFE**

**or
How I Can Put My Life Back
Into The Order That God Created For Me**

I am told that the female deer, which is called a hind in the Bible, is the most perfectly coordinated animal in creation. Her hind feet track so perfectly with her front feet that wherever her front feet touch down, her hind feet will touch down in exactly the same spot. Her legs follow one another in perfect unison without missing an inch. When she races like the wind up the mountainside, jumping from ledge to ledge, she doesn't fear that she's going to stumble and fall and be injured or plunge to her death. Her steps track so perfectly that no mountain can stop her, no ledge can frighten her, and no enemy can catch her.

The Psalmist David says that God makes OUR feet like the female deer's feet, and like her, He sets us upon high places (Psalm 18:33).

When you read the Bible and see the men and women who obeyed God and reached their "high places," you see that they learned how God made their SPIRIT and their MIND to work together as hinds' feet. They discovered God's tracking system which He placed inside each one of us — a way of living where our minds "track" or follow our spirits in perfect harmony so that we can reach God's highest for our lives.

King David was a man who was destined by God to be set in high places from his very childhood. His spirit and mind were so perfectly coordinated that he could race with abandon toward new heights.

When David was a young shepherd and the lions and bears would spring out to take his sheep, they were no match for the power of God in him. Not even the giant Goliath or the mad, demon-possessed King Saul and his most sure-footed army could harm David when his mind and spirit were tracking with God's system.

HOW YOU CAN "TRACK" WITH GOD

How can this tracking system work in your life and mine today?

First, you must recognize that God created you for "high places." The high places are where God is. And where God is, He wants you to be. He has "high hopes" for you, high desires, high standards.

Second, you must recognize that man lost his original position in the high places with God when Adam fell, because man chose to put his mind above his spirit. He got God's tracking system into reverse order. And since then, man has wanted to order his life by his mind.

When I think of my own life, how as a young man I brought upon myself a terrible disease and nearly lost my life, it was because my MIND had turned against my parents, against their faith, against the Church, and against the Bible. I ran away and lived in my mortal mind, totally disregarding my spirit.

When I look back from the time I was converted and filled with the Spirit to this moment, I can see that every mistake I made was when I was not tracking with God — and when my spirit was not leading my mind. Today when I let my mind dominate my spirit, my failures begin to pile up. But when I allow God's Spirit to work through my spirit to lead my mind, I can accomplish the things God has called me to do.

MAKE YOUR MIND FOLLOW YOUR SPIRIT

When God established His Church on the day of Pentecost, He gave us the way to get back into His tracking system. And that way is to "repent" (Acts 2:38). Peter said, "Change your mind." That's what the word *repent* means — to change the position of your mind, to elevate your spirit so that your mind follows in God's divine order. And then, Peter said, "You shall receive the gift of the Holy Ghost."

When the first 120 people were "filled with the Holy Ghost, and began to speak with other tongues, as the Spirit gave them utterance" (Acts 2:4), the door was opened to people everywhere so they could once again track with God's system. Suddenly through the Holy Spirit, they began to speak in a new language. It was not a language such as the one we speak every day, which is stored in our intellect or in our mind. It was a language that came out of the spirit, allowing them to bypass their minds and pray directly to God from their spirits, their innermost beings.

THE PRAYER LANGUAGE OF THE SPIRIT

The prayer language, which is what I call this language that comes from the spirit, is critically important to you in the needs you face right now... *today.*

You are, first of all, a spiritual being. You are spirit made in the image of God, with a mind and body attached to you and enveloping you. The real YOU is your spirit. And there's a language stored up in your spirit. Remember Christ said, "He that believeth on me... out of his belly shall flow rivers of living water" (John 7:38).

The Holy Spirit is in every child of God, no matter what his denomination is. He comes in the moment you believe on Jesus Christ. All you have to do is bring up the language of the Spirit, stored in you by the Holy Spirit. The moment you believe on Jesus, the Holy Spirit's work in your life is like a flowing river erupting in your innermost being. Suddenly you have a new language, the language of the Spirit. Through it you can pray directly to God and then ask God to open your understanding and help you interpret back to your mind so your spirit and mind can move in perfect unison like the feet of the hind.

Oh, how I wish somebody had told me on the night I accepted Jesus that I could begin right then to track with God's system by using my prayer language and then interpret back to my mind. I felt the Spirit flooding up inside me, but I didn't know how to let it

417

out. I didn't understand that I would pray in the Spirit BY MY WILL.

In 1 Corinthians 14:15 Paul says, "I *will* pray with the spirit, and I *will* pray with the understanding also." In other words, he is saying that he will pray in his spiritual prayer language and then he will interpret what God has said back in response to tongues.

GOD IS READY WHEN YOU ARE

Some people say, "When God is ready, I'm ready to speak out my prayer language." But God is not going to MAKE you speak in tongues or use your spiritual language. In order to pray in your spiritual language, when you feel the Holy Spirit stirring inside you, you must first stop speaking in your everyday language. Then you open your mouth and start to speak when the Spirit prompts you to speak out of your own spiritual depths.

Recently it was my honor to talk with an outstanding medical doctor about the prayer language. I asked him, "Doctor, how sharp is your mind?"

I had his credentials. He is one of the top ten people in his field in the entire world and his credentials are about ten pages long. So when I asked, "How sharp is your mind?" it threw him for a moment.

"What are you saying?" he asked.

"Do you know how sharp your mind can be?" I asked.

He said, "I've often wondered."

"Are you really born of the Spirit of God?" I asked.

"I am," he said.

"Do you remember in Acts 2:38 that Peter said repent and be baptized in the name of Jesus and you *shall* receive the gift of the Holy Ghost?"

"Yes," he said, "I have the Holy Spirit."

"Why don't you let His language come out?"

"How?" he asked.

"By placing your mind and your will in submission to your spirit," I said.

"You mean it's not some big overpowering experience that comes upon me?" he asked.

THE HOLY SPIRIT IS IN YOU

"No," I said, "the Holy Spirit is in you. But if you want to release your spiritual prayer language, then let the Holy Spirit language come up and out to your tongue and then ask God to interpret to your mind so you can also pray with your intellect."

"Do I have to wait?" he asked.

"No," I said. And just like that, he opened his mouth and began to speak, and the language of the Spirit came out in a flood stage. Then I said, "Now, doctor, by your own will, stop and pray in English. Don't let it be just an emotional experience."

We prayed in tongues together — stopping, interpreting, praying in tongues, then stopping and praying in our understanding for about 30 minutes. We were into God's tracking system!

Let me tell you, no power on earth can stop men and women who have learned how to pray in the Spirit, walk in the Spirit, and live in the Spirit. These are people who are leading with their spirits and tracking with their minds — interpreting back the desires of God and the methods of God that really WORK.

The gift of the Holy Spirit has been present in you from the moment Christ came into your life. In fact, you could not have received Jesus without the Holy Spirit enabling you to receive Him. He has come as a gift from God, to lead you by your spirit over the

419

obstacles that stand between you and God's highest and best for you.

SPEAK OUT YOUR PRAYER LANGUAGE

As you let your spirit come into harmony with the Holy Spirit, and as you speak out your prayer language, stop and then ask God to open your understanding and help you interpret back to your mind what you were saying in tongues. Then speak out in your everyday language. The more you practice this, the more your mind and spirit will begin to move together in harmonious motion just like the deer's feet. God's perfect tracking system will come forth and be developed in your life.

And, friend, no power can stop you when you're moving in unison with God's tracking system!

YOUR GOD-GIVEN KEY FOR TODAY

"I Can 'Track' With God By Using My Prayer Language And Interpreting Back To My Mind."

**Key:
THE PRAYER
LANGUAGE
IS A GREAT
KEY TO
HEALING**

WEDNESDAY

**or
How I Can Be Healed In My Innermost Self By
Praying In The Spirit And Interpreting Back**

Several years ago I had the opportunity to help a young minister friend of mine, Terry Law, who has literally held crusades around the world, including a ministry behind the Iron Curtain and private meetings with the pope. Terry is a graduate of Oral Roberts University and had been our close associate for many years.

This experience that we shared together was a deep and meaningful one, and I believe it has bearing on your life and what you are facing today. Here is what happened in Terry's own words...

"Two years ago I was in London preparing for a crusade. I had arrived on Monday and had been busy making arrangements for the meeting. But on Tuesday night my world came crashing down when someone awoke me and told me that my wife had been killed in an automobile accident. I immediately went into shock and said, 'No, it can't be! I'm going to go back to sleep and when I wake up this will all go away.'

"But it didn't go away...and the next day I flew home to Tulsa. I told the Lord at least a hundred times on the airplane that I was through with the ministry. I said, 'Lord, I've done everything I know to do. I've been interrogated by the KGB in Russia on five different occasions. I've put my life on the line in serving You. This is not fair!'"

"I'M GOING TO SHOW YOU SOMETHING"

"After the memorial service for my wife, I went into a spiritual collapse. I moved into a cocoon and I didn't know how to get out. During this horrible time Oral Roberts called and said he wanted to talk to me. I went to his office and he shared some of the trauma of his own life. I cried and opened my heart up to God. Then he said to me, 'Terry, I'm going to share something with you that will save your life but you've got to do what I say.' I asked him what it was and he said, 'I want you to go home and pray in the prayer language. I want you to get on your knees and start to praise and worship the Lord and then let God speak back to you. First Corinthians 14:13 says, *Let him who speaks pray that he may interpret.*'

"At first I said, 'I can't do it. I hurt too bad.' There was anger in me, a bitterness, a hurt so bad I couldn't even go to God. But Oral Roberts said, 'Go home and do it.'

"The next morning I woke up before daybreak, got on my knees, and started to pray. I tried to say 'Hallelujah' but it seemed to hit the roof and bounce right back at me. I felt as if the devil were sitting on my shoulder saying, 'Terry Law, you're a hypocrite. You don't mean what you're doing. How can you praise God after what's happened?'

"I came to the point where I had to make a decision whether to continue to praise God or not. The words of Psalm 34:1 came to me. King David said, 'I *will* bless the Lord at all times: his praise *shall* continually be in my mouth.' And I said to the devil, 'Shut up! I refuse to listen to you! I *am* going to bless

God! I *am* going to pray in the Spirit and allow that bitterness to be taken out of me.'

"Nothing happened to me immediately. But after I had prayed for about two and a half hours, a dam in my spirit broke and an incredible feeling came over me. Then I began to interpret back to my own mind what I had been praying in the Spirit. I prayed for my own healing and sensed the Holy Spirit pouring the oil of healing over my fractured emotions.

"After about two months of praying in the Spirit like that each day, the presence of God filled my room one morning and I felt God speaking to me, *Terry, I've taught you to praise and worship. Now I'm going to have you lead My people in praise and worship...and I will heal the sick, I will deliver those who are oppressed with demon spirits, and you will see more people saved than you have ever seen before.*

THE HEALINGS START

"What has amazed me is that ever since that time, about ten percent of all the people who attend our healing crusades are getting healed and helped!"

Friend, what happened in Terry Law's life can happen in yours.

Is there bitterness in your heart?

Are you wounded?

Is something stirring up your emotions all the time?

God has made a way for you to be healed. He has built it right into your system.

That way is for you to pray in the prayer language often, and to praise and worship the Lord and listen to God's response. Allow the Holy Spirit to give you the interpretation of what you said to God — even if you don't feel like it. Don't be discouraged in doing this. Don't let the devil talk you out of it. It is critical for your health and your ability to get on with your life in the way God wants you to! This will not be easy at first but remember...

In the darkest times of your life, God is there. He wants to heal you. He has given you the best way to *be* healed — by using your prayer language. Talk to God and let Him talk back to you. Praise Him today for His healing power! Open up your life and begin to pray in your spiritual prayer language today...for as long as it takes...day after day. Every day! Start today....

YOUR GOD-GIVEN KEY FOR TODAY

"I Will Praise And Worship God And Pray In My Spiritual Language Every Day... Starting Today... And I Will Expect God's Healing Power To Flood My Innermost Being."

THURSDAY

Key: GOD HASN'T FORGOTTEN YOU

or
How You Can Rest Assured That God Remembers You And Is Working On Your Miracle This Very Moment

Do you ever feel as if God has forgotten you?

Do you wonder at times if God even remembers your name?

When I get down, I get down, down…down! I get down so low that you'd have to jack me up to bury me. And when I really get down I have the feeling that God has forgotten Oral Roberts.

When my finances are drained and it seems like I can never get enough money to pay the bills that have piled up, it feels like God has forgotten me. When my body is struck with sickness and hurts from the crown of my head to the soles of my feet, the devil whispers, "God has forgotten you."

You know what I mean. You've experienced the same feelings. We're all the same. Every one of us has the same kind of blood pulsing through our veins…we live on the same earth…we face the same devil…we have the same types of problems.

But in the midst of the darkest hours of your life, God says to you and me, "I remember you."

Hebrews 6:10 speaks to you and me at those moments, "For God is not unrighteous to forget your work and labor of love, which ye have showed toward his name, in that ye have ministered to the saints, and do minister."

DON'T BUY THE DEVIL'S BILL OF GOODS

The devil tries to sell you a bill of goods by claiming that God doesn't know your name. The truth is He *does* know your name! He knows all about you. He's aware of every good seed you've planted. And He's aware of the pain that hits you in the pit of your stomach. He's aware of your WHOLE life. God remembers you!

In Genesis 37-47 we read the story of a young man named Joseph who thought God had forgotten him. Joseph was the favorite of his father's twelve sons. He loved God more than the other children loved

Him. He was the "dreamer" who had visions of what God was going to do for people. His brothers turned against him because they couldn't stand the faith that he had. They accused him falsely to his father and finally sold him to a caravan of traders on their way to Egypt.

When Joseph got into Egypt, he was sold to Potiphar, an officer of the Pharaoh. His wife fell in love with Joseph and tried to get him to commit adultery with her, but he wouldn't sin against God. Then one day when he refused her advances, she grabbed the sleeve of his jacket. He slipped out of his clothes and ran, but she convinced her husband of Joseph's guilt and he threw Joseph into prison.

WHAT DOES THE DREAM MEAN?

Then one day Pharaoh got mad at his butler and threw him into prison where Joseph was. The butler woke up one morning a while later with a dream on his mind that he could not interpret. He turned to Joseph because he sensed that God was in that boy. "Joseph, what does this dream mean?" he asked.

Joseph said the dream meant that in three days the butler would be released from prison and restored to his position. He said, "When it happens and you are restored to the king's favor, remember me." The butler was released as Joseph had said he would be, but he made no mention of Joseph to Pharaoh. He forgot Joseph...for two miserable years.

Then Pharaoh dreamed a dream. It confused him, disturbed him. He slept, and he dreamed the same dream again. He called for the wisest men in Egypt to interpret the dream but they failed. Suddenly the butler said, "Oh, King! I forgot! There is a young man in prison who once interpreted my dream. Send for Joseph."

Joseph was brought out and, sure enough, he could interpret the dream because God gave him the meaning. The king said, "There is nobody this wise in all of Egypt. Joseph, I will promote you to my right hand." Joseph went from being a prisoner to being prime minister in one day!

As a result, he was able to save the nation in a time of severe trouble, and also to save his own family, despite what his brothers had done.

GOD REMEMBERS YOU — ALWAYS

Friend, Joseph's brothers may have disdained him and forgotten him...Potiphar may have believed lies about him and forgotten him...the butler may have gone on his way and forgotten him. But God remembered Joseph. And when God remembers, God acts.

Has someone turned on you today?

Has someone spread lies about you?

Has someone forgotten to mention the good things you are doing...at home...at your job...to your friends?

GOD REMEMBERS YOU.

If you think nobody knows your name...GOD DOES.

If you think God doesn't care about you...HE DOES.

If you think God doesn't remember you...HE DOES.

If you think God isn't working RIGHT NOW to prepare a miracle from the good seeds you've planted...HE IS.

If you think God isn't planning your best and desiring your highest...HE IS.

GOD REMEMBERS YOU.

And, friend, that's a principle you can stake your very life on today.

Say it over and over until it sinks deep within you…

YOUR GOD-GIVEN KEY FOR TODAY

"God Remembers Me…Me…Me!"

FRIDAY

**Key:
YOU ARE A "LIGHTED"
WITNESS OF
GOD'S POWER TODAY**

or
How You Can Catch A Glimpse Of
God's Purpose For Your Entire Life On Earth

One of the most wonderful examples in the entire Bible of a human being truly used of God is the story of Moses.

As a man, Moses was rejected by his people and forced to live in exile. Yet it was at that point that he met God in a personal encounter that changed his life forever. From that encounter with God, Moses became a LIGHTED person…and even so, you and I today as followers of Jesus Christ, can also be a LIGHTED people.

In Exodus 3 we read how Moses came to encounter the light of God:

> "Now Moses kept the flock of Jethro his father in law, the priest of Midian: and he led the flock to the backside of the desert, and came to Horeb, the mountain of God. And the angel of the Lord appeared to him in

a flame of fire from the midst of a bush. So he looked and, behold, the bush burned with fire, but the bush was not consumed. And Moses said, I will now turn aside to see this great sight, why the bush does not burn.

"So when the Lord saw that he turned aside to look, God called to him from the midst of the bush and said, Moses, Moses. He said, Here am I. Then he said, Do not draw near this place. Take your sandals off your feet, for the place where you stand is holy ground. Moreover, he said, I am the God of your father, the God of Abraham, the God of Isaac, and the God of Jacob. And Moses hid his face; for he was afraid to look upon God.

"And the Lord said, I have surely seen the oppression of my people who are in Egypt and have heard their cry because of their taskmasters; for I know their sorrows. I have come down to deliver them out of the hand of the Egyptians, and to bring them up from that land to a good and large land, to a land flowing with milk and honey; to the place of the Canaanites...

"Come now therefore, and I will send you to Pharaoh, that you may bring my people the children of Israel out of Egypt."

How does this relate to you and me today?

YOU ARE ONE OF THE CALLED OF GOD

You and I, as Christians, are also a CALLED people, a CHOSEN people, a people who are sent out into this world with a mission.

Moses was conceived and born in a time of great adversity when all of the children of Israel had lost favor with Pharaoh. A new Egyptian ruler had come on the scene and he didn't remember how Joseph had once spared the land. He only knew that he saw a fruitfulness among the Israelites that he was determined to stop.

He laid heavy burdens upon the Israelites and increased their burdens until he had reduced them to slave status in Egypt. The Israelites were ostracized…friendless…and alone in a land of cruel taskmasters.

They cried out to the Lord for deliverance. And the more they were oppressed, the more they multiplied their numbers.

Then the king moved even further to annihilate them. He gave an order to the Hebrews' midwives to kill every male baby born to the Hebrew women. But the midwives, in their wisdom, feared God. They saved the lives of the babies and God blessed them for it and allowed them to have children of their own.

It was during this time that a Hebrew woman named Jochebed and her husband Amram, descendants from the tribe of Levi, had a son named Moses. His mother was forced to hide him in the bulrushes of the river so the Egyptians wouldn't find him. She built a little bassinet-type container out of the reeds and put it out upon the river with her baby inside, just in the place where the princess of Egypt often came to bathe. And while the princess was bathing, the baby cried.

The princess responded to Moses' cry and had him taken to the palace, where she raised him as her son. Meanwhile, Moses' sister Miriam came out from behind the river brush where her mother had stationed her and she asked the princess, "Would you like to have a wet nurse for the baby?" And when the princess said yes, Jochebed came to the palace. She was allowed to nurse and be with her own baby.

YOU CAN DREAM A DIFFERENT DREAM

And while the princess dreamed dreams of her little boy one day becoming the king of Egypt, Jochebed dreamed another dream...that one day God would touch her son's life and use him for His glory.

Do you think that was just an accident? Do you think *your* life today is just an accident?

No. Somewhere along the line someone heard the voice of God. Somebody listened and obeyed. Somebody dreamed a dream...and acted upon it. Somebody faced the enemy so you could one day be born on this earth and have your life count for God.

One of the strengths of the American Indian has always been that they fought not for greed or for lust, but for the *glory* of taking one more enemy. That's why they called themselves Indian *braves*.

And in a spiritual sense, Jochebed passed that kind of warrior faith on to Moses. The Bible says that Moses learned all the wisdom of Egypt, but from his real mother and father, he also heard about God.

Moses listened to his parents and he eventually faced a choice. Would he stand up for God or would he continue with the Pharaoh's policy of placing heavier and heavier burdens on God's people?

YOU ARE FACING A CHOICE

What choices are you facing today? Are you willing to make the choice for God and for God's people? Are you willing to be a warrior Christian *brave?*

Moses began to identify with those who were being persecuted and he was eventually forced to run for his life.

While he was in exile, Moses married the daughter of a Midianite priest who was a shepherd. He began to care for his father-in-law's flock on top of Mount Horeb. And it was there he encountered the LIGHT OF GOD.

A bush on fire was not an uncommon sight on the mountain where Moses had gone with his sheep. The sun beat down so hot there at times that shrubs and bushes would spontaneously spring into full flame. But this bush was different, and Moses could not turn his eyes away. This bush burned, BUT IT WAS NOT CONSUMED BY THE FIRE. Its flame came up out of itself and lighted the bush and made it flame and shine to give a man a vision of God. But it was not the bush that gave Moses the vision; it was the unique LIGHT that enabled him to see.

You know, people often think, *I'm frightened for God to fill me up so that His will for my life is above my own.* I've even felt that way at times as a minister of the gospel. We're frightened to be engulfed by God. But this little bush was engulfed by the unique flame of God and yet the flame did not consume the bush. It remained whole.

What does that mean to you?

It means that YOU can let God engulf you and use all of the choices that happen in your life and still not consumed. You can be a LIGHTED PERSON...a person lighted by God's power…a person who glows with God's Holy Spirit that flows out to others and heals their hurts and needs.

Moses…born in adversity, persecuted by his former people, forgotten by the world…still heard God speak to him miraculously out of a flame in a bush. Friend, God's miracle-working days aren't over!

God has a plan for your life. He has a purpose. And part of that purpose is to be His LIGHT to your family…your friends…your generation. As my Partner in this ministry, you are to be God's LIGHT to this nation and others…to the sick and needy and desperate people of this world…to those who have never heard the gospel and do not know about a loving, healing God who is good and who wants only their good. You are chosen to be a LIGHT in a world where God's voice is heard dim and His light is seen small. What will you do about it? Will you purpose in your heart to allow God to shine through you? You have a choice.

YOUR GOD-GIVEN KEY FOR TODAY

"I Am A Lighted Person!"

SATURDAY

**Key:
I HAVE
THE AUTHORITY
TO REFUSE
TO GIVE UP**

or
How To Keep Going On
Even When Every Obstacle Tries To Trip You Up

I vividly recall a time in my life when I closed my Bible and said, "I'm through."

It was six months after I had launched out into the ministry of healing evangelism — November 1947. I was preaching a city-wide crusade in Kansas and people had come from a three-state area. Many were accepting Christ as Savior and Lord and many were receiving healing. There was only one thing wrong — the crusade expenses were not being met.

As we neared the end of the crusade, the money we needed to pay the rent on the auditorium was not in hand and I became very distressed. Many times Evelyn and I had done without in order to pay bills in connection with our ministry. It was a habit that I knew God didn't want us to continue. He wanted to MEET our needs — both in the ministry and in our personal lives.

I made the mistake of starting to brood and worry instead of looking to God as the Source of my *total*, complete, down-to-the-last-cent-needed supply. The thought of not being able to pay that bill totally filled my mind and I became more and more disturbed by our lack of funds. I felt if I could not trust God for finances, how could I continue to trust Him to save and heal the people?

WHEN YOU THINK YOU'RE THROUGH

One evening I was waiting behind the curtain to be announced to preach. My brother Vaden was standing nearby. All at once something broke within me and I said, "I'm through."

Vaden was the brother closest to me in age. We were almost like twins and he could tell when I was deeply troubled in spirit. He said, "What's wrong?"

I said, "I don't have the faith and God is not helping me."

"Why, Oral," he said, "this is a wonderful crusade!"

"Yes," I said, "but we can't pay the bills. We were taught to pay our bills and be honest. I can't continue and be honest. I am giving up and going home."

Vaden knew I was serious and he quickly turned and went to get Evelyn. She was as white as a sheet. She too knew that when I said something, I meant it.

"Oral, I know it's hard, but you can't quit now," she said. "The services are too good and the people are turning more to the Lord every day."

"Evelyn, you know my vow. You and I both promised God that we would never touch the gold nor the glory, but we have to have enough to meet our budget. If I am to continue in this ministry, God will have to meet our needs. If He doesn't, I am going home."

She said, "Oral, why don't you tell the people how you feel?"

I said, "No. God knows my needs. If I can't trust Him for this, how can I trust Him for other things?"

"Are you going to preach tonight?" she asked.

"No," I said. "It's all over."

She and Vaden left.

EVELYN SAVED MY MINISTRY

Pretty soon I heard her voice over the loud-speaker as she spoke to the crowd. I was startled because she had never done this before. She always said, "When I stand up in front of an audience, my mind sits down." But this time she was really talking. I heard her say:

"Friends, you don't know what it means for me to stand up here tonight in my husband's place. And I am sure you don't know him as I do. He came here by faith. No one is responsible for the financial needs to be met except him and God. He has preached and prayed for you and tonight he feels like quitting. Some of you have not realized your responsibility in supporting this ministry and we can't even pay the rent on the building. Whatever you may think of Oral, he is honest and if he cannot pay the rent, he will not go on. He won't blame you. He'll just take this as a sign that God wants him to end this healing ministry. I'm asking you to help him. Together we can save this ministry tonight."

As she spoke, big tears splashed down her face.

Then she said, "I want some man here to lend me his hat, and I'm going to take a freewill offering for the rent."

A JEWISH FRIEND HELPED ME

Several men volunteered their hats and Evelyn selected a big-brimmed black one. She prayed and then just as she was starting to pass the hat, a Jewish businessman who had attended the services stood and asked permission to say a word. He said, "Folks, you all know me. I am not a Christian but if I ever am one, these people have what I want. I have some money I owe the Lord. I'm starting this offering with ty dollars."

Evelyn just stood there and waited. And then she started through the crowd. I finally had the courage to step to the platform. I had no idea whether enough had been taken to raise the rent on the building or not. But a new feeling had taken control of me. My wife had done something few wives would have had courage to do for their husbands. A team of wild horses could not have pulled her up there. She had gone willingly because she knew that the ministry God had given me was endangered.

I read my text and began to preach. And I tell you the power of Niagara Falls seemed to be released. I knew the tide had turned. The crusade ended with a packed house and the audience standing en masse urging us to return for another series of meetings.

I am sure that when God gives out the credit for the souls that were saved and the lives that were changed during that crusade, more of the credit will go to Evelyn than to me. *Because Evelyn did not give up.*

TWO IMPORTANT LESSONS

I learned two important lessons from that experience that I want to share with you today.

First, I learned that it isn't wrong to tell somebody when we are hurting and in need. God works through people. In fact, He doesn't have any other way to work on this earth. He doesn't rain money out of the skies. No, He gives us ideas, and we work those ideas with and through people. It isn't wrong to share our problems with other people and to be open to RECEIVING their help — their ideas, their advice, their opinions, their practical assistance.

If you are facing a difficult decision today, don't shut out other people. Don't keep your problem or worry all bottled up inside. Talk it out with someone you trust and who can give you good support and advice.

Second, I learned that there isn't any way you can get through life without having your very existence threatened. The devil knows your weak points and he hits you there. Money, on that particular night, was our weakest point. And the devil was striking at the money issue to try to destroy our commitment.

The devil is also determined to keep striking at us. We are in a struggle with the devil that doesn't end as long as we are alive. Oh, we may win one round. But we need to know that the battle goes on…and we can fight with courage knowing that eventually we win the war!

What am I saying to you? I'm saying that you are going to face struggles. You need God and other people to get through them. But the really good news is that Jesus promised, "He who ENDURES TO THE END shall be saved" (Matthew 24:13, caps added).

You can be an "endure-er." You can be someone who LASTS in your faith.

YOU'RE CLOSE TO YOUR MIRACLE — SO DON'T GIVE UP

Don't give up! Don't give up! Don't give up! For if you give up, how can you ever know how close you might have been to your miracle? Don't let the devil badger you. You have been given power over Satan in Jesus' name, and in Jesus' name you can command him to leave you and not come back.

The Bible tells how the Apostle Paul escaped with his life one night shortly after his conversion experience on the road to Damascus. Saul — as he was n — had been a great enemy of the early Church.

He had consented to the death of Stephen, the first Christian martyr, and had actually stood by while he died.

Then when he encountered the living Christ in a blinding light on the road to Damascus, Saul was dramatically and soundly converted to Christ. Although blind, he was led to Damascus where a lay leader in the church there, a man by the name of Ananias, came to pray for him that his sight might be restored.

Saul remained with the believers in Damascus for some time. These were the very people Saul had persecuted and now he was one of them. Soon the Jews began to hear reports that Saul was actually preaching Christ and they took counsel to kill Saul. They planned to ambush him as soon as he left the city.

The disciples learned of the plot and by night they put Saul in a basket and let him down over the wall. He fled into the wilderness, where he continued to grow strong in his faith.

Can you imagine how those disciples felt as they held on to the ropes that were attached to the basket carrying Saul? Surely they must have wondered about this man on the end of their rope.

Friend, are you holding the rope for a situation in your life — believing that it's about to turn around?

Let me encourage you today.

You don't know how close your basket is to touching the ground. You may be only inches away from the answer you need.

DON'T GIVE UP! You may have a very important person on the end of your rope so hold on to that rope in Jesus' name.

YOUR GOD-GIVEN KEY FOR TODAY

"I Can... And Will...
I Am Determined To Endure To The
End And Receive My Miracle Harvest!"

THIRTEENTH WEEK

SUNDAY ROSES WILL BLOOM AGAIN IN MY LIFE!

MONDAY I CAN RUN FASTER THAN I CAN RUN…WITH GOD'S HELP!

TUESDAY I CAN "TRACK" WITH GOD BY USING MY PRAYER LANGUAGE AND INTERPRETING BACK TO MY MIND

WEDNESDAY I WILL PRAISE AND WORSHIP GOD AND PRAY IN MY SPIRITUAL LANGUAGE EVERY DAY…STARTING TODAY…AND I WILL EXPECT GOD'S HEALING POWER TO FLOOD MY INNERMOST BEING

THURSDAY GOD REMEMBERS ME…ME…ME!

FRIDAY I AM A LIGHTED PERSON!

SATURDAY I CAN…AND WILL…I AM DETERMINED TO ENDURE TO THE END AND RECEIVE MY MIRACLE HARVEST!